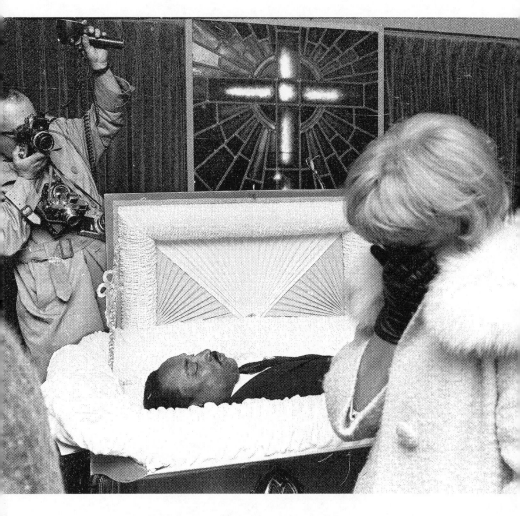

On the morning of April 5, 1968, a woman mourns as she views the body of Martin Luther King Jr. at the R. S. Lewis & Sons funeral home in Memphis. Hours later, the body was flown to Atlanta. *AP Photo/Charles Kelly*

BURIAL FOR A KING

Martin Luther King Jr.'s
Funeral and the Week That
Transformed Atlanta
and Rocked the Nation

Rebecca Burns

SCRIBNER

NEW YORK LONDON TORONTO SYDNEY

Scribner
A Division of Simon & Schuster, Inc.
1230 Avenue of the Americas
New York, NY 10020

A few passages in this book previously appeared in a different
format in the *Atlanta* magazine articles "Funeral," April 2008, and
"Atlanta Student Movement: 50 Years Later," March 2010,
and in the master's thesis "Mourning and Message"
(Georgia State University, 2008), all by the author.

First Scribner hardcover edition January 2011

SCRIBNER and design are registered trademarks of The Gale Group, Inc.,
used under license by Simon & Schuster, Inc., the publisher of this work.

For information about special discounts for bulk purchases,
please contact Simon & Schuster Special Sales at 1-866-506-1949 or
business@simonandschuster.com.

The Simon & Schuster Speakers Bureau can bring authors to your
live event. For more information or to book an event contact the
Simon & Schuster Speakers Bureau at 1-866-248-3049 or
visit our website at www.simonspeakers.com.

Book design by Ellen R. Sasahara

Manufactured in the United States of America

1 3 5 7 9 10 8 6 4 2

Library of Congress Control Number: 2010029980

ISBN 978-1-4391-3057-5

CONTENTS

BURIAL FOR A KING

Tuesday, April 9, 1968, morning

Mourners in King's funeral procession march past the gold-domed Georgia capitol
on the morning of April 9, 1968. *AP Photo*

THE WINDOWS ON THE second floor of City Hall provided a clear
view of Georgia's state capitol, and Mayor Ivan Allen could plainly
see what Governor Lester Maddox was up to. Dozens of state troopers
climbed out of armored trucks and marched up the wide walkway toward
the capitol. Although the April morning was a drizzled gray, the troopers' bayonets gleamed, as did the capitol's gold dome. Mayor Allen and
Vice Mayor Sam Massell watched silently as soldiers took their positions.
There was no sign of Maddox, but they knew he was in the capitol. *He's
showing his strength*, thought Sam Massell. *He's drawing a line and daring
anyone to cross it.*

Directly across the street from the capitol, people streamed in and out
of the double arched doors of Central Presbyterian Church. For days the

church had served as a makeshift shelter, kitchen, and hospitality center for tens of thousands of mourners. Some gathered on the lawn in front of the sanctuary now. They wore neat church dresses and dark suits and clutched umbrellas, rain hats, and Bibles. Bolder mourners looked over at the troopers. Some soldiers stared right back. In just a few hours, the mourners at Central Presbyterian would be joined by many more; police predicted today's crowd would reach 150,000 by noon. That mass of grieving humanity would move down Central Avenue—right between the church and the capitol, and right behind the coffin of Martin Luther King Jr.

The mayor turned from the window and walked out of his office. In the anteroom a few staff members manned phone lines. Everyone appeared subdued, exhausted after five days and nights of anxiety. In 110 other cities, the reaction to King's April 4 assassination had been arson, looting, and deadly riots. In response, 57,500 National Guard troops deployed around the country, the largest domestic military mobilization since the Civil War. By contrast, the 160 troopers positioned at the perimeter of Georgia's capitol seemed a puny force—except that the mayor knew Maddox had thousands more soldiers on alert just outside of the Atlanta city limits. There had been no rioting in Atlanta—yet. But on that Tuesday morning, no one in City Hall could predict how the day would unfold. All of the racial tension of the city's past replayed at fast speed, triggered by the death of a thirty-nine-year-old Atlanta preacher whose pulpit was just a mile from the governor's fortified base of operations.

Mayor Ivan Allen left City Hall and headed to King's church, Ebenezer Baptist, for the day's first event, a service organized by King's widow and family members. The big procession through downtown Atlanta and past the capitol would follow a few hours later.

Lonnie King arrived at the church early, but tens of thousands of people already jammed into the blocks around Ebenezer Baptist Church.* People slept in nearby vacant lots; others appeared in the predawn gloom to stake out spots with prime views. Scanning the crowd, Lonnie King saw police officers discreetly positioned at every intersection, and he knew FBI and

---

*Lonnie King and Martin Luther King Jr. were not related.

Secret Service agents were interspersed among the mourners, crouched on rooftops along Auburn Avenue, and hidden in the choir loft and aisles of the church. At the time the funeral duties were divvied up, Lonnie King's task—monitoring guests at the church door—had not seemed too challenging, and the assignment was certainly appropriate for a former prizefighter. But with each minute the crowd grew larger and surged threateningly closer to the sanctuary. He checked his list again. Robert Kennedy. Michigan governor George Romney. Sammy Davis Jr. Jackie Kennedy. Rabbi Abraham Heschel. Thurgood Marshall. Diana Ross. John Lewis. Vice President Hubert Humphrey. It was an unlikely gathering.

But then, Lonnie King was in the unlikeliest of situations. Eight years ago, he had been the leader of a student group that held sit-ins to protest Atlanta's segregated lunch counters and department stores. The sit-in movement grew, and adults joined the student protesters, and blacks boycotted downtown businesses for months. During the boycotts, Lonnie King had sat in on negotiation sessions with Police Chief Herbert Jenkins, white business leaders, and black lawyers and pastors. Now, less than a decade later, Lonnie King, Mayor Ivan Allen, and Chief Jenkins were working together—along with hundreds of other Atlantans—to strategize about how to keep the city from erupting in the kind of violence that overwhelmed more than a hundred other cities. Less than a decade earlier, Lonnie King and Martin Luther King Jr. were photographed as police officers took them to jail for staging a protest at Atlanta's venerable Rich's department store. Today Lonnie King stood with a walkie-talkie in front of historic Ebenezer Baptist Church as thousands of people crowded close to pay tribute to Martin King, killed by an assassin's bullet five days earlier.

As a little boy, Lonnie King came to this part of town almost daily, attending after-school programs at the Butler Street YMCA and services at Ebenezer. He knew Martin Luther King Jr.; *everyone* in black Atlanta knew Martin King, the pastor's son they all called M.L. Now a quarter century later, everyone in the *world* knew M.L., and it seemed they were all desperate to be part of his funeral rites. The crowd got bigger. The cops in front of the church stood up straighter and looked around more alertly.

It was early in the morning. The funeral services were scheduled to last almost eight hours. No one knew how the day would end.

ONE

Thursday, April 4, 1968

Coretta Scott King and Mayor Ivan Allen return to the King home from
the Atlanta airport on the night of April 4, 1968. *AP Photo*

The Marriott Motor Hotel, downtown Atlanta, early evening

O F ALL THE weird ideas you've had for me, this is one of the weird-
est," Martin Luther King Jr. told Xernona Clayton when she
approached him with a request: Calvin Craig, Grand Dragon of the Ku
Klux Klan, wanted to meet him. Would he consider? King eventually
agreed, and so on this Thursday, the day after she took King to the airport
to catch a flight to Memphis, Clayton had lunch with Craig to finalize the
details.

While they ate in the Marriott's tropical-themed dining room, Clayton realized they drew attention. It was still odd in late 1960s Atlanta to
see a black woman and a white man sharing a meal—especially in a hotel

restaurant. On top of that, she and Craig were minor local celebrities, which contributed to the raised eyebrows, sideways glances, and outright stares.

She was the star of *The Xernona Clayton Show* on the local CBS affiliate—the first television show in the South to be hosted by a black woman. Her husband, Ed Clayton, had directed public relations for Martin Luther King and the Southern Christian Leadership Conference (SCLC),* and after Ed died, she had filled in when needed. She frequently traveled with King's wife, Coretta Scott King. Diminutive and feisty, Clayton was recognized by her trademark hairstyle—a tall, tightly pinned topknot anchored by a shiny headband. She had a flair for fashion and an enviably taut figure; she had met Ed when he begged her and her identical twin, Xenobia, to model bikinis for the centerfold of *Jet* magazine.

In contrast to the chic Clayton, Calvin Craig was a burly construction worker, mustached and with arms and a neck reddened from a lifetime of outdoor labor. Like Clayton, Calvin Craig was familiar to television viewers—but as the subject of news stories, not a polished anchor. He notoriously appeared in full Klan regalia to lead anti-integration protests through the streets of Atlanta or on the steps of the Georgia capitol. He traveled throughout the South to attend cross burnings.

Craig and Clayton met through Model Cities, the urban component of President Lyndon Johnson's War on Poverty. Craig was named to the program as the representative from Adair Park, a neighborhood of mostly working-class whites not far from its predominantly black counterpart, Pittsburgh. Their first encounter was prickly; Clayton watched as Craig scooted from chair to chair to avoid sitting next to any black participant in the meeting. Not long after, Craig visited Clayton's office and rattled her as he revealed he had compiled a dossier on her. He knew that her husband, Ed, former executive editor of *Jet*, helped launch the *Atlanta Voice*, a black newspaper, and served as public relations coordinator for Martin Luther King and the SCLC. Furthermore, the Grand Dragon knew all about Xernona's travels with Mrs. King and about her early work as an

*The story of the civil rights era brings with it a host of acronyms and abbreviations designating various movement organizations. To help keep track of them all, I have added a glossary on page 222.

activist with the Urban League.* The Klan leader unnerved Clayton, but she forced herself to remain composed.

Clayton and Craig sparred at subsequent Model Cities meetings. She chided him for taking payments to stage Klan protests at the behest of white businesses that opposed integration. Craig criticized Clayton for socializing with whites, saying such intermingling would lead to a dilution of racial purity that both races ultimately would regret. Eventually the two reached an uneasy détente and developed, if not a friendship, at least a cordial working relationship as they tackled the task of finding jobs for members of their respective constituencies. Atlanta was transforming in the 1960s, with the erection of a new stadium, skyscrapers, and hotels such as the Marriott. But Atlanta's poor and uneducated residents—white and black—struggled to keep up with the changing economy. Urban-renewal programs made space for gleaming new hotels and office towers by flattening cheap housing, forcing working-class Atlantans farther from the city center and jobs.

Despite the changes she'd witnessed in Calvin Craig over the years, Xernona Clayton still worried about arranging for Martin Luther King to meet with the Grand Dragon. The Klan remained a visible presence in Atlanta; just three years earlier, robed and masked Klansmen protested the dinner given to honor King's Nobel Peace Prize win. Stone Mountain, the looming granite dome fifteen miles east of the city, was the birthplace of the modern KKK and the site of Klan rituals for decades. The call "Let freedom ring from Stone Mountain of Georgia" in King's famous "Dream" speech carried a special significance for Atlantans, who knew of the mountain's connection to the Klan. Five years after King gave that speech, a black woman might have been able to walk into a restaurant in downtown Atlanta and get a table, but on the rocky face of Stone Mountain, stonecutters were still completing the mammoth carving of

---

*Xernona Clayton's career as a civil rights activist had started a few years back in Chicago, when she and Xenobia were recruited by the Urban League to go undercover to investigate job discrimination. Day after day they responded to help-wanted ads, and night after night they trekked to the Urban League offices to report how they had instantly been rejected when they went to job interviews—often told as soon as they walked in the door that positions had been filled.

Confederate heroes Jefferson Davis, Stonewall Jackson, and Robert E. Lee—bankrolled in part by the KKK.*

Xernona repressed her uneasiness, said good-bye to Craig, and prepared for her next meeting, a dinner with Sam Caldwell, Georgia's labor commissioner. On the agenda: more Model Cities business—employment for ten young men King and Clayton identified as prospects for a summer-jobs program.

As Caldwell and Clayton ate dinner, the hostess approached with a discreetly folded slip of paper. Clayton opened it and glanced at the cryptic message: *Have you heard about Dr. King?* She refolded the note and kept chatting with Caldwell.

After a few minutes the hostess returned. "Did you read my note?"

"Yes," said Clayton distractedly.

"Don't you understand?" the hostess pressed. "He's been shot."

Clayton nodded and nonchalantly returned to her dinner. In the years she had known King she had received reports he had been attacked, even killed—sometimes as she sat directly in his presence. She chalked up the message as another rumor or distasteful prank. *It's not like you say good-bye to someone at the airport and then the next day they're dead*, she thought. Only twenty-four hours ago, dropping King off at the terminal, she reminded him, "Call your mother." On a recent Sunday, she, the King family, and other friends had gathered after church for games and singing. Mama King longed for more afternoons like that and asked Xernona to make them happen. As she tried to focus on her conversation with the labor commissioner, Clayton thought about that carefree afternoon and remembered sitting at the piano to play as the King family sang. She wondered if King had made the call to his mother. (Indeed, he had. From the Lorraine Motel in Memphis on the afternoon of April 4, M.L. and his brother, A.D., called their parents and talked for almost an hour.)

---

*The carving on Stone Mountain was started in the 1920s under the direction of Gutzon Borglum, the sculptor of Mount Rushmore. Borglum withdrew and the project passed on to two other sculptors and stretched out over five decades. The carving was not dedicated until 1970, and the final details completed in 1972. "Inevitably, mountain, memorial, and kitsch blend together," wrote Peter Range in a 1972 *New York Times* travel story. "The rest of the South is no longer fighting the Civil War; at the foot of Stone Mountain is where it belongs."

The hostess came back. She looked distressed.

"Maybe you should check," said Caldwell. "I'll wait."

The hostess offered the use of the restaurant phone. Clayton called the King home; the line was busy. She called the family's unlisted number; busy, too. She went back to Caldwell, who offered to drive her over to the Kings' to make sure everything was all right. As they pulled out of the drive in front of the sleek motel and headed into the rainy night, Xernona Clayton could not resist a twinge of amusement. Who would have predicted that she, a black woman with Native American blood who grew up in segregated Oklahoma, would be chauffeured through the streets of Atlanta by a middle-aged white man who held one of the highest positions in Georgia government?

Any bemused reflection vanished as soon as they approached the Kings' modest redbrick house just a few miles west of downtown. Two police cars blocked a large Chevrolet in the driveway. Louise Allen, wife of Atlanta mayor Ivan Allen, sat behind the wheel of the Chevrolet while the mayor crouched in the passenger seat of one of the police cars talking into a radio transmitter. In the front seat of the other police cruiser was Coretta Scott King, a gold damask cap hurriedly pulled over her loose curls. Her face was barely made up and she looked uncharacteristically young, anxious, and frazzled, a marked difference from her usual calm demeanor and immaculate grooming.

Mrs. King rolled down the window and called out to Xernona Clayton, "Martin's been shot in Memphis. We are going to the airport. Can you stay with the children?"

Sam Caldwell and Xernona Clayton hurried into the house. The youngest King child, Bernice, whom everyone called Bunny, was already in bed. The three older children—Yolanda, twelve; Martin III, ten; and Dexter, seven—sat in the front room watching television newsmen talk about their father.

Less than an hour earlier, the kids had been lounging in the living room when SPECIAL BULLETIN flashed across the television screen and an announcer said their father had been shot. Dexter raced to his mother's room to tell her what they had seen, but she was already on the phone. Jesse Jackson, the twenty-six-year-old activist who had been at the Memphis motel with King, called minutes after the shooting.

"Doc just got shot," Jackson said to Coretta. "I would advise you to take the next thing smoking."

Mrs. King pulled out her overnight bag. Both she and Juanita Abernathy, wife of King's closest friend, Ralph David Abernathy, kept bags stocked and ready so they could leave at the shortest notice if trouble arose while their husbands were on the road or if, as had happened so many times before, they needed jailhouse essentials after being arrested on civil disobedience charges. As she was checking the contents of her bag with the help of Yolanda, the phone rang again; it was the mayor, who said the 8:25 flight to Memphis would be held for her and he would bring a police escort to help her get to the airport as quickly as she could.

Northside Drive, Atlanta, around 7:30 p.m.

Mayor Ivan Allen and his wife, Louise, had been watching television in their bedroom when the special bulletins aired.

Immediately, the mayor said, "I'm going to his wife."

Without hesitating, Louise replied, "I'll go with you."

Before they headed out, Allen called his chief of police, Herbert Jenkins, and asked him to meet them at the King house. He also called local newsrooms, the Atlanta bureaus of national papers, and network television affiliates. During his six years in office, the mayor had become acutely sensitive to the symbolic weight attached to his actions. He was shrewdly aware that news he'd rushed to help King's wife would be significant to Atlanta's black residents, and equally sensitive that it would make for good press beyond the South. Allen did not only worry about public relations; he could not predict what the response to an attempt on King's life would be and wanted to prepare for any outcome. Atlanta had not experienced large-scale riots like those that ravaged Los Angeles, Detroit, and Newark in the summers of 1965, 1966, and 1967, but during the past few years a few outbursts had been triggered by racial tension. From experience, Mayor Allen and Police Chief Jenkins had learned that the most effective way to keep violence from accelerating was to insert themselves bodily into a situation and remain visible until trouble dissipated. He hoped that his swift response tonight would prevent trouble from even starting.

Allen's actions were not merely political calculations. His esteem for

King had grown over the past years. Both men—Allen, heir to a multi-million-dollar business, and King, third in a line of activist preachers—were influential in Atlanta. But typical of the chasm that existed even between the most elite blacks and whites, their early lives barely intersected. Although they had encountered each other during segregation protests in the early 1960s, their first personal interaction came in January 1965, when Allen helped to organize a dinner in honor of King's being awarded the Nobel Peace Prize. Most white business leaders initially resisted the idea of the banquet. Angered by his counterparts' reluctance to honor King, Allen, along with Paul Austin, president of the Coca-Cola Company, convened a meeting at the Piedmont Driving Club, the city's old-money retreat. Allen goaded the men, telling them even if they disagreed with King's philosophies and methods, it would look bad for Atlanta's image if they did not show up at a dinner honoring Georgia's first Nobelist. He cautioned that should they make excuses, go out of town, or send underlings in their stead, *he* would be at the dinner and taking note of who attended and who did not. There would be consequences was the implication from City Hall and Atlanta's other civic force, Coca-Cola.

In the end virtually every man Allen and Austin summoned to the meeting at the Driving Club was among the fifteen hundred Atlantans attending the banquet at the Dinkler Plaza Hotel.* Addressing the dinner guests, Rabbi Jacob Rothschild said, "You gather to honor a man but you honor a city as well, a Southern city that has risen above the sordidness of hate and prejudice."

After the event, architect Cecil Alexander of Atlanta sent the rabbi a letter, thanking him for "the difficult role you played from the rostrum and (among those who know) your efforts prior to the event." Acknowledging the initial reluctance of the white community—businessmen in particular—to get behind the Nobel banquet, and the struggles that Ralph McGill, Ivan Allen, himself, and others had encountered while garnering

---

*The Nobel Prize banquet represented a microcosm of Atlanta's changing racial dynamics. Just four years earlier, Secretary of Defense Robert McNamara spoke to a segregated audience at the Dinkler Plaza, and black college students and the NAACP picketed the hotel in protest. A few years, later when the Dinkler family decided (reportedly at the direct request of Robert Kennedy) to make theirs one of the first whites-only hotels in Atlanta to integrate, the family received bomb threats.

white buy-in, Rothschild wrote to New York rabbi Sidney Regner confiding, "After the dinner ended, those of us who had been involved in it for so long a time felt like singing 'We did it!' from *My Fair Lady.*"

There had been bomb threats on the night of the banquet, the Klan picketed outside, and police squads swept the area, delaying the start of the dinner. Ivan Allen waited in the foyer with civil rights activist the Reverend Sam Williams, the pastor of Atlanta's influential Friendship Baptist Church, one of Martin Luther King's professors at Morehouse College, and later one of King's Southern Christian Leadership Conference cofounders. A hotel staffer apologized for the delay. "Don't worry about that," said the mayor. "My friend Sam Williams has been waiting for a hundred years to get into that ballroom, and forty-five minutes one way or the other isn't going to bother him much."*

These recollections flashed through the mayor's mind as he and Louise left their home on Northside Drive and made their way along the tree-lined streets that wound from their neighborhood, Buckhead—a hilly enclave of mansions and graceful estates—to the King home at 234 Sunset Avenue in Vine City. Six blocks to the south, Sunset dead-ended at Hunter Street, the main thoroughfare through Atlanta's cluster of historically black colleges. City planners considered Sunset the western boundary of Vine City, commonly referred to in the white press as a "Negro slum," an area where just a few years earlier Coretta and Martin King, along with Ralph and Juanita Abernathy, led protests against negligent slumlords, rat infestation, and crime. In 1966, Vine City had been described by a writer for the *Georgia Bulletin*, a Catholic newspaper, as "generally forgotten by civic leaders, the Christian churches, and well-to-do Negroes." As the Allens' car drew closer to Vine City, it seemed as though the night got darker, visible evidence of the city's historic neglect of black neighborhoods: fewer streetlights—if any at all—were installed in black residential areas.

As he drove, the mayor clung to the scattered radio bulletins delivering more details about the shooting. King stood on the balcony of the

---

*In an understatement, *Newsweek* editors in New York sent a telex to their Atlanta bureau asking reporters to "please include any controversial bits should there be any" along with "background on the dinner and whether it shatters any precedent" in a report of "200 words . . . including best King quotes plus menu of dinner and any color details."

Lorraine Motel when a shot was fired. Police were searching for the shooter. Authorities believed the gunman to be the young white man spotted leaving a boardinghouse across from the motel. An ambulance rushed King to St. Joseph Hospital, accompanied by members of his inner circle, including Andrew Young and Ralph David Abernathy. Buford Ellington, the governor of Tennessee, had mobilized the National Guard. Memphis authorities feared riots.

When the Allens reached the King home on Sunset Avenue, police cars were already there. The mayor had planned to ride along with Mrs. King, but realized that the best way to stay in touch with City Hall would be to take a police car, where he could use the radio, so he took one cruiser and asked Mrs. King to ride in the second police car, along with her sister- and brother-in-law Christine King Farris and Isaac Farris, who had come to the house as soon as they heard of the shooting. Louise Allen followed—driving the Allens' car and taking other King family friends. The convoy headed toward the airport, police lights flashing in the rain as the cars made their way south.

They arrived at the terminal to find reporters already clustered around the doors. The group evaded the reporters' shouted questions as they made their way through the rain and into the lobby. There, Dora McDonald, the King's close friend and personal assistant, waited. She, Mrs. King, and Christine King Farris went into the ladies' room while the mayor headed to the Eastern Airlines counter to check on the flight. Before the mayor reached the counter, an airline staffer stopped him and asked him to take a call—the official notification from Memphis that King was dead.

Allen went into the ladies' room to find Mrs. King. In a quiet, formal tone, the mayor said, "Mrs. King, I have to inform you that Dr. King is dead."

The mayor and the three women stood there, silent, weeping, for a while. They held hands.

"Coretta, do you want to go to Memphis or what?" the mayor finally asked.

The widow decided to go home to be with her children rather than fly to Memphis that night. As they exited the restroom and walked down the airport hallway, television crews tracked their movements and news cameras flashed. Ignoring the barrage of questions, Mrs. King stared stoically straight ahead, the camera bulbs created a harsh glare on her glasses. The mayor strode purposefully, posture erect, close-cropped silver hair glinting, his mouth rigidly set.

By the time they returned to the house on Sunset Avenue, reporters, police, relatives, and curious neighbors surrounded it. Mrs. King pushed through the crowd to make her way in, Mayor Allen walked a few steps behind, holding an umbrella. Mrs. King went straight to her bedroom at the back of the house. Xernona Clayton came to ask what she could do to help.

"I can't reach my parents because all of the lines here are busy. Can you go to your house and call them for me?" Coretta asked.

Xernona paused. "Well, my car is at the hotel downtown."

Once again, the labor commissioner stepped in to serve as her chauffeur, and Caldwell and Clayton left Coretta's house and went back to the Marriott.

When she finally walked into her own home, Xernona found it packed. People had come to see what she knew, and her housekeeper had let them all in. They crowded around Xernona asking questions. Where was the body? How was Coretta? What were the plans for the funeral?

"I don't know any of that yet," she said. "I have to call Coretta's parents."

Before she could make the call, her phone rang. Coretta. "I need you here. Can you come back? The phones are ringing nonstop and I need help with the children."

Xernona shooed everyone out of her home, packed an overnight bag, and drove back to Sunset Avenue.

Morehouse College student Marvin Mangham Jr. sat in the living room of his parents' home on Collier Ridge Drive watching television with his mom, dad, and girlfriend, Mary, a student at Spelman College. They were aghast when they saw the news of King's shooting. Marvin senior, Morehouse '48, was a classmate of Martin King's. Marvin junior grew up seeing the King family regularly; his paper route included the home of Martin Luther King Sr., known to Atlantans of all ages and races as Daddy King, the formidable patriarch of Ebenezer Baptist Church.

Like other members of Atlanta's black middle class, Marvin's parents migrated to the suburbs from older, inner-city black communities such as Sweet Auburn, where Ebenezer Baptist stood; Vine City, close to the Atlanta University Center; or Summerhill, built on land designated for former slaves during Reconstruction. The Manghams and the elder Kings lived in Collier Heights, a postwar development created by blacks for blacks, one of the few of its kind in the country.* Marvin's newspaper delivery customers included Christine King Farris, Martin's older sister, and Dr. Frederick Earl McLendon, a physician whose massive home took up an entire block and famously housed an indoor swimming pool.† The Manghams' neighbors included teachers, professors, lawyers, and Atlanta's first black city alderman, Q. V. Williamson. In the early 1960s, Ralph Abernathy, Martin Luther King's best friend and cofounder of the SCLC, bought a house on nearby Laverne Drive, a low-slung ranch with a curbside mailbox encased in cut stone. A black, cast-iron banner heralded ABERNATHY across the top.

The Mangham family and Mary watched in horror as the news reports came in from Memphis. "Let's go check on the Kings," Marvin senior said after a while, so the family got in their car and drove over to the elder Kings' home on nearby Dale Creek Road. Neighbors and friends already clustered on the front lawn.

Marvin knew he had to get Mary back to her dorm before curfew, so the Manghams went home, and Marvin took his dad's car and he and Mary headed out. They drove in near silence through the rain-slicked curving streets, leaving behind Collier Heights' cul-de-sacs, wide front lawns, and streamlined, modern homes. A few miles east, closer to the Atlanta University Center, exuberant middle-class ranch houses made way for tidy cottages, square duplexes, narrow shotgun shacks, and the stolid brick apartments of the University Homes housing project.

---

*In 2009, Collier Heights was named to the National Register of Historic Places, one of the few postwar developments to be so honored. The neighborhood is known for distinctive midcentury modern ranch homes. One house is entirely pink; another is completely circular. One of the most idiosyncratic homes is designed to look like a Japanese pagoda.

†In the 1940s, Dr. McLendon opened a private health clinic serving Atlanta's black community, which had limited access to any health services, public or private.

Marvin dropped Mary off at her dormitory. True to its roots as a female "seminary," Spelman maintained stringent rules for students and strictly enforced its curfews. After saying good-night to Mary, Marvin headed up Chestnut Street, where students from nearby Morehouse and Clark colleges streamed out of dorms and classrooms to gather in the campus quadrangle. At the corner of Chestnut and Parsons, teens threw rocks at the window of a small store owned by a white couple. As a boy, Marvin helped out in the store at the request of his grandmother, who lived nearby and knew the owners. Boys and young men crowded the intersections, peering through the windshields of passing vehicles. Marvin watched as they pulled a white driver out of his car, pushed him to the street, and shoved and kicked him.

Marvin headed back to Collier Heights. The scenes near the university center seemed surreal. He remembered the John Kennedy assassination four and a half years earlier, when it seemed as though everything moved in slow motion; an "out of body experience" is how he would later describe it. He had been in high school then, and his parents urged him to go about business as usual, insisting he take a scheduled driving lesson.

"You were awful," the instructor said at the end of the session. "Can't you focus?"

"No, of course not. Think of what happened today," Marvin had said.

Oval Office, the White House, Washington, D.C., 7:24 p.m.

President Lyndon Johnson chatted with visitors from Atlanta: Robert Woodruff, the retired president of Coca-Cola, and Carl Sanders, the former governor of Georgia. Sanders had been a workhorse on LBJ's behalf in the 1964 presidential campaign, and Woodruff was a substantial donor. A onetime University of Georgia football player and World War II bomber pilot, Sanders had been elected to the top Georgia post in 1962 at the age of thirty-seven, the youngest governor in the country. Tall, with an athlete's natural grace and the rich cadences of his native Augusta, Sanders presented a glamorous figure. As governor, he riled Georgia whites by cooperating with the federal government on integration after the passage of the 1964 Civil Rights Act, presenting a marked contrast to segregationist governors of neighboring states such as George Wallace of Alabama and Ross Barnett of Mississippi.* After leaving office because of term-limit rules, Sanders was succeeded in 1967 by segregationist Lester Maddox.

Considered a rising star in national Democratic politics, Sanders had declined several job offers from the LBJ administration, but now speculation about his national political future continued—with a twist. Five days earlier, President Johnson had made a surprise announcement in a televised address: "I do not believe that I should devote an hour or a day of my time to any personal partisan causes or to any duties other than the awesome duties of this office. . . . Accordingly, I shall not seek, and I will not accept, the nomination of my party for another term as your president."

The president's withdrawal from the 1968 race had been preceded by plans to pursue peace talks in Vietnam—"I am taking the first step to deescalate the conflict"—and to curtail bombing. While this meant the United States would scale back fighting in civilian areas and reduce bombing in enemy territory (above the twentieth parallel), it did not mean reduced troop deployment; another 13,500 Americans forces, both active and reserve, would head to the conflict. To accomplish all this, budgets would certainly be slashed and taxes might be raised. The president conceded that this was happening at a time of domestic strain, largely over racial issues:

> In these times as in times before, it is true that a house divided against itself by the spirit of faction, of party, of region, of religion, of race, is a house that cannot stand. There is division in the American house now. There is divisiveness among us all tonight. And holding the trust that is mine, as president of all the people, I cannot disregard the peril to the progress of the American people and the hope and the prospect of peace for all peoples. So, I would ask all Americans, whatever their personal interests or concern, to guard against divisiveness and all its ugly consequences.

---

*This also presented a marked change from Sanders's earlier stance on integration. Although he eventually became a moderate on race and enforced the Civil Rights Act, he previously had testified before Congress against portions of the act.

The exit of Johnson, who won a landslide in 1964, shifted the dynamics of the election year and opened a rush of speculation. On the day of Sanders's meeting with the president, the *Atlanta Journal* ran a front-page story suggesting that the handsome former governor—"one of the best acts-of-God men in the business"—was prime vice-presidential material, an essential Southerner to balance the ticket in a Democratic field that, following Johnson's withdrawal from consideration, was dominated by senators from the Northeast and the Midwest, including antiwar candidate Eugene McCarthy, who had rattled LBJ with strong New Hampshire results; Robert Kennedy, who had entered the race a few weeks earlier; and LBJ's vice president, Hubert Humphrey. On the Republican side, former vice president Richard Nixon vied against governors Ronald Reagan of California and Nelson Rockefeller of New York.

Tom Johnson, a White House special assistant, interrupted president Johnson's Oval Office conversation. He had an urgent bulletin for the president. A Georgia native and former staffer of the *Macon Telegraph*, Tom Johnson instantly recognized the guests from Atlanta. After President Johnson took the bulletin, he turned to Woodruff and Sanders and said, "I'm sorry you have to hear this." He initialed the note and handed it to Sanders, saying, "This is history."*

Looking at the slip of paper, Sanders and Woodruff read about the King shooting in Memphis. As the president conferred with aides, the two men from Atlanta found another phone in the Oval Office and tried to reach Mayor Ivan Allen. Unsuccessful, they went to say good-bye to Johnson, and found the president already huddled with Attorney General Ramsey Clark and other advisers. They were debating what Johnson should do in light of King's shooting. The president had been slated to fly from Washington to Honolulu at midnight for talks with General William Westmoreland about Vietnam War strategies. Would it be appropriate or politically expedient to stick to the schedule after America's best-known civil rights leader had been shot?

Ramsey Clark had long feared that King would be killed. He first

---

*Sanders kept the slip of paper LBJ gave him that night. When I talked with him in early 2008, the former governor said that he still kept it secure in a lockbox.

became anxious about King's safety when, as an assistant attorney general, he was assigned to monitor the Selma-to-Montgomery voter registration march of 1965 and witnessed the constant threats against King and his SCLC cohorts. Clark's fears escalated over the subsequent years.

Clark flew to Memphis that night to oversee the investigation into King's shooting. Before Clark left the White House, assistant FBI director Cartha "Deke" DeLoach made a wager with the attorney general: the shooter would be found and caught in twenty-four hours. If not, DeLoach said, he would buy Clark a bottle of sherry.

The Henry Grady Hotel, Atlanta, 8 p.m.

For years, the bar, lobby, and guest suites of the Henry Grady Hotel were considered the auxiliary workspace of the good old boys of the Georgia legislature. The once magnificent redbrick hotel on the former site of the governor's mansion at the corner of Peachtree Street and Ellis was getting shabby, but the clubby atmosphere remained intact.* Tonight, in the hotel ballroom, the Georgia meeting of the American Independent Party was under way. Its immediate goal: to gather enough signatures to allow George Wallace, the segregationist governor of Alabama, to run as a third-party candidate in the November presidential election.

Roy Harris, Georgia's American Independent Party chairman, was direct in his introductory remarks. Nothing will get better in this country, he said, "until we have someone in the White House who recognizes the viewpoints of white people in the South." Peter Zack Geer, the former lieutenant governor of Georgia, drew cheers when he said that Wallace would "save us from Stokely Carmichael, Martin Luther King, Ralph McGill, Eugene Patterson, and, yes, little Bobby Kennedy."

The next day, one of the men mentioned by Geer, *Atlanta Constitution* editor Gene Patterson, published a column that contrasted Lyndon Johnson, a "Southerner who turned away from the ancestral vices," with Wal-

---

*The Henry Grady was demolished in 1972 to make way for the Westin Peachtree Plaza, a 723-foot, glass-and-steel cylinder topped by the Sundial revolving restaurant. The John Portman–designed building was Atlanta's tallest for years and is still one of the tallest hotels in the Western Hemisphere.

lace, whose politics "bound the South in the ignominy of its vices instead of giving free run to its virtues as Johnson tried to do."

In the column, Patterson quoted an interview with Harris in which the Independent Party operative outlined his tactics for Wallace's Georgia campaign. "It's going to be states' rights and the right to run your own schools," Harris said. "But when you get right down to it, there's really going to be only one issue and you spell it *n-i-g-g-e-r.*"

Indianapolis Municipal Airport, just after 8 p.m.

Robert Kennedy spent the afternoon of April 4 traveling and learned of King's death as he rode from the airport to an Indianapolis campaign rally. From the car, Kennedy radioed to campaign staffer John Lewis, former head of the Student Nonviolent Coordinating Committee (SNCC) and a King protégé. When Kennedy told him about King's death, the young activist forced himself to remain stoic. He stayed that way even when Kennedy arrived from the airport, looked at Lewis directly, and said, *"You've* lost a leader. *We've* lost a leader."

When Kennedy reached the rally, a crowd waited—loud, excited, and largely oblivious of the news about King. A band played on the campaign stage, and some audience members danced. A few people on the edges of the crowd listened to pocket radios and talked about King's death. Some campaign staff members were worried that Kennedy would be shot in retaliation; a gang was rumored to have staked out the rally site.

Television camera crews were focused on Kennedy as he was greeted by campaign staff. "Do they know about Martin Luther King?" he asked. "We left it up to you to tell them," a staffer said. Kennedy solemnly walked up to a microphone. He looked out over the crowd and said, "I have bad news for you, for all of our fellow citizens and people who love peace all over the world."

Many in the crowd continued to chatter and laugh, not aware that the candidate had started speaking. Kennedy looked down at the notes he'd written on the back of an envelope en route from the airport.

"Martin Luther King was shot and killed tonight," Kennedy stated. From the back of the rally, Lewis watched the news travel in a wave across the audience. Those closest to Kennedy broke down in sobs. Word passed from row to row, and excited conversation turned into wails. People abruptly stopped clapping. Kennedy then delivered an extemporaneous eulogy:

> Martin Luther King dedicated his life to love and justice for his follow human beings, and he died because of that effort. . . . For those of you who are black—considering the evidence there evidently is that there were white people who were responsible— you can be filled with bitterness, with hatred, and a desire for revenge. We can move in that direction as a country in great polarization. . . . Or we can make an effort, as Martin Luther King did, to understand and to comprehend and to replace that violence, that stain of bloodshed that has spread across our land, with an effort to understand with compassion and love.
>
> For those of who you are black and are tempted to be filled with hatred . . . I can only say that I feel in my own heart the same kind of feeling. I had a member of my family killed, but he was killed by a white man. We have to make an effort to understand, to go beyond these rather difficult times.*

John Lewis was astounded; in the years they had spent together, Lewis never heard Kennedy publicly discuss his brother's assassination. Lewis watched as the now hushed spectators listened to Kennedy:

> We've had difficult times in the past. We will have difficult times in the future. It is not the end of violence. It is not the end of disorder.
>
> The vast majority of white people and the vast majority of black people in this country want to live together, want to improve the

---

*Describing Kennedy's speech as an example of "the rhetoric of control," Karl Anatol and John Bittner of Purdue University deemed his master touch to be creating empathy with the audience by drawing on his own experience. Kennedy's phrase "I feel in my own heart" was repeatedly quoted when people in the audience were interviewed that night. The speech, carried on TV and radio, was a pivotal moment in the 1968 campaign. "Kennedy created a new, or accentuated an already existing 'image' that appealed to the Black community," write Anatol and Bittner.

quality of our life, and want justice for all human beings who abide in our land.

Let us dedicate ourselves to what the Greeks wrote so many years ago: to tame the savageness of man and to make gentle the life of this world.

Let us dedicate ourselves to that, and say a prayer for our country and our people.

After Kennedy's speech, the campaign team went to their hotel. Lewis watched as Kennedy lay facedown on a hotel bed and wept. After a while the candidate got up, spoke with some of his staffers, and went to the phone—attempting to reach Mrs. King.

Atlanta Symphony Hall, 8:15 p.m.

Just before the Atlanta Symphony Orchestra started their evening performance, the conductor announced the news of King's death to the audience. Over at the Martel Homes housing project in East Point, Charles Weltner, the congressman who gave up his seat rather than support the gubernatorial bid of Lester Maddox,* was meeting with a group of resident activists. "There was stunned silence," he told the *Atlanta Constitution*, describing the reaction to news of King's death. On Auburn Avenue, the audience leaving a show at the Royal Peacock Lounge heard about the assassination and immediately made their way across the street to the offices of the black-owned newspaper *Atlanta Daily World*, desperate for updates.

Ron English, a student at the Interdenominational Theological Center and the associate pastor at Ebenezer Baptist Church, was driving to the library at Emory University to do some research. When a radio bulletin announced King's death, English instinctively wanted to drive to the airport and get to Memphis; he had flight privileges thanks to a part-time job at Delta. Instead he drove to Ebenezer, where he found grieving congregants clustered around the front door.

---

*Georgia's political rules at the time required all Democrats to sign a "loyalty oath" supporting the gubernatorial bid of their party's nominee. Weltner refused to support Lester Maddox and as a result lost his seat in Congress.

Ron English had known Martin—whom he and most friends and family members called M.L.—all his life. The Englishes were stalwarts of the Ebenezer congregation. Ron's parents, Jethro and Auretha, sang at the senior Kings' wedding ceremony. Ron drew on his long relationship with the family as he navigated the tricky terrain as the junior pastor in a church dominated by the older, politically powerful Daddy King and his charismatic, celebrity son.

As Ron consoled congregants at the doors of Ebenezer, he recalled words he'd exchanged with M.L. just days earlier. English and Daddy King disagreed about the church's youth ministry and Ron asked M.L. to weigh in. "As soon as I'm back from Memphis, we'll talk," Martin had promised. As Ron comforted others, he tried to grasp the reality that he would never have that conversation.

In the Burge Apartments near the campus of Georgia Tech, where her father was an architecture professor, Maria Saporta heard the news on the radio. Maria's parents had both survived the Holocaust and, after moving to Atlanta, actively supported the civil rights movement. Maria and Yolanda King were classmates at Spring Street Elementary School, and Maria often spent the night at the King home.

The Saporta family listened quietly to the radio. No one had the energy to make dinner, so they headed out to a restaurant. On their way down in the elevator, they met a neighbor from the apartment building, also on his way out. He was accompanied by a group of friends.

"Martin Luther King has been shot!" the neighbor shouted to the Saportas. "We're going out celebrating!"

By just after eight that evening, 60 percent of Atlanta residents knew King had been shot. By eight the next morning, 97 percent of the city would know he was dead, according to Emory University researchers, who declared it the fastest dissemination of news Atlanta had ever experienced.

Kathryn Johnson idly watched the windshield wipers as her date drove to the movie. When the news came on the radio, her date, without pausing to ask, turned the car around and headed for Sunset Avenue. The only female reporter in Atlanta's Associated Press bureau, Johnson had become friends with the King family when she was assigned to cover a strike at Atlanta-based Scripto Pen Company that started during Thanksgiving weekend 1964. King, by then internationally famous as an activist, kept a relatively low profile in his hometown, through an agreement with his dad and other lions of the local black leadership. However, when the mostly female workforce at Scripto—whose leaders included Mary Gurley, an influential congregant at Ebenezer Baptist Church—went on strike demanding better wages, Martin Luther King Jr. had got involved.*

On a cold night, as she left the picket lines, Kathryn was surprised when King approached and offered to walk her to her car.

"This is not a good neighborhood," he warned.

The neighborhood was, in fact, where King grew up—the pen factory operated just blocks from Ebenezer Baptist Church.† In return for the company, Johnson offered to drive King home. When they reached the house, Coretta invited Kathryn in for coffee and cake. The three of them talked into the night.

The next morning Kathryn and her mother sat in their den watching television, and Kathryn saw jerky news footage of herself and King walking away from the picket line. Her mother turned to the young reporter and said, "Someday, someone is going to try to kill that man."

Now, as her date dropped her off at the Kings' home, Kathryn Johnson saw that other reporters, including one from the *New York Times*, were there already, and she had to push her way toward the door. Coretta King spotted her from inside the house. "Let Kathryn in," she said. Johnson followed Mrs. King—who had changed from her dress, coat, and gold hat into a pink robe and slippers—to the back bedroom, where Yolanda sat on her parents' bed watching television. Yolanda's hair was tightly rolled in plastic curlers. Kathryn could tell that the girl struggled to not cry. When a photographer came in the room, Kathryn rolled off the bed and

---

*Among the critics of King's actions during the Scripto strike had been KKK Grand Dragon Calvin Craig, who said King was "overstepping the bounds of Christianity" by getting involved.

†The former site of the Scripto plant is now part of the King Historic District near downtown Atlanta. The land where the factory stood is now the parking lot for a visitors center operated by the National Parks Service.

hid on the far side, making sure she was undetected behind the bedspread. As a reporter, she did not want to make herself part of the story.

After the photographer left, Kathryn got back on the bed and watched the breaking news from Memphis. It was eerie. Kathryn knew King's daughter must ache inside, but unsure of what to say to the girl, Kathryn simply sat with her in companionable silence.

Walter Cronkite opened the CBS evening newscast with a forthright statement: "Dr. Martin Luther King, the apostle of nonviolence, has been shot to death in Memphis, Tennessee. Police have issued an all-points bulletin for a well-dressed young white man seen running from the scene."

The newscast cut from Cronkite to the White House press office. The black-and-white film exaggerated President Johnson's deeply creased cheeks, heavily lidded eyes, and somber expression. "America is shocked and saddened by the brutal slaying tonight of Dr. Martin Luther King," he said.

By the time late-night news aired, cameras were at the Lorraine Motel. Police moved out across the crime scene, and King's stunned colleagues could be seen entering the motel. Networks played clips of King's famous speeches and the dramatic sermon he had given just the night before, when he had arrived in Memphis in support of a sanitation workers' strike.

King's April 3 journey to Memphis was his second visit to the city in less than a week. On March 28, King had taken part in a march at the request of Memphis pastors and union leaders. That march was poorly planned and devolved into violence. More than one hundred people were arrested, and a black teenager, accused by police of looting, was shot and killed. Chaos escalated as businesses were looted. Some suspected that government plants had instigated the disorder. In the aftermath of the failed march, FBI director J. Edgar Hoover—who had for years spied on King and his colleagues, convinced King was embroiled in Communist plots and engaged in moral lassitude—leaked reports to the media that triggered increased controversy over King's antiwar activities and his crusade against poverty.

King had returned to Memphis to lead a second march scheduled for April 5. He was determined to prove that it could be nonviolent and successful. Expectations were high. Arriving late on the evening of April 3 (his plane had been delayed by a bomb threat), King spoke to the strikers and their supporters. Creating a comparison between his experience as a civil rights leader with that of the biblical Moses,* King told the audience:

> We've got some difficult days ahead. But it doesn't really matter to me now, because I've been to the mountaintop. . . . Like anybody I would like to live a long life . . . but I'm not concerned. . . . I've looked over, and I've seen the Promised Land. I may not get there with you. But I want you to know tonight, that we, as a people, will get to the Promised Land. So I'm happy tonight. I'm not worried about anything. I'm not fearing any man. Mine eyes have seen the glory of the coming of the Lord.

Now that King was dead, news programs aired that speech repeatedly. Watching as King's impassioned face filled the television screen and the lighting cast a halo about his head, Ron English thought, *A Hollywood director could not have staged this better.*

Governor's Mansion, Atlanta, 9 p.m.

It still rained hard, and a drenched reporter waited at the guard station at the front gates of the mansion, a twenty-four-thousand-square-foot Greek Revival behemoth on Buckhead's West Paces Ferry Road. The reporter pleaded with the guards to let him in so he could get a comment from Governor Lester Maddox. The voluble chief executive of Georgia usually handed out sound bites eagerly. Tonight he was refusing to talk to the press about King's shooting. You have to wait, the guards instructed.

Reticence from Governor Maddox was surprising. For decades, he made no secret of his rabid commitment to segregation and his disagree-

---

*After leading the Israelites out of slavery and through the wilderness for forty years, Moses came close to the promised land of Canaan, but was punished by God and not allowed to complete the journey. "Yet thou shalt see the land before thee; but thou shalt not go thither unto the land which I give the children of Israel," God told him (Deuteronomy 32:52). On God's instructions, Moses climbed to the top of Mount Nebo, which offered a view of Canaan. Shortly after he saw the promised land from that mountaintop, Moses died. Joshua, one of Moses' aides, led the Israelites into their new homeland.

ment with King's methods and philosophy. But the reporter would get no outrageous statement tonight, and after an hour he left the soggy mansion guardhouse.

At almost midnight Maddox finally issued a statement. He said although he condemned King's assassination, the civil rights leader's death was not a surprise. Civil disobedience as practiced by King and his followers, said the Georgia governor, "builds the foundation" for "launched disorder and lawlessness."

Memphis Police Department, between 9 and 10 p.m.

Police reports would describe a "bundle" left in the doorway of Canipe's Amusements, a bar whose South Main Street entrance faced the Lorraine Motel. Members of the Tactical Squad dug through the bundle and found a Remington 760 Gamemaster rifle, underwear, toiletries, two cans of beer, a pair of binoculars—and a receipt for their purchase from York Arms Company in Memphis. After they made notes of these items, the Tactical Squad shipped the bundle of evidence to Washington, D.C.

A white Mustang was reported heading away from the Lorraine at a high speed within a half hour of the shooting, and witnesses reported seeing a sharp-faced, puny white man in the area. Within days, the main suspect was a thin, dark-haired white man who'd registered at a rooming house under the name John Willard, paying $8 up front for a week's rent on a room. The communal second-floor bathroom in the rooming house provided an almost direct shot to the balcony outside King's room at the Lorraine at a distance of just 205 feet.

Police were on the scene within seconds of King's being shot. Plainclothes officers had tailed King and his cohorts from the moment they arrived in Memphis, staking out the motel, church, and other places on King's itinerary. When Ralph Abernathy, Andrew Young, and King's brother, A.D., arrived at St. Joseph after following the ambulance, cops were already everywhere, lining the halls outside King's hospital room and standing guard at the ER entrance.

After King was pronounced dead and his body taken to a funeral home, the inner circle went back to the Lorraine. Bright lights flooded the parking lot as crime scene investigators moved through the area. Spectators gawked from the far side of South Main, and news and television cameras captured the tableau. FBI agents worked the scene as well. Despite the presence of all these investigators, Theatrice Bailey, brother of motel owner Walter Bailey, was vigorously scrubbing the balcony, trying to clean up the blood that had puddled everywhere.

Young, Hosea Williams, Abernathy, King's brother, King's assistant Bernard Lee, and other supporters crowded into King's motel room, number 306, smoking, drinking coffee, and eating potato chips. They debated what to do next. They agreed to try to place as many media calls as possible, asking that King's commitment to nonviolence be stressed. "The dreamer has been killed, but not the dream" was the message they crafted, said Andrew Young. But they struggled to get through to newsroom switchboards. "No one wanted to hear from us," said Young decades later. "They had made up their minds about the story." And as Young and the others could tell from watching the news, the preferred story was about rioting in response to King's death.

Hosea Williams, the brash and boisterous field coordinator for the Poor People's Campaign, did get a call through to the *Atlanta Constitution*, where he recounted the shooting and the SCLC's pledge to move on with the campaign. "Let's not burn America down," he stated.

But overall, there was little media coverage of the SCLC team in Memphis. A staffer with the *Memphis Commercial Appeal* photographed Jesse Jackson—the charismatic and youthful organizer of SCLC's Chicago Operation Breadbasket program—talking with detectives. Later that night, Jackson flew back to Chicago and from the airport gave a television interview. Blood was on his brown suede jacket and splattered on his green turtleneck.*

"The black people have lost their Moses," Jackson said. "The white people have lost their best friend."

----

*Later, some SCLC members accused Jackson of calling a press conference while the others accompanied King's body to the hospital. The Reverend Samuel "Billy" Kyles, the local minister who had been at the Lorraine to gather King and his cohorts for dinner, insisted that Jackson had merely been at the motel when the detectives and the press appeared. Reporters approached Jackson, Kyles said; the minister had not summoned them. Likewise, Jackson was en route to Chicago—alert to the potential for riots there and to organize a contingent from Chicago to Atlanta for the funeral—when press flocked around him at the airport.

Seventeenth Street area, Washington, D.C., around 10:30 p.m.

While the plane circled for landing, Bernard LaFayette looked out the cabin window and saw fires dotting the cityscape below. As he left the airport, he learned that King had been shot and killed. LaFayette, SCLC national field-operations director, was returning to the organization's D.C. headquarters from Memphis to continue planning for the convergence of protesters on the U.S. capital that would be part of the upcoming Poor People's Campaign. LaFayette had started his civil rights work as a student organizer and Freedom Rider and spent eight years with the movement, during which he was beaten, jailed, and once pursued by the Klan. Instrumental in organizing the Selma voter-registration campaign, LaFayette became a logistics expert and coordinated dozens of sit-ins, marches, protests, and rallies. The Poor People's Campaign was to be his biggest project yet. In addition to wrangling thousands of protesters in Washington, D.C., the campaign was to feature dozens of mule wagons, symbols of rural poverty. While LaFayette had experience organizing marchers, he still was unsure how to get ninety pairs of mules from the rural South to the Washington Mall.

Mules seemed beside the point when he walked through Washington, D.C., tonight. Rioting overwhelmed this section of the city. Windows were shattered. Buildings were aflame. People ran down the center of the street clutching armloads of looted food, clothes, shoes, and liquor bottles.

LaFayette passed a storefront that a young man had just shattered with a Molotov cocktail. As flames licked through the shop, the man screamed hysterically, "My grandmother is inside that building! She's on the second floor. I was so angry I didn't think before I set the fire."

The man screamed for passersby to help him put out the fire that he had started. LaFayette kept walking. He could not believe that King, whom he had seen just a few hours earlier, was dead. He could not believe the reaction erupting around him. King's death was announced by radio at 8:19 that Thursday night, and by 9:25 rioters shattered the first window. By midnight, the fire department logged at least a hundred blazes.

Rioters moved south down Fourteenth Street like "killer bees in a horror movie," remembered Bob King, a short-order cook who watched from his home near the intersection of Fourteenth and Harvard streets.

In a "live mass," the mob swarmed down the street "charging and chanting 'burn this mother down.'" Bob King stayed up all night guarding his home. He resisted the temptation to join the looters, although the free-wheeling chaos created an almost party-like atmosphere that was alluring.

As Bernard LaFayette strode through Washington, D.C., he spotted a familiar figure amid the turmoil: Stokely Carmichael. Lithe, elegant, and commanding, Carmichael moved through the congested streets and called for people to be calm. The irony that Carmichael—proponent of the Black Power slogan and reviled by most white media as a threatening symbol of black militancy—was urging rioters to keep their cool was not lost on LaFayette.

When he reached his hotel, LaFayette called Memphis.

"Get to Atlanta as fast as you can," he was told. "We've got to get ready for a funeral."

Atlanta Police Headquarters, 11 p.m.

The bulletin about King's being shot arrived just as Police Chief Herbert T. Jenkins met with his senior staff to finalize strategies for defusing riots that were expected to occur in the coming summer, exacerbated by heat and bored kids out of school for the long vacation. While Atlanta had seen less destruction, damage, and loss of life than such cities as Detroit, Newark, or Los Angeles, Jenkins wanted to be prepared. Jenkins was a tall, sturdy man grown stout in middle age, whose shock of white hair and emphatic black eyebrows framed a sturdy face and a quick, broad smile. The consummate city cop, he had dropped out of high school to join the force in 1931, following the path of his father, an Atlanta motorcycle officer. Jenkins moved into the top job in 1947. The year after becoming chief, he hired Atlanta's first black officers. The initial recruits were not issued weapons and had no authority to arrest whites. Because facilities were segregated, the black officers used the changing rooms at the Butler Street YMCA to get ready for duty. Over the next two decades, Jenkins would move closer to true integration, giving black officers the authority to arrest whites, and making sure officers shared the same facilities.

Like Mayor Ivan Allen, Police Chief Jenkins underwent a gradual evolution in attitudes about race. Hiring the first black officers in the 1940s had been a response to pressure from leaders such as John Wesley Dobbs, the Grand Master of the powerful Prince Hall Masons fraternal organization, and the Reverend William Holmes Borders, pastor of the influential Wheat Street Baptist Church. By the time Jenkins retired in the early 1970s, almost a quarter of the Atlanta force was black.*

As soon as he learned of the shooting in Memphis, the police chief dispatched officers to guard the King home in Vine City and the Collier Heights home of King's parents, with orders that officers were to be stationed twenty-four hours a day. He then called heads of his crime prevention (CP) division to get a sense of the mood of the city and to gauge the best way to respond. Assigning officers to communities where they lived, interacted with residents, and hosted sporting events and picnics was one of Jenkins's innovative tactics. The concept of the CP program was to foster better relations between the police and low-income communities. Generations of mistreatment of blacks, especially poor blacks, at the hands of the city's white police force had created rifts. As part of their mission to transform attitudes toward the police from fearful and confrontational to cooperative and respectful, the interracial team of CP officers had, for instance, started eight baseball teams in communities that had few recreational facilities, let alone leagues for kids. "These policemen also speak to PTAs, church and civic clubs, talk to people in their homes, in the groceries, laundries, and bars. They may know all of the gamblers and bootleggers in the neighborhoods, but they still make no arrests," declared a statement issued by Captain Morris Redding six months into the CP program. While progress occurred on the Atlanta police force, racial discrimination was far from eliminated. In 1968, police arrested blacks under seventeen for burglary and larceny at more than double the rates for white youths and arrested adult black men on weapons charges at three times the rate for white men.†

---

*Jenkins's retirement was controversial. Law required the police chief to step down at age sixty-five; Sam Massell, who succeeded Allen as mayor, created a loophole by giving Jenkins a new title—police commissioner.

†According to the Atlanta Police Department annual report for 1968, 247 white youths under the age of 17 were arrested for burglary, compared to 661 blacks, while 510 white youths were booked on larceny charges compared to 1,173 blacks. Only 357 white men

Jenkins had a personal stake in avoiding conflict. He had been the only Southerner, and only police officer, on the eleven-person commission on urban riots appointed by President Lyndon Johnson and headed by Otto Kerner, governor of Illinois.* The National Advisory Commission on Civil Disorders—commonly referred to as the Kerner Commission—had released a report on its findings just weeks before King's death. The Kerner Report affronted white America by placing the blame for urban riots on white racism and entrenched patterns of discrimination. "Segregation and poverty have created in the racial ghetto a destructive environment totally unknown by most white Americans," the commission members concluded. "What white Americans have never fully understood—but what the Negro can never forget—is that white society is deeply implicated in the ghetto. White institutions created it, white institutions maintain it, and white society condones it." The commission offered prescriptive suggestions for alleviating urban problems that focused on employment, education, and housing. Their recommendations also included law enforcement tactics based on Jenkins's experiences in Atlanta, including keeping arrests to a minimum and reducing outward displays of force, such as carrying large weapons or wearing excessive riot gear.

Following the publication of the *Kerner Report,* Atlanta's top cop was pleased to receive a telegram from Martin Luther King:

> You, as a member of the President's Commission on Civil Disorders, deserve the gratitude of the nation because you had both the wisdom to perceive the truth and the courage to state it. The

---

were arrested on weapons charges, compared to 1,133 black men, although double the number of white men (26,149) were charged with drunkenness compared to blacks (13,074).

*The other nine commission members included only two African-Americans—Roy Wilkins, director of the NAACP, and Senator Edward W. Brooke, a Republican from Massachusetts. The one woman on the panel was Katherine Graham Peden, Kentucky commissioner of commerce. The rest of the commission members were I. W. Abel, president of the United Steelworkers of America; Charles B. Thornton, chairman of Litton Industries, then a major military manufacturer; John Lindsay, mayor of New York City; Senator Fred R. Harris, a Democrat from Oklahoma; Congressmen James C. Corman, a Democrat from California; and William M. McCulloch, a Republican from Ohio.

commission's findings that America is a racist society and that white racism is the root cause of today's urban disorders is an important confession of a harsh truth. My only hope is that white America and our national government will heed your warnings and implement your recommendations. By ignoring them we will sink inevitably into a nightmarish doomsday. God grant that your excellent report will educate the nation and lead to action before it is too late.

Days after the report was released, the *New York Times* and Bantam Books produced a paperback version that became a bestseller. By the week of King's assassination, *The Complete Text: The Kerner Report*—six-hundred-plus pages including dense charts documenting poverty, housing, and crime statistics—was already in its eighth printing; there would eventually be twenty-one. (A hardcover version from E. P. Dutton also sold well.) The government data was accompanied by a pictorial supplement titled "Eyewitness to Crisis." Some thirty pages of photographs depicted ghetto conditions, riot scenes, and National Guard deployments in the streets of Newark and Detroit. In an introduction, the *Times*'s Tom Wicker noted that the composition of the commission, mostly white and mostly moderate, raised questions at first. "Where, the critics demanded, were Stokely Carmichael, Floyd McKissick, Martin Luther King, such white radicals as Tom Hayden or such fiery evangelists as James Baldwin?" Wicker wrote. Jenkins, top cop in a Southern city, was assumed to be conservative, but Wicker observed, "The policeman surprised other members with his acute sensitivity to such matters, and his progressive and compassionate approach."

Wicker concluded that hearing criticism from one of their own such as Jenkins might serve as a better wake-up call for middle-American whites than if the message came from more radical sources. He noted, "Reading it is an ugly experience but one that brings, finally, something like the relief of beginning. What had to be said has been said at last, and by representatives of that white, moderate, responsible America that alone needed to say it."

As Chief Jenkins received bulletins about the riots starting in Washington, D.C., he feared that the "nightmarish doomsday" King prophesied in his telegram would become true. Jenkins put into action the antiriot plan formulated as a preventative measure for the summer. Police went on twelve-hour shifts; members of Jenkins's CP units went into black neighborhoods and offered help to community groups. Although the Atlanta Police Department had vetted the plans for months, the chief felt there was "no rule book." He urged his officers to be flexible.

Atlanta City Hall, close to midnight

When Mayor Ivan Allen arrived at his office after leaving Coretta King's home, he found a flurry of activity. In addition to the city staff, employees from the mayor's family-owned business, the Ivan Allen Company, an office-furniture and supply company, came to help. One of these was Marie Dodd, director of advertising. She arrived to find a "wild" scene. Phones rang constantly and reporters crowded into the pressroom down the hall. Vice Mayor Sam Massell manned the switchboard along with Linda Mullá, an administrative assistant barely in her twenties. Calls came in from all over the world. Everyone wanted to know how Atlanta would respond to King's death. What were the plans for the funeral?

From City Hall, Allen tried repeatedly to reach the president. By the time he was patched through to the Oval Office at 11 p.m., he knew about the riots in Washington, D.C., He felt compelled to assure the president there would not be rioting in Atlanta.

"We've been through these situations before; I think we can cope with them. We're doing everything we can to hold our house in order," Allen told President Johnson.

"Well, you're mighty good and I have confidence in you," said LBJ. "I called Mrs. King—"

"I was with Mrs. King when you called," the mayor interrupted. He told the president about his trip to and from the airport.

"You've done a wonderful job," said the president. "I hope you let me know if you have any suggestions. We have a little problem in Durham and one here in Washington."

They talked for a while about the president's decision not to run for reelection. Allen sent his regards to Mrs. Johnson, and the president put her on the phone.

"Mayor?" said Lady Bird Johnson.

"Hello, Mrs. President. How are you?" asked the mayor.

"Troubled and sad. But God bless those who keep on strivin' and tryin', and you're surely among 'em."

"Thank you, ma'am."

Shortly afterward, the mayor took a call from Robert Woodruff and Carl Sanders. They had tried to reach him ever since learning, at the Oval Office, that King was shot.

"Whatever you need will be taken care of," Robert Woodruff told the mayor.

Years later Woodruff would be revealed as "Mr. Anonymous," the secret benefactor of many Atlanta nonprofit and civic fund-raising efforts. But he was better known to his contemporaries in the Atlanta business community as "the Boss"—the city's most influential corporate citizen. Woodruff promised the mayor that he would help with any expenses that King's funeral would create outside the scope of the city's regular budget.

Before he hung up, the soft-drink tycoon cautioned the mayor, "Ivan, the minute they bring King's body back tomorrow—between then and the time of the funeral—Atlanta, Georgia, is going to be the center of the universe."

TWO

Friday, April 5, 1968

President Johnson and civil rights leaders meet in the Cabinet Room of the White House on April 5 to discuss ways to thwart the spread of riots. *LBJ Library photo by Yoichi R. Okamoto*

The White House, 1:05 a.m.

LYNDON JOHNSON'S STAFF canceled the president's planned trip to Honolulu for talks about the Vietnam War. Instead, aides worked the phones late into the night, preparing a home-front strategy. The riots in Washington, D.C., were threatening enough. What would happen if this kind of violence spread beyond a few large cities? The White House staff organized a meeting with civil rights leaders, looking for ways to quell riots. The last call LBJ made before going to sleep was to Whitney Young, executive director of the National Urban League, top on the list of leaders invited to the meeting. Young, a skilled mediator who maintained a careful nonpartisan stance, became an adviser the president trusted—a biographer would later write that LBJ "adored" the politically savvy Young, who had vowed that the Urban League would keep its distance from organizations that "formally adopted black power as a program, or which [tied] in domestic civil rights with the Vietnam conflict." In other words, distance from both militant Stokely Carmichael and pacifist King.

While the president slept, his staff continued to place calls. Conspicuously absent from the invitee list were the names of any of King's inner circle—either those who had been with him in Memphis or back in Atlanta. King's increasingly vocal criticism of the Vietnam War and his plans for the Poor People's Campaign were branding him a radical, a label that extended to his associates. The Poor People's Campaign intertwined the issues of poverty and the war.

In a press conference a few days before his death, King suggested that negotiations with the government might prevent the need for the Poor People's Campaign. "I would be glad to talk to President Johnson or anyone else. But I wouldn't say that a mere statement that just something will be done—just a pat on the back—would cause us to call off the march," he told reporters. On that same Sunday King delivered his antiwar sermon and held the press conference, the influential *New York Times Magazine* ran a lengthy article about the campaign, which it referred to as "King's March on Washington, Part II," an allusion to the famous 1963 march and King's "Dream" speech.

Those invited to the president's meeting represented the old-guard civil rights movement, the people and organizations Johnson felt most comfortable with, including Roy Wilkins, executive director of the NAACP; Clarence Mitchell Jr., the NAACP chief lobbyist, and his son, Clarence Mitchell III, a SNCC cofounder and Maryland state senator; Leon Higginbotham, the Philadelphia district judge; the Reverend Leon Sullivan of Philadelphia's Zion Baptist Church; and Bishop George Baber of Detroit's Ebenezer AME Church. Of course, many of those leaders also had ties to King. Sullivan's economic boycott and self-help techniques were the foundation of SCLC's Operation Breadbasket economic empowerment program, and Higginbotham had, along with Coretta Scott, been among the first black students to attend Antioch College. But the roster excluded King's closest colleagues, like Andrew Young and Ralph Abernathy. As *Jet*'s Simeon Booker noted, the leaders summoned to the emer-

gency gathering were heads of "traditional" organizations, and many
opposed King's planned Poor People's Campaign or, as Booker dubbed it,
"camp in."

One person close to King—his father—did make the guest list. At
around 2 a.m. White House staff assistant Jim Gaither reached Daddy
King. Gaither, at the president's instruction, said that the president's
prayers were with the King family and asked what the president could do
to help. Daddy King replied, "That's not the question. The question is,
what can I do for the president?" The senior King said that at the advice
of his wife, daughter, and nurses, he would decline the invitation. He was
quite ill, and his family pleaded with him not to travel. Also, he wanted to
be in Atlanta when his son's body was returned from Memphis.

The King home on Sunset Avenue, about 2 a.m.

The two phones in the King home rang constantly. Xernona Clayton
screened calls using the phone in the front of the house; if the caller proved
to be someone she thought should be put through, Mrs. King would
answer the line in the back bedroom. Clayton thought, *Everyone is working
from the same script.* It seemed she took the same call over and over: "This is
Senator So-and-So. This is Mr. So-and-So. I'm just calling to say we heard
the news, we're so sorry, let us know if there's anything we can do to help."

After hours of fielding messages, Clayton picked up the receiver to
hear a familiar and distinctive voice. Without preamble the caller said,
"This is Robert Kennedy. It's obvious you need more phone lines; we've
been trying to call you since six o'clock."

Before Clayton could respond, the senator informed her that a telephone technician was being sent to the King home and would resolve the
problem. "He'll be there this morning to install adequate phone lines,"
said Kennedy, going on to give Clayton the technician's name and the
work-order specifics. Then he continued, "I heard on the news that Mrs.
King would like to go to Memphis. So we've arranged for a private plane.
It will be at hangar two of the Atlanta airport in the morning."

He gave Clayton the tail number and the pilot's name. She listened,
thinking, *Everyone else said, "If there is anything I can do, let me know." He isn't
waiting for us to ask; he knows what we need.* Before hanging up, Kennedy

instructed Clayton to call every hotel in downtown Atlanta and ask that blocks of rooms be reserved for diplomats and international dignitaries. He offered to help manage the needed protocols. "My family has experience in dealing with this kind of thing," he added in a matter-of-fact understatement.*

Clayton directed the next call to Mrs. King without hesitation. Harry Belafonte. Long before King earned national notoriety leading the 1955–56 Montgomery bus boycott, Belafonte openly criticized the Jim Crow South by refusing to perform in segregated venues. An early supporter of the Kings, the singer-actor put up bail for King's 1963 arrest in Birmingham. Belafonte spoke at the March on Washington that summer, and at King's request took on another role—"Coordinator of the Celebrity Plane," marshaling well-known faces and voices to D.C. to boost media attention. Over the past decade, Belafonte's New York apartment had served as a refuge for King—particularly as King's outspoken criticism of the Vietnam War and his calls for economic justice led to intensified scrutiny by the FBI and escalating tension with the White House. Belafonte shared King's antiwar stance; in April 1967, he joined King and famed pediatrician Benjamin Spock to lead one hundred thousand antiwar protesters on a march through New York City. In February 1968, just weeks before his death, King joined Belafonte for an appearance on the *Tonight* show.

Belafonte's outspoken conviction was no secret to the millions of Middle Americans who loved his calypso-tinged hits and recognized the lankily handsome performer from movies and television specials. He frequently took to the stage at civil rights rallies. But it would surprise most Americans to later learn that Belafonte shared another distinction with King's inner circle: Belafonte had also been wiretapped by the government.†

---

*In a 2009 interview, I asked Clayton if it struck her as odd that Kennedy would arbitrarily send phone technicians to the house, given the FBI wiretapping of the Kings' phone lines that Kennedy had, as attorney general, authorized. No, Clayton said. The installation of extra phone lines during a crisis seemed to be simply a "practical necessity." As for wiretapping, her experience traveling with Mrs. King and being close to the family was that by this time they had come to see bugging as an inevitable consequence of public life and assumed few conversations were private.

†"We knew we were wiretapped by J. Edgar Hoover and his boys, and this fact gave us no end of inventive ways to pass along sensitive information," Belafonte would later say

Belafonte, the first black man to win an Emmy (for the 1959 special *Tonight with Belafonte*), had bonded with Coretta King over a shared passion for music. Mrs. King had studied at the New England Conservatory of Music in Boston and had, before getting married, planned a career as a performer. Coretta King and Belafonte first met at a 1956 fund-raising concert held in New York in support of the Montgomery Improvement Association. At the concert, Mrs. King sang classics and spirituals including "Your Hand on the Plow" and "Honor, Honor," while Belafonte and Duke Ellington also performed. From then on, Mrs. King considered Belafonte "one of our truest friends." The singer provided practical and financial support for Mrs. King. Recognizing the strain faced by a young mother of four children whose husband was constantly on the road (when he was not in jail on civil disobedience charges), Belafonte paid for a maid and a housekeeper to assist Coretta.

Now, in a late-night call, Belafonte promised that he would once again help in any way needed. "I want to come down there tomorrow to be with you and the children. I just want to be there at your side and do any little menial thing," he said. "I want to share this sorrow with you, and I want you to know you can call on me for anything you need."

in an interview that was part of the *Eyes on the Prize* PBS series. "However, in some cases there were people who we saw as allies to our cause, who we thought were people of fundamental goodwill, who were involved in wiretapping. . . . To learn that the Kennedys, Bobby Kennedy and people in the Justice Department's civil rights division, were wiretapping us was a painful discovery."

Asked if he thought that Hoover's monitoring of King represented a "vendetta," Ramsey Clark would say, "I think there's something to that. I think it's something of great concern. Dr. King had really incurred some very ill feeling from Mr. Hoover. . . . And there were months and months, even several years, where you couldn't talk very long with Mr. Hoover without him bitterly criticizing Dr. King as being an immoral person, a bad person." Lyndon Johnson had, in June 1965, prohibited wiretapping. That did not stop the FBI from continuing to request permission from Ramsey Clark to install bugs—including on King and his associates. "I never granted any," Clark would say in a 1969 oral history interview recorded at the Lyndon Johnson Library. However, Hoover's vendetta persisted. "My recollection is that there was a request as late as April 2, 1968," Clark said.

Khesanh, the mountains of South Vietnam,
early morning (local time)

About two miles from base camp, a marine patrol crested a hill. North Vietnamese army (NVA) soldiers charged and the marines fired back. On the way back to camp, the U.S. Marines counted ninety-three NVA corpses trapped in the makeshift barbed-wire fence erected around base camp. It was one of the first sorties on foot attempted since the siege at Khesanh* had started January 21. Soldiers decided to risk the sortie because a few days earlier the military had announced Operation Pegasus, an effort to relieve the besieged fighters at Khesanh. Some twenty thousand to thirty thousand forces were headed to Khesanh by the road dubbed Route 9, which wound through the hills and rough terrain in the remote area near the Laotian border.

Over the past seven weeks, six thousand marines and South Vietnamese soldiers had been under siege, as forty thousand NVA forces surrounded their hilly fortress. Bridges on the road to camp were destroyed, and the thick jungle and red clay hills around Khesanh were riddled with mines and trenches. By March, 90 percent of supplies had to be airlifted in, and injured fighters were evacuated under enemy fire. It became so treacherous that one of the last C-130 cargo planes to arrive at Khesanh did not even land, but just grazed the airstrip as its cargo door opened and a marine drove a truck out of the hold while the plane continued at fifty-five miles an hour. The trench-warfare conditions hearkened to World War I, but a modern aresenal made the fighting more deadly. In two months, the twenty-four thousand American bombing missions around Khesanh dropped more explosives than had been used in all of 1942 and 1943 across Europe in World War II.

The longest and deadliest battle of the war, Khesanh dominated newspaper and television reports throughout the winter and early spring of 1968. In early 1968, Khesanh coverage represented a quarter of all broadcast news segments, and fully 50 percent of reporting on CBS. At home,

---

*Today's histories of the Vietnam War refer to the location as *Khe Sanh*. Most media reports in the 1960s used the Americanized spelling *Khesanh*. I have opted for the latter form because it is consistent with news sources cited, making for easier readability.

Americans tracked the experience of troops in Khesanh and learned about improvisations such as the Super Gaggle, a complex but speedy maneuver that required coordinating helicopters, fighter bombers, Huey gunships, and a command-and-control airship to deliver supplies. Television viewers watched as young men hunkered in underground bunkers, ate cold rations out of tin cans, and ducked at the sound of explosions. In Washington, Lyndon Johnson kept a model of the battleground—complete with sand and mud—in his Situation Room.

Political commentators and military analysts expressed fear that Khesanh could be "another Dien Bien Phu," referring to the 1954 siege of a French camp in the Vietnamese hill country that resulted in a French surrender to Viet Minh Communist forces. After the battle of Dien Bien Phu, Vietnam was divided into North and South. During the Dien Bien Phu siege, more than five thousand wounded French soldiers crammed into a base hospital designed for forty-two beds. At the end of the battle, ten thousand soldiers were taken captive; most died on death marches before reaching prison camps.

Echoes of Dien Bien Phu were easy to find in Khesanh. As in the first siege, North Vietnamese fighters created treacherous trenches around the Western force's base camp and fired at airborne reinforcements. Vo Nguyen Giap, NVA commander in 1968 and director of operations at Khesanh, was the same man who'd orchestrated the French defeat at Dien Bien Phu. Back then, Giap said, "The only military academy I have ever been to is that of the bush." His skill at maneuvering in the jungle was a reason the Khesanh siege was so brutal and so lengthy.

The ongoing siege at Khesanh contributed to public dissatisfaction with how the war was being waged. In February 1968, newsman Walter Cronkite traveled to Vietnam and in a break from objective reporting editorialized that the effort seemed "mired in stalemate." By March, a national poll showed 49 percent of Americans saying it was wrong to have sent U.S. troops to the conflict, and 69 percent supporting a "phase-out" plan to bring U.S. military back and turn the war over to South Vietnam. By March, just over a quarter of Americans gave LBJ a positive rating for his handling of the war.

Meanwhile, the number of U.S. forces in Vietnam surged from some fifteen thousand in 1964 to more than half a million by the end of 1967.

Reports that General Westmoreland thought the war was at a positive turning point were diminished by his request for more troops.

The national antiwar movement was gaining momentum and followers. Martin Luther King had simply been one of the most visible.

SCLC headquarters, Atlanta, early morning

Tom Houck, an SCLC field coordinator, was in Appalachia, assigned to recruit impoverished whites to join the Poor People's Campaign. When he learned of King's death, Houck drove all night to reach Atlanta. The scene he discovered at the SCLC office on Auburn Avenue was "discombobulating." Some people were drunk. Some were simply bewildered and trying to figure out what would happen next. Messages poured in from the bank of telex machines; rolls of paper cascaded to the office floor.

"Andy is in Memphis. Abernathy is in Memphis. Who's in charge?" Houck asked.

No one knew. Meanwhile, people lined up outside, desperate for news. Willie Bolden, who had been leading a protest in Social Circle, Georgia, also instinctively returned to Atlanta to man the SCLC headquarters. He stood at the office door with tears running down his face.

"I really don't know what to say," he told reporters.

Houck, a stocky Irish Catholic with a loud voice and thick South Boston accent, had dropped out of high school in 1964 to go to work for the SCLC's public-facilities protests in St. Augustine. Later he moved to Atlanta and worked as a driver for the King family, then became a field coordinator for SCLC. He was accustomed to the fluid concept of organization that defined movement activities, but had never seen such chaos. He pitched in, answering phones and organizing messages spitting out of the telex machines. He was relieved when Bernard LaFayette arrived from D.C. a few hours later and took charge. *Somebody needed to start coordinating things*, Houck thought.

It was no accident that both SCLC and SNCC were headquartered in Atlanta. The SCLC offices were on Auburn Avenue. The street had been dubbed Sweet Auburn decades earlier by John Wesley Dobbs, the Prince

Hall Masons grand master and an early black-voting-rights advocate. Dobbs and his wife, Irene, raised their six daughters in a big house on Houston Street, just a few blocks from the two-story Victorian home on Auburn Avenue where Daddy King raised M.L., A.D., and Christine. All six Dobbs daughters graduated from Spelman College, as did Christine King.

Known in the early 1950s as "the richest Negro street in America," Auburn Avenue was home to a network of black-owned shops, banks, businesses, concert halls, churches, funeral homes, insurance agents, restaurants, and hotels. The entrepreneurial spirit of Auburn Avenue and the educational richness of the Atlanta University Center helped Atlanta develop the largest, wealthiest, and best-educated black middle class in the country, providing the foundation of economic support for civil rights efforts as well as the talent pool to staff them. Long before Martin Luther King Jr. was born, Atlanta fostered civil rights pioneers, from one-time Atlanta University professor W. E. B. Du Bois, who cofounded the NAACP in 1909, to the Reverend William Holmes Borders and Grandmaster Dobbs, who led voter-registration campaigns and lobbied for police integration in the 1940s.

Unlike other Southern cities, without the educational and social infrastructure for a black community to thrive in spite of racial oppression, or cities in the North or West, where relatively new black populations were ghettoized by de facto segregation and economic oppression, Atlanta's African-Americans had the resources and infrastructure to function autonomously. For decades, black and white Atlanta existed in essentially parallel societies.

"What I noticed when I moved here was how proud black Atlanta was," recalled Bunnie Jackson-Ransom, who moved to the city with her fiancé Maynard Jackson Jr., grandson of John Wesley Dobbs. "Everything was here, banks, stores, restaurants, movies. We didn't have to worry about Peachtree Street or downtown; Hunter Street was our downtown. There was a feeling of pride and of independence."

The city's black community thrived in spite of huge obstacles, and in the 1960s Atlanta was by no means a place of equal opportunity. In the century since the Civil War, legal segregation and extralegal intimidation had kept the city's black population oppressed; data from 1961 showed that the average black family in Atlanta had a $3,307 annual income, less than half the average white family's $6,984. While 57 percent of whites were homeowners, only 19 percent of blacks were. More than three-quarters of the city's whites owned cars, but less than a third of blacks did. Law, custom, bank redlining, and zoning policies kept Atlanta's African-Americans in certain geographic areas—close to downtown, in the southwest part of the city, or near the black college campuses. Hiring policies kept most blacks restricted to blue-collar jobs and work as domestics. Over the preceding decade, white Atlantans had seen their incomes rise by a half, while African-Americans had seen an increase of less than a third.

From Auburn Avenue, looking toward downtown, the futuristic blue-glass Polaris restaurant on the top of the Regency-Hyatt hovered like a spacecraft over a skyline surging upward. In his City Hall office, Mayor Allen kept a growing collection of shiny decorative spades from ground-breaking ceremonies he'd presided over as mayor.* Many of those projects came at the expense of Atlanta's black community. The Downtown Connector expressway that routed Interstates 75 and 85 through Atlanta's core was created by demolishing a swath of Sweet Auburn, replacing street-front shops and family homes with an imposing concrete overpass that bisected the community and left rubble-strewn vacant lots amid the historic homes and businesses.

Breakfast tables across Atlanta, morning

Subscribers to the *Atlanta Constitution* woke up to a front-page editorial by publisher Ralph McGill titled "A Free Man Killed by White Slaves." Known as an advocate for civil rights, McGill wrote, "White slaves killed Dr. Martin Luther King in Memphis. At the moment the triggerman

---

*The new skyscrapers were dominated by the work of young architect John Portman, whose interconnected Peachtree Center towers were touted as the future of the modern workspace. Portman designed the Hyatt—Atlantans arriving for the grand opening were astounded by his innovative "indoor garden," a soaring atrium where interior balconies from the hotel's floors overlooked an expanse of potted plants and shiny tile, all accessed by a glass elevator that transported hotel guests for a see-and-be-seen rise upward. The radical design embraced the innovation that some sociologists claim transformed Atlanta more than any other—air-conditioning. Lingering on the balconies inside the Hyatt was for many a far more comfortable way to spend an evening than on the humid porch of a traditional Southern home or hotel.

fired, Martin Luther King was the free man. The white killer (or killers) was a slave to fear."

An angry subscriber called and told McGill's secretary, "I just want to say that the death of old King is the greatest news since the Second World War ended." Then he hung up with a bang. "That one symbolic call was, of course, from a spiritual brother in madness and hate to the killer," McGill would write in his next day's column.

McGill's mailbox would overflow with letters from readers in Atlanta and around the country (his columns were widely syndicated). A high percentage shared a view similar to that irate caller. "Many of us peace-loving, God-loving humans today unite in thanks to our God for delivering us and ridding humanity of one who has caused so much violence, bloodshed, and discord," stated one unsigned missive dated April 5. "We thank God that King is dead." On the same date, a writer from Mattapan, Massachusetts, wrote, "I hope your daughter, if you have one, gets raped by some godamn Niger [*sic*]." Joe Boozer sent McGill a telegram: "Your column accusing white people of racism has done more to bring about hate and violence than anything in this country." Douglas Williams of Toccoa, Georgia, wrote, "It is sad that Dr. Martin Luther King Jr. was shot in cold blood in America, but also he reaped exactly what he sowed. He taught people to disobey laws, and his assassin simply disobeyed the law against murder."

Other readers submitted tributes to King. Charles Gunter, a clerk at the Atlantic Steel mills, told McGill he was appalled by the comments from his white colleagues. "In the past week, I've tried not to hear the hate spewing out of the mouths of some of the workers here," he confided. Some people shared attempts at poetry. Mrs. Frances Isrel of Chamblee, an Atlanta suburb, wrote, "Why am I in mourning for a man I never knew? Why do I feel guilty when nothing I did do? . . . But wait! Instead of a parting let this be a gathering call to the black and white together, to each one and to all."

McGill was not the only media commentator to seize on the symbolism of King's death. Television reports of violence and fiery destruction in Washington, D.C., and other cities were intercut with equally dramatic footage of King's last speech in which he spoke of seeing "the promised land" of equality—even if he would not be able to complete the journey before dying. Commentators eagerly seized on the prophetic metaphor of the "mountaintop" speech and portrayed King as a martyr slain before his time. A barrage of media reports referred to King using terms such as "apostle," "Messiah," and "Moses."*

Editorial writers and commentators contrasted King—prophet of peace—and Stokely Carmichael—militant advocate of Black Power—as shorthand for the complexities of the debate within the civil rights movement over nonviolent civil disobedience versus militant activism and black nationalism. A story that ran on the front page of the *Atlanta Journal* the day after King's death suggested to readers that the assassination occurred when "[King] was locked in a life-and-death struggle to keep nonviolence as the major weapon in the Negro's arsenal." In a lengthy *New York Times* article the same day, Steven V. Roberts wrote, "The strategy of Dr. King and the conference has varied little, no matter what the issue. They have steadily espoused the ideal of nonviolence and have depended more on moral than political influence to win their battles." Roberts contrasted the SCLC credo of nonviolence with "angry statements by such young Negroes as H. Rap Brown and Stokely Carmichael."

City Hall, Washington D.C., early morning

Overnight, police arrested more than two hundred rioters and reported fifty injuries and one death. Disorder would escalate throughout Friday; by midday police logged 238 instances of vandalism and 153 looters, and the arrest total crept up to 274. City health-care centers overflowed; Freedmen's Hospital, the historic institution erected to serve blacks during the final days of the Civil War, became so crowded that it had to implement its disaster protocol. At one point, fifteen triage rooms operated simultaneously.

Smoke clogged the air and sirens wailed nonstop. By noon five thousand army troops and a thousand members of the National Guard moved into D.C. chanting, "March! March! March!" as they made their way

---

*For a fascinating analysis of the biblical metaphors applied to King—both when he was alive and after his death—read the Scott W. Hoffman essay "Holy Martin: The Overlooked Canonization of Dr. Martin Luther King, Jr.," *Religion and Culture*, 2000. "As the mantle of Moses and the cloak of Christ were placed on King's shoulders during his lifetime, the trappings of sainthood popularly were placed around his memory after his death," Hoffman writes (p. 137).

into rubble-strewn blocks congested by traffic jams and looters. Tourists took snapshots and home movies. Police officers fired tear gas to clear the streets so firefighters could approach burning businesses; in response, just-dispersed rioters pelted firemen with rocks. To avoid more retaliation, authorities rented U-Haul trucks to drop off police officers in the worst riot areas; the cops dubbed the trucks "Trojan horses."

Mayor Walter Washington issued a 5:30 p.m. to 6:30 a.m. curfew. The next day he would move the curfew up to 4 p.m.—by then 4 deaths had been reported, along with 2,686 arrests, 860 cases of looting, and 510 fires. The number of troops in the city doubled. The riot zone extended to within two blocks of the White House.

As he flew back to Washington from Memphis that Friday night, Attorney General Ramsey Clark asked the pilot to get as close to the scene as possible. The pilot flew low and circled the city several times. "It was one of the saddest sights you'll ever see," Clark would later say of the smoldering buildings and smoke-clogged air.

The White House, 9 a.m.

As soon as President Johnson woke up, he reviewed a fourteen-item talking-point memo that staff had prepared for his meeting with the civil rights leaders. They suggested opening with a strong statement about King's death (Talking Point 1: "We are meeting in the wake of a national tragedy. Martin King's voice has been stilled. What a bigot's word could never do, his bullet has done") and reminding the leaders about the president's work with King on civil rights legislation (Point 2: "I remember the time, three years ago, when Martin King's voice and presence raised the first right of freedom at Selma—the right of men to vote. And I remember the night in the Hall of the House when I spoke the words of the movement he led at Selma: 'We shall overcome.' And we did").

The staff advised Johnson to be candid about King's war dissension (Point 6: "He held deep convictions about the great issues of our day. Some of them did not agree with mine. But on the issue of human dignity, there was no difference between us").

But the real focus of the meeting was to plead with the black leaders to help quell further riots (Point 8: "Let us be frank about it. It can mean that those—of both races—who believe that violence is the best means of settling racial problems in America will have had their belief confirmed. That will be nothing less than a catastrophe for our country"; and Point 13: "Despite what we have done together in these years, the division remains. The riots of last summer proved that, for those who needed proof").

Anxiety about rioting had been prevalent even before King's death became a catalyst for outraged violence. A month earlier, the *New York Times* had run a front-page story on the lack of response in New York, New Jersey, and Connecticut to trigger factors behind riots. "The approach of another summer finds conditions as explosive as ever," warned writer Homer Bigart in the introduction to the survey of tristate cities from Rochester to New Haven. Alarmingly, in Newark, where riots in the summer of 1967 left twenty-six people dead, the *Times*'s reporters found that white vigilantism was on the upswing, and both blacks and whites were circumventing gun laws by bringing in weapons from Pennsylvania and Maryland. The Kerner Commission had criticized the aggressive way law enforcement responded to riots, and the *Times* found that Newark mayor Hugh Addonizio had done little to adopt recommendations made by the commission. For example, a citizens' complaint board had not yet been set up.

The riots shifted focus from legal segregation and abuses in the South to the economic plight of blacks in the North and West. This opened a broader dialogue about opportunity. In the South, blacks had legally been banned from voting booths, restaurants, parks, schools, and water fountains. In other parts of the country, they were ghettoized under de facto segregation. Riots revealed the appalling conditions of slums in such cities as Newark and Detroit, but the violence mitigated white culpability for the oppression, a point King himself made frequently. "Riots increase the fears of the whites and relieve them of their guilt," King had repeatedly said in the weeks before his assassination and following the release of the *Kerner Report*. Two days before his death, the April issue of *Look* carried an article in which King predicted, "If rioting continues, it will strengthen the right wing of the country."

Finally, Johnson, the consummate political dealmaker and experienced legislator, wanted to enlist help in passing the civil rights housing act that was working its way through Congress (Point 9: "It can—on the other hand—mark a time when men of both races, determined to avoid a catastrophe, decide to meet their responsibilities. When Negro Americans determine to press forward—non-violently—to fulfill the rights Martin King helped to win. When White Americans determine to pass the legislation that has been waiting too long in Congress and to root out every trace of racism from their hearts").

The staff added a parenthetical note that reminded Lyndon Johnson—known for a tendency to lecture—to solicit comments from his guests.

Sidewalk in front of the Lorraine Motel, Memphis, early morning

Hotel staff dragged a table outside to the pavement and threw a cloth over it. Ralph Abernathy, tired and unshaven, stood behind the table and addressed the television cameras and reporters. Directly above him was the balcony where King had stood the moment he was shot. Behind Abernathy loomed a row of police officers in white helmets holding guns.

"No man can fill Dr. King's shoes," said Abernathy, who was preparing to do just that. Abernathy had just been named temporary president of the SCLC (a formal board meeting was scheduled in Atlanta for later in the week to officially declare King's successor). "Martin Luther King is no longer with us, but his marvelous loving spirit has been unleashed across the length and breadth of history."

Abernathy announced that SCLC would complete the march King had been slated to lead in Memphis in support of the striking sanitation workers. The march would be rescheduled for the next Monday, April 8. The Poor People's Campaign also would carry on, he said: "We have decided that as he died for the poor, so must we work for the poor."

Georgia State Capitol, early morning

Three state troopers flanked Governor Lester Maddox and his regular bodyguard/driver, serving as props for the governor's announcement to reporters. The Georgia National Guard had been put on alert in case the kind of trouble overwhelming Memphis and Washington, D.C., erupted in Atlanta. "We have to take whatever precautions are necessary," said Maddox.

The governor spent most of the rest of the morning trading calls with Georgia's secretary of state, Ben Fortson. Maddox refused to lower the flags at the Georgia capitol in honor of King. Finally, when Fortson emphatically stated lowering the flags was a federal mandate, Maddox capitulated.

In contrast to Atlanta's well-bred Mayor Ivan Allen, Governor Maddox came from a blue-collar family. A high school dropout, he worked a variety of jobs, including a stint in the mills at Atlantic Steel, before opening a cafeteria called the Pickrick, which specialized in fried chicken ("You 'pick' and we 'rick' it up"), where he, his wife, Virginia, and their four children worked long hours.

As early as the 1940s, Maddox advertised his restaurant in weekend editions of the *Atlanta Journal,* and as the civil rights movement gained momentum, he took out a series of full-page ads that doubled as vehicles to espouse his segregationist views. The ads touted chicken-dinner specials at the Pickrick alongside lengthy screeds that decried King as "Martin Luther Coon." During the 1964–65 Scripto strike, Maddox ran an ad that labeled King and SCLC supporters of the strikers "Communist inspired racial agitators" and cautioned, "What a shame if the 'Great Black Father' and the Communists should lead them [the strikers] to fight until there is no more Scripto," and suggested King's support might be motivated by Maddox's own stance at the Pickrick. "To the 'Great Black Father,' stop taking it out on other companies because you are mad in not being able to get any of our fried chicken."

In 1961, Maddox ran against Allen in the Atlanta mayoral election. In the runoff, Maddox placed an ad in the *Atlanta Journal* headlined "Actual Scene Photographed in the Ivan Allen Jr. Headquarters." A picture showed Allen's biracial campaign staff at dinner, and the ad copy cautioned, "Inter-racial parties and gatherings were held all over Atlanta during the campaign. ... If you love your family, church, home, school, and your city, vote for Lester Maddox." In another ad Maddox vowed to white voters, "I will close down the public swimming pools before I will allow white and Negro children to integrate in them."

Allen, who had grudgingly admitted to being the "silk-stocking" candidate in contrast to the rest of the field, was taunted by his own self-description. Once, when he and Maddox met to debate, Allen's opponent said, "In that you are the silk-stocking candidate, I am presenting these silk stockings to you as a gift." Maddox then proffered a pair of Virginia's panty hose to Allen.

Maddox lost the mayoral race to Allen, and three years later, following passage of the Civil Rights Act, Maddox closed the Pickrick rather than comply with the law. When African-Americans tried to enter the restaurant, the wiry restaurant owner chased them off with a pistol. Behind him, Pickrick staff menacingly clutched ax handles, ready to be used as clubs. In August 1964, Maddox told a *New York Times* reporter, "We're closed for good. I can't integrate. God forbid." After Maddox shut the restaurant, he opened a segregationist souvenir stand and sold replica ax handles called Pickrick Drumsticks. This enterprise netted him more than $130,000 in 1964.* To raise funds for his gubernatorial campaign, Maddox peddled $1 novelty license plates emblazoned with a Confederate flag and the slogan "I stand with Pickrick."†

The New School of Afro-American Thought, Washington, D.C., early morning

Reporters and photographers were frisked as they entered the building; student volunteers confiscated nail clippers, penknives, and other sharp objects. Herded into a small office, the press listened as Stokely Carmichael delivered a diatribe that *Washington Post* reporter Phil Casey described as "strange and hostile."

Carmichael stood in front of enlarged photographs of assassinated Nation of Islam leader Malcolm X and of SNCC president H. Rap

---

*In the 1970s, Maddox opened another souvenir business. Located in Underground Atlanta, the downtown tourist destination, the shop carried merchandise such as the Wake Up America Lester Maddox Alarm Clock.

†Whether noisily shuttering his restaurant or leading a 1965 march in support of segregation through downtown Atlanta, demagoguery earned Maddox regular front-page coverage and television news segments. Without press attention, Maddox might have been an unremarkable Southern segregationist and a footnote in Georgia history, famous perhaps for his crowd-pleasing campaign stunt of riding a bicycle backward. As a biographer would eventually note, "If not for his well-publicized ranting about integration and Communist influence, few people other than Atlanta-area fried chicken aficionados would ever have heard of Lester Maddox."

Brown.* Carmichael told the journalists, "When white America killed Dr. King, she opened the eyes of every black man in this country. He was the one man in our race who was trying to teach our people to have love, compassion, and mercy for what white people have done. When white America killed Dr. King last night, she declared war on us." Carmichael warned the gathered reporters, "The final showdown is coming," and predicted an escalation of street violence:

> We die in Vietnam for the honkies. Why don't we come home and die in the streets for our own people? We die cutting and fighting ourselves in our own communities. We cut and fight and kill each other off. Let's kill off the real enemies. Black people are not afraid to die. We die all the time. We die in your jails. We die in your ghettos. We die in your rat-infested homes. We die a thousand deaths every day. We're not afraid to die, because now we're going to die for our people.

Carmichael concluded, "Black people are going to have to find ways to survive. The only way to survive is to get some guns, because that's the only way white America keeps us in check, because she's got the guns."†

Carmichael's press conference played directly into the image of him cultivated by white media. If King symbolized the nonviolent civil rights movement, Stokely Carmichael symbolized its militant wing. But Carmichael's rise to this position was more complex than the shorthand of news stories allowed; he had a years-long relationship with King and the nonviolent civil rights movement. Born in Trinidad and raised in the United States, Carmichael attended historically black Howard University. As a student, he joined a campus chapter of SNCC and, like Bernard LaFayette and John Lewis, volunteered in the Freedom Rides and voter-registration

---

*Brown, who changed *nonviolent* in SNCC's name to *national*, famously coined the phrase "Violence is as American as cherry pie." He left SNCC in 1968 to join the Black Panther Party. At the time of King's death, Brown was in jail on weapons charges.

†Over the next few days, some papers, including the *New York Times*, reported that Carmichael actively urged young men in D.C. to riot. Other papers stressed his attempts to calm the crowds, such as those Bernard LaFayette had witnessed.

drives in the Deep South. He was intrepid and had been arrested many times.

Carmichael was as brash as he was bold. As John Lewis, who had been SNCC chairman when Carmichael joined the organization, recalled, "Stokely was very visible. He loved nothing more than to scare the hell out of people, especially white people. And he was good at it. He had a sharp tongue, and he knew how to use it, to poke and prod and provoke. . . . He either mesmerized you or irritated you; there was no middle ground." Gordon Parks, the *Life* magazine photographer and writer, said Carmichael had such charisma one could imagine watching him "stroll through Dixie in broad daylight using the Confederate flag for a handkerchief" without reprisal.

In 1966, Carmichael orchestrated a takeover of the SNCC chairmanship from Lewis. A year later, he cowrote the book *Black Power* with political scientist Charles V. Hamilton and went on a campus speaking tour. His calls for militancy increased. He was ousted in turn from SNCC in 1967, and in 1968 was named honorary prime minister of the Black Panther Party. Carmichael had become such an incendiary figure that the Kerner Commission actually plotted his itinerary into a computer model, attempting to see if he could be linked to riots. The commission dubbed him an "inciter" but found no concrete evidence that he instigated riots; no Carmichael conspiracy existed, they concluded.

One reason for Carmichael's "instigator" label was the volatile relationship he had with Ivan Allen and Herbert Jenkins, Atlanta's top cop. As an officer and then president of SNCC, Carmichael spent considerable time in Atlanta in the early 1960s, and open conflict between him and City Hall erupted in the fall of 1966. On September 6, Carmichael went to City Hall in the morning, met with Ivan Allen, and accused him of "police brutality" for arresting antiwar activists. Later in the day, police shot and injured a black man accused of stealing a car. Among the gawkers at the scene was Carmichael, who called for everyone to return to the spot at four that afternoon to "tear this place up."

At four, whether spurred by anxiety, Carmichael's agitation, curiosity, or a blend of all three, more than two thousand people gathered in the street. Many of those present were Atlanta police officers, sent as a precaution by a wary Jenkins. Ivan Allen and police captain George Royal walked through the throng, asking people to be calm. At one point, the mayor climbed on the roof of a police cruiser, grabbed a bullhorn, and begged the crowd to disperse.

Charles Black, the former student activist, was then working for Economic Opportunity Atlanta (EOA) in the Summerhill area. He watched as Ivan Allen, spotting a distinguished-looking man in a clerical collar, pulled him up to the car roof. *He's picked the wrong preacher,* Charles Black thought. *That's Rob Hunter.* The Reverend Mr. Hunter had more than a little sympathy for urban rioters. He grabbed the bullhorn from the mayor and, with a sardonic grin, yelled, "Burn, baby, burn!" Hearing the rallying cry of the 1965 Watts riot, people surged closer to the police car, rocking it so hard that the mayor was knocked off. Officers fired tear gas as residents threw bottles, bricks, and rocks. By the time the riot broke up, sixteen people had been hurt and seventy-three were arrested.

Later that night, Allen and Police Chief Jenkins went back to Summerhill and walked through the streets, talking with residents. City Hall's official word on the episode, repeated in the Atlanta papers and the national media, was that Carmichael instigated the episode; *Time* headlined its report on the event "Stokely's Spark." The magazine quoted Chief Jenkins calling SNCC the "violent, nonstudent committee," a laugh line he would use over the next few years on the law-and-order luncheon circuit.

In the fall of 1966, SNCC responded with a fund-raising letter claiming the organization was being "attacked from all quarters" and falsely accused of "insurrection" in Atlanta. "Powerful white forces" were colluding to force SNCC out of business, wrote Carmichael to supporters.

A more nuanced assessment of the Summerhill incident came in a September 9, 1966, report by the biracial Council on Human Relations (CHR), which put out a statement saying that "no one group, including SNCC, can be held responsible." Rather, CHR asserted, the trigger for unrest was "Atlanta's lack of concern over the miserable conditions in the slum areas." The CHR insisted, "SNCC members are not responsible for the fact that the leadership of metropolitan Atlanta has refused to acknowledge" poor living conditions that "require continuous, professional attention." The problem, according to CHR, "does not lie with 'Negro leadership' or with 'white leadership.' It lies with 'community leadership,'" and inner-city tensions "will continue to plague us all until we admit that we are all equally involved."

Don Bender, a volunteer living in the Atlanta Mennonite House not far from Summerhill, reported to the Mennonite Central Committee, "The civil rights movement has not touched these slum dwellers' lives significantly. It has primarily affected the Negro middle class. The Negro middle class community reacted strongly to the riots and condemned the rioters. They spoke from the viewpoint of the privileged and showed they were as out of touch with their brothers in the slums as were the 'white' people."

Less than a year later, Carmichael made another cameo appearance in an Atlanta racial incident. One evening in June 1967, a teen and a security guard scrapped over a can of beer outside a supermarket in Dixie Hills—a poor neighborhood between Collier Heights and the Atlanta University Center, known for cheap, new apartments and old, crumbling streets. In response, police stepped up patrols in Dixie Hills, and residents became tense. The next evening, Carmichael and a group of friends defied police orders to stay away and were arrested.

On the third day, Carmichael came back to Dixie Hills and talked to a group of kids hanging out near the supermarket, telling them that the police targeted them. Don't clap, he told his audience when they started to applaud his speech. Clapping dispels your frustration. "That's our trouble. We've been letting off steam when we should have slapped some heads." By that night, rocks and bottles were thrown, police cars damaged, and arrests made. (Carmichael, *Time* magazine claimed, left ahead of the trouble and was "dancing the boogaloo at a downtown nightclub when the rock-throwing in Dixie Hills started.") Later that night, the explosion of a Molotov cocktail thrown at police prompted gunshots. One person died and three others were hurt.

After the Dixie Hills episode, state senator Leroy Johnson, the first black elected to Georgia's statehouse since Reconstruction, helped residents craft a petition demanding better services, including a playground, which would provide Dixie Hills youngsters a better place to congregate than parking lots. Few parks were built in black sections of Atlanta, and even after ostensible desegregation there was no parity when it came to recreational facilities. The petition read, "We favor nonviolent, peaceful demonstration," and outlined seven demands, including playgrounds, sewers, and garbage collection to address "long-standing social needs in our community."

After the Summerhill and Dixie Hills events, a pamphlet called "Perspective on the Atlanta Rebellion" was produced by the Afro-American News Service in Atlanta and distributed by the Movement Press in San Francisco.

Julius Lester wrote:

> In Atlanta, the Marriott Hotel, a deluxe accommodation for those who can afford to be deluxely accommodated, stands in the heart of what used to be a black slum area, Buttermilk Bottom. Urban renewal is nothing more than evicting poor black people from their homes, razing the area, and "renewing" it with high-cost apartments, hotels, and expressways. No matter how many times the city of Atlanta and the press scream that SNCC was responsible for the rebellion, the black people of Atlanta know that SNCC did not destroy homes for hotels, motels, expressways, and a ball stadium. They know that SNCC did not force these people to move into Summerhill, Mechanicsville, and other already crowded areas of the city.

Ivan Allen was able to get away with urban renewal projects with the help of "black men he has bought off with tea and cookies. These leaders are the sort of people who say, 'Our main concern is Stokely Carmichael,'" wrote Lester, adding, "The black community will continue to fight until a society is created in which the black man will be able to fulfill himself. In that society there will be no place for the Ivan Allens who think a city's image and progress can be separated from the people of that city."

Atlanta University Center, 9 a.m.

Alerted that protests were planned at the city's historically black colleges, Mayor Ivan Allen went to the Atlanta University Center, taking with him

Atlanta Constitution editor Gene Patterson. When they got to the cluster of colleges just west of downtown, they found that more than a thousand students had gathered on Hunter Street, the main road through the campus complex.

Allen offered to march with the students to show his support for them and his sympathy with their outrage over King's death, but Arthur Burghardt, student organizer, turned him down. As a compromise, Allen, Patterson, and Allen's driver, police captain Morris Redding, drove a short distance ahead of the marchers in a police car. As the student march made its way through Vine City, just blocks from the King home on Sunset Avenue, the six college presidents of the Atlanta University Center joined the procession. Some students chanted "Black power!" while others chorused "We're hip, black, and angry!"

When the students returned to the University Center, they sat for hours in "rap sessions" discussing how to respond. At first "people were talking about 'How can we get violent?' They were mad and wanted to burn Rich's [department store] or go to white neighborhoods and show some reaction," recalled James Wilborn, then a Morehouse sophomore, and a friend of Marvin Mangham's. "But nothing materialized. In general at that time, students were searching for leadership, trying to find their place in the civil rights arena." Classes were canceled and the campus essentially shut down while faculty, staff, and students talked about their reactions.

"There was a real sense, and I don't know if this came from the school administration, or students, or leaders, or some combination, that we were going to be the center of a lot of attention and what we needed to do was remember that all this would reflect on Morehouse [and the other schools]," remembered Marvin Mangham.

Eventually, students formed a number of committees to contain violence. A group called the Black Action Committee circulated a statement saying, "Violent retaliation is out!" Clark College students formed a group called Operation Respect and handed out flyers asking for young Atlantans on campus and in other parts of the city to resist the urge to riot.

The university presidents, student leaders, Police Chief Jenkins, and Mayor Allen found a way to defuse potential campus violence: recruit students to directly help prevent riots. They would be trained as marshals for the day of King's funeral and during events leading up to it. Their work would start on campus. To help train the students, City Hall called in help from people with an unusually close affinity for the project—former leaders of the Atlanta student movement of the early 1960s. One of those summoned was Morehouse alumnus Charles Black. He drove over to campus in a car he had impulsively purchased that morning. After hearing about King's death he was initially stunned, then decided, *If the world is falling apart, it's as good a time as any for a splurge.* So he bought a red Pontiac LeMans with a black vinyl top and it was in that car that he headed toward campus.

Charles Black hoped to have black armbands for the marshals, but a thousand could not be found on short notice. He enlisted the help of Shirley Ashley, a home economics teacher at Crim High School. Ashley and her students sewed armbands out of gray flannel, the only muted fabric that could be located in large enough quantities.

Cooperation between former student leaders and City Hall represented a milestone in Atlanta's racial politics and paralleled Ivan Allen's personal evolution from passive segregationist to pragmatic integrationist to ardent civil rights supporter.

Student movement activities in Atlanta began in 1960. Calling themselves the Committee on the Appeal for Human Rights (COAHR), Atlanta University Center students took out a full-page ad in the March 9, 1960, editions of the *Atlanta Constitution, Atlanta Journal,* and *Atlanta Daily World.* The ad announced the students' plan to boycott segregated restaurants and cataloged racial discrimination in the city that had touted itself as "too busy to hate." Under the headline "An Appeal for Human Rights," the student statement read, "We want to state clearly and unequivocally that we cannot tolerate, in a nation professing democracy and among people professing Christianity, the discriminatory conditions under which the Negro is living today in Atlanta, Georgia—supposedly one of the most progressive cities in the South."

The appeal went on to document seven areas in which discrimination persisted: education; jobs; housing; voting; hospitals; access to movies, concerts, and restaurants; and law enforcement. "If a Negro is hungry, his hunger must wait until he comes to a 'colored' restaurant, and even his thirst must await its quenching at a 'colored' water fountain." Also on the list of grievances: many children traveled more than ten miles each way to attend segregated schools; blacks accounted for 32 percent of Atlanta's population but were restricted to living in 16 percent of the city's area; and just 35 African-Americans were on the city police force of 830.

The day the sit-ins started, seventy-seven protesters were arrested, most students, but a few older volunteers, including Martin King's brother, A. D. King. Charles Black, who had led a group into the Terminal Station waiting room along with A. D. King, was sent to Atlanta's prison farm. In prison, he and dozens of arrested students were awakened at 4 a.m. and sent to hoe fields of collards. They spent nights on "putrid mattresses" that had to be shared because the jail was so crowded.

The sit-ins continued throughout 1960. Some of Atlanta's established black businesses and institutions lent support to the students. Employees of Atlanta Life Insurance helped to staff picket lines. Restaurants near the Atlanta University Center, such as Paschals and Frazier's Café Society, served as meeting places for the students and the owners often put up bail money. The movement spawned a newspaper, the *Atlanta Inquirer*.

By the fall, Lonnie King and student leaders persuaded Martin Luther King to get involved. On October 19, 1960, King agreed to take part in a massive sit-in that COAHR organized at Rich's, Atlanta's old and venerated department store. King was arrested alongside Lonnie King and other protesters. The students were released a few days later, but Martin Luther King was transferred to the state prison in Reidsville, Georgia, after Judge Oscar Mitchell ruled that his arrest violated his probation on a traffic violation from earlier that year. King was slated for a prison work gang.

Learning of King's sentence, Harris Wofford, a civil rights coordinator on John Kennedy's presidential campaign and an ally of King's, put in a call to Morris Abram, an Atlanta lawyer, asking for help. Abram went to meet with Mayor William Hartsfield and mentioned the call. The mayor, ever politically canny, told boycott negotiators that Kennedy supported King's release. This was, of course, news to the Kennedy campaign, which worried about association with King. Wofford worked within the campaign, and eventually candidate John Kennedy called Coretta Scott King to express sympathy, while Robert Kennedy called Judge Mitchell. Shortly afterward, King was released.

The Kennedys had assistance from an unlikely and unreported source, Georgia governor Ernest Vandiver, who had been elected on an anti-integration platform (although he was more moderate than other Georgia politicians). John Kennedy called asking for help with the situation. Vandiver's brother-in-law called George Stewart, a Georgia Democratic Party leader, and asked him to call Mitchell. Vandiver, in the meantime, called Robert Kennedy to confirm the campaign's interest in King's case. Although Stewart's call to Mitchell was reported in the Atlanta press, the calls by the Kennedys achieved national attention.* After his son's release from jail, Daddy King told the congregation at Ebenezer Baptist Church that he would be voting for JFK—even if Kennedy *was* a Catholic. Later, Daddy King would brag he had delivered the decisive "suitcase full of votes" that clinched the presidency for JFK.

The Kennedys earned a victory, but the Atlanta students could still not sit at the lunch counter in Woolworth's, enter the tearoom at Rich's department store, or use the dressing rooms of most downtown stores. The boycotts and sit-ins continued over the Christmas shopping season, hurting businesses and creating a public relations mess for Mayor William Hartsfield, famous coiner of Atlanta's "too busy to hate" slogan, and Ivan Allen, then head of the Atlanta Chamber of Commerce. Allen was attempting to launch the Forward Atlanta marketing campaign, a $500,000 advertising program touting Atlanta as a good place to run a business and raise children, praising its booming airport, new high-rises, and low labor costs.†

---

*Atlanta historian Clifford Kuhn recounts the story of Vandiver's little-known involvement in the events in the article "'There's a Footnote to History!'" Sifting through oral histories by Robert Kennedy and Vandiver, Kuhn found that the story was consistently told by both men, but probably downplayed at first out of political consideration for Vandiver and later overlooked because "the episode, linking the Kennedy and King families for the first time, occupies a central place in the country's modern political history, memory, and legend."

†The mayor's father, Ivan Allen Sr., had also served as head of the Atlanta Chamber of Commerce and had headed its first Forward Atlanta campaign in the 1920s, writing the text for the "Atlanta from the Ashes" brochure distributed as part of the program. In the younger Allen's campaign, print ads ran in magazines such as the *New Yorker,* and

In early 1961, a compromise was negotiated between Daddy King, other old-guard black leaders, Mayor William Hartsfield, and white business leaders that would allow for desegregation of schools in August of that year, followed by desegregation of restaurants by early 1962. Some students felt betrayed by the deal.

Tellingly, the Atlanta Chamber of Commerce, working with Mayor William Hartsfield and Police Chief Jenkins, coordinated integration efforts. The chamber saw the undertaking as a way to distinguish Atlanta from other Southern cities such as Birmingham and Little Rock. Atlanta's white business leaders did not want racial tension to scare off investors and corporate relocation scouts. The chamber ran dozens of newspaper, radio, and television ads with the theme "How Great Is Atlanta?" encouraging peaceful integration. Community organizers in the biracial coalition of parent and church groups called OASIS (Organization Assisting Schools in September) helped. Churches—black and white—held prayer services during "Law and Order Weekend" before the first day of integrated classes in the fall of 1961, and OASIS prepared a briefing document for reporters and television crews who came to cover the event. The successful integration was touted by the Chamber of Commerce in follow-up ads and in articles in *Atlanta* magazine. These actions helped Atlanta earn a reputation as a racially harmonious city. The *New York Times* called Atlanta's school integration "a new and shining example of what can be accomplished if the people of good will and intelligence, white and Negro, will cooperate to obey the law."*

---

the chamber reprinted the ads in *Atlanta* magazine with notes explaining the campaign to its readers. A 1963 ad, for example, headlined "Atlanta has everything, including vast lakes for family fun," noted, "Because Atlanta lies inland, newcomers are usually somewhat startled to find the city so close to such large bodies of water as Lakes Allatoona and Lanier."

*In the year schools in Atlanta integrated, 1961, Marvin Mangham Jr. started high school. Although his parents picketed in support of integration, they did not want him to be one of the token few breaking the color barrier. They worried about their children; Marvin in turn worried about his dad. News of picketers being arrested was frequent, and Marvin could not imagine his dad in jail. Almost a decade later, it was a different story. Marvin became the third black student to attend the University of Georgia's law school. "My dad told me I had to 'tough it up.' He said this was a public school, funded by taxpayers, and that included him." For Mangham, the experience was

When it came time to implement the postponed integration of restaurants and lunchrooms, representatives of the Atlanta student movement met with Police Chief Jenkins to administer the agreement, including plans for the first day of legal integration. "We decided who to send to which restaurant," recalls Charles Black. "We didn't let the hoity-toity people from Auburn Avenue go to the Magnolia Room [the famous lunchroom at Rich's department store]," he said.

The emergence of a student movement in Atlanta altered the delicate balance maintained for the past half century between City Hall, the white business community, and black civic leaders. Cooperation between the elite of both races traced its roots to the 1906 Atlanta race riot, a four-day massacre during which rampaging whites killed at least twenty-five blacks and destroyed black homes, businesses, and property. In the aftermath of the riot, a series of unprecedented biracial meetings took place, laying the foundation for Atlanta's uniquely open channels of communication across racial lines. While by no means as progressive as city fathers would like to claim (stricter Jim Crow laws were, after all, quickly enacted after the riot), this pattern of cooperation helped Atlanta avoid some racial conflict experienced by other cities and contributed to its burgeoning black middle class.

As Charles Black and other young activists of the 1960s saw it, the power structure of black Atlanta contained three strata. The "old guard" were represented by heads of fraternal organizations—such as Benjamin Davis Sr., editor of the *Atlanta Independent*, the organ of the Odd Fellows organization, and John Wesley Dobbs of the Prince Hall Masons—or reverends such as Daddy King, William Holmes Borders, and Sam Williams. The "young Turks" rose through professions and business and included attorney Donald Hollowell, state senator Leroy Johnson, and entrepreneur Herman Russell. The "militants" were radicalized students such as themselves.*

---

brutal. Decades later, his son also went to UGA Law School. "A very different experience than mine," Mangham said in 2009. "My kids and grandkids have no clue of what we went through."

*Charles Black, Julian Bond, and Amos Brown were among the handful of students in a class that King taught at Morehouse College. "It was a seminar in modern social philosophy," recalled Black. As electrifyingly eloquent as King could be in front of a crowd,

The school and restaurant integration efforts played out against the backdrop of the 1961 mayoral election. Lester Maddox ran on a segregationist platform. Milton "Muggsy" Smith was the candidate initially favored by Atlanta's black community. Ivan Allen was supported by moderate whites and, of course, the business community.

Coca-Cola chief Robert Woodruff was an adviser to Allen's 1961 mayoral campaign and, along with a small inner circle of other supporters, regularly received updates on the campaign progress, ranging from financial records to the candidate's schedule. Allen's campaign included an innovative technique of visiting shopping centers and stopping at all small businesses, black and white. The week of July 24, 1961, for instance, he went to the Seller Brothers Funeral Home, the Pittsburg Civic League, the West End Businessmen's Association, and Parkview Plaza. (The campaign briefing included a parenthetical note that the plaza was on Memorial Drive in a section of town Woodruff and other white backers were unlikely to visit.) In a memo telling "The Boss" (Woodruff) about a June kickoff meeting at the campaign headquarters, Allen enclosed a bumper sticker and added, "P.S. Hot dogs and Coca-Cola will be served."

In August, candidate Allen met with black leaders including C. A. Scott of the *Atlanta Daily World* and attorney W. T. Alden. In December, after winning the election, thanks to the black vote that gave him an edge over Maddox, Allen was a guest at Woodruff's Ichauway Plantation in Newton, Georgia. "The glories of the Old South are gone—except here," Allen wrote in his thank-you note. Allen and Woodruff may have been progressive for their time, but they enjoyed their privileged status, and their private lives occupied a sphere that black Atlanta rarely entered.

Allen's pragmatic attitude toward civil rights compliance as a PR tactic was evolving into sincere conviction. On the day he took office in January 1962, he removed all the WHITE and COLORED signs from City Hall's drinking fountains and restrooms. In 1963, he testified in support of the Civil Rights Act—the only white Southern elected official to do so. In 1965, he organized the dinner to honor King's Nobel Prize victory. In

---

as a professor he was didactic at best, plodding at worst. "He'd talk in a monotone. Staying awake was a major challenge."

1966 and 1967, he supported economic development as a preventive measure against riots and advocated gentler tactics for police.

Leveraging the power of elected office and the persuasion of the Chamber of Commerce, Allen forged a coalition of business leaders in support of civil rights efforts. He recognized that for many of his counterparts support for abolishing Jim Crow laws was grounded solely in self-interest. "The top fifty business and civic leaders in the city have backed me to a man all the way through the civil rights issue," he would tell *Atlanta* magazine in a January 1969 interview, adding candidly, "That doesn't mean they liked it." Allen reflected, "I think many of them would prefer the old segregated practices because it was personally more convenient, and it was an easier way of life. But they have faced up to the necessity of making these changes."

Ivan Allen's conversion may have been authentic, but the majority of Atlanta's white business leaders abandoned Jim Crow under duress. The perception of Atlanta as a beacon of progress was just that, a perception, wrote James Townsend, founding editor of *Atlanta* magazine, which had been launched by the Chamber of Commerce in 1961 to promote the city.* He wrote that Atlanta

> was hailed in the world press as "the city too busy to hate." We were no such thing. There were as many "haters" in Atlanta as Birmingham or any other major Southern city. We were merely luckier—and smarter—than Birmingham. Without Birmingham's awful example of race relations, and there could have been no worse in the world, Atlanta almost surely would have erupted into the same kind of image-tarnishing riots. And instead of being known nationally as a good city for rearing children and locating industry, the distinction of being the foremost city in the South might have been seized by, say, Charlotte or Jacksonville.

---

*I should disclose that I was editor in chief of *Atlanta* magazine from 2002 to early 2009. The Chamber of Commerce sold the magazine decades ago, and it is now an independent general-interest magazine with no formal ties to the chamber or any other civic organization in Atlanta.

Townsend credited Atlanta's image to "a combination of good luck" and "excellent leadership," combined with "a benign and benevolent power structure—those business leaders, all white, who ran the banks and major industries and who belonged to the Piedmont Driving Club."

As mayor, Allen continued to highlight the relationship between peaceful integration and economic prosperity. In the early 1960s, Morris Abram, then a member of the United Nations' Subcommission for the Prevention of Discrimination and the Protection of Minorities, decided to showcase Atlanta as an example of racial harmony—in part a result of President John Kennedy's urging to stave off criticism from other countries that American blacks were mistreated. Abram, a Georgia native, took a contingent of U.N. representatives to Atlanta. They stayed at the Riviera Motel and toured the city. At the same time, the Klan staged protests, which Abram made part of the tour. "We drove the multicolored, multiracial, multinational subcommission by to see the Ku Klux Klan."*

But progress was not as dramatic as Atlanta's PR machine would have it. In June 1962, after Atlanta restaurants officially integrated, singers Harry Belafonte and Miriam Makeba, along with a group of friends both white and black, were turned away from lunch service at the King's Inn Restaurant. Belafonte and Makeba had performed for President John Kennedy just weeks before and were in Atlanta for an SCLC benefit.† King and SCLC put out a statement saying that in "ordinary circumstances" he would have asked SCLC members and supporters to stage a sit-in at the King's Inn. Because the incident happened just weeks after a fatal plane

---

*In a later interview, Abram would recount, "I remember going through the section of the city that had these wonderful black homes, acres and acres and acres, some with tennis courts and swimming pools, and Mr. Boris Ivanov, the Russian, comes up to me, and he says—we were at the home of a black woman who was entertaining us for coffee—'Are all these homes we've been seeing black?' I said, 'Every one of them, and I want to tell you something, Mr. Ivanov. This will sort of break up your rather unified image of what capitalism is and what socialism is. These are all black capitalists. The mayor is a capitalist, and all of these people who have been so good to you and who are interested in improving race relations are capitalists, and they are for equal rights. This afternoon we're going to see the Ku Klux Klan demonstrating downtown, and I want you to know that under every one of those sheets beats a proletarian heart.' He turned and walked away."

†Belafonte and Makeba's performances had been overshadowed at the event by a rendition of "Happy Birthday" by Marilyn Monroe.

crash killed 106 Atlanta arts patrons (many close friends of Mayor Allen's), action would be postponed until "a more propitious time."

During the transition, the Greater Atlanta Council on Human Relations kept lists of integrated facilities. In October 1963, knowing Belafonte's personal interest in the status of facilities in Atlanta, council head Eliza Paschall sent a memo to the singer that listed integrated businesses and services. The list included some twenty freestanding restaurants in addition to lunch counters and tearooms in stores such as Sears Roebuck, Woolworth's, and Davison's. Only three hotels—the Peachtree Manor, the Hilton Inn, and the Air Host Inn—were fully integrated. Others said they would accept black convention attendees, but only up to the percentage of delegates at the convention. Paschall explained that while some hotels had privately changed policies, "they will not publicly say this, and if you call and ask if they will make a reservation for a Negro, they say no."

The suburban city of Decatur had integrated public facilities—except swimming pools. Catholic schools and Trinity Presbyterian school were integrated, but no other private schools were yet. Tellingly, of the sixteen hospitals in metro Atlanta that belonged to the Georgia Hospital Association, ten did not admit black patients, and of those that did, some, such as Grady, still segregated health-care services, and others, such as DeKalb General, segregated wards. One hospital—St. Joseph's—was fully integrated. Paschall added a note saying, "It is safe to say that fewer than 20 Atlanta restaurants are 'open.'"

Five year later, Atlanta had made progress and most facilities were integrated. But the changes had brought with them a shift in the city's power structure. Atlanta's black and white leaders had worked together through a number of crises. In 1968, they would need to bring a new group to their alliance, the young men and women of the Atlanta University Center.

Memphis, R. S. Lewis & Sons Funeral Home, 10:15 a.m.

The funeral home had opened its doors early for public viewing, and several hundred people came by to see King's body. Ralph Abernathy, Andrew Young, Hosea Williams, and other members of the inner circle drove over from the Lorraine and stood around the casket, offering a silent salute to King while news cameras clicked. Then, they followed the hearse that took the casket to Memphis airport.

Coretta Scott King had just arrived in the American Electra airplane chartered by Robert Kennedy. She was accompanied by Juanita Abernathy; King's secretary, Dora McDonald; the Reverend Fred Bennette; and her sister- and brother-in-law, Christine King Farris and Isaac Farris. At the airport, National Guard soldiers carried bayonets and nightsticks, fending off onlookers. The military presence distressed Christine Farris. "They stood there, unflinching, with their bayonets fixed and trained on the people," she wrote later. "The mourners were there purely out of respect for my brother, and they were as torn up and in as much pain as we were. They represented no threat to us." She vowed never to return to Memphis.

Attorney General Ramsey Clark, who had been in Memphis overnight meeting with local police and FBI agents, entered the plane and briefed the family on what had been learned so far. Afterward, Clark held a brief press conference on the ramp of the jet as King's casket was loaded behind him. The lanky Texan told reporters he was confident the assassination was the "work of just one man" and the killer would soon be caught. "Real progress is being made," he said. He dismissed reporters' suggestions that a conspiracy was behind the killing.

When he got back to Washington, the attorney general collected on his bet with Deke DeLoach; the killer had not been caught in a day, and Clark won the bottle of sherry the assistant FBI director had wagered. Undeterred, DeLoach bet another bottle on a new wager: the killer would be identified and caught within a week.

The Cabinet Room of the White House, 11:10 a.m.

White House staff spent the morning preparing for the meeting, down to the detail of strategically seating the attendees. The president sat at the center of a long, wide oval table, flanked by Thurgood Marshall, whom the president had nominated in 1967 to be the first black judge on the U.S. Supreme Court, and NAACP lobbyist Clarence Mitchell Jr. Seated around the table in high-backed leather chairs were Whitney Young; Bayard Rustin, executive director of the A. Philip Randolph Institute; Roy

Wilkins, executive director of the NAACP; Walter Washington, mayor of Washington, D.C.; Richard Hatcher, mayor of Gary, Indiana; Clarence Mitchell Jr.'s son, Clarence Mitchell III, an SNCC cofounder and Maryland state senator; Leon Higginbotham, the Philadelphia district judge; the Reverend Leon Sullivan of Philadelphia's Zion Baptist Church; and Bishop George Baber of Detroit's Ebenezer AME Church. Dorothy Height, head of the National Council of Negro Women, sat at the end of the table, her pale suit and jaunty pillbox hat providing a contrast to all the dark suits of the men in the room. White House staff and administration officials squeezed into chairs pushed along the wall or stood near the doorway. Aide Tom Johnson sat in the back of the room furiously taking notes. The table was cluttered with notebooks, ashtrays, and water pitchers. Fingerprints smeared its shiny surface.*

The top levels of government were represented by Warren Christopher, deputy attorney general; Robert Weaver, Department of Housing and Urban Development secretary; Stephen Pollak, assistant attorney general in the Civil Rights division; Mike Mansfield, the Senate majority leader; Thomas Kuchel, the Senate minority whip; John McCormack, Speaker of the House; Oklahoma congressman Carl Albert; and Ohio's William McCulloch, the key Republican supporter of fair-housing legislation that LBJ was working to get through Congress.

In the Cabinet Room, the president looked around at the group. "I asked you here for your support as responsible Negro leaders," he said. High on the agenda: Stokely Carmichael. Before going through his fourteen talking points, the president read from an Associated Press bulletin reporting Carmichael's statements calling King's death a "war" on black America.

---

*Floyd McKissick, then head of the Congress for Racial Equality (CORE), was invited to the meeting. At first he told the White House that he was in hiding in Cleveland, afraid for his life after learning of King's death, and would not be able to attend. Over the next few hours, CORE leader Roy Innis would call the White House several times on McKissick's behalf, wanting to know the exact agenda and who was going to be invited—specifically whether Stokely Carmichael, H. Rap Brown, Nation of Islam president Elijah Muhammad, or Adam Clayton Powell were on the list. In a 4:05 a.m. memo to the president, White House staffer Jim Gaither advised, "It seems apparent that McKissick will not come, and that he may well denounce the meeting, saying that he had been invited but had refused."

"I hope my department will not be required to enter this situation," said Secretary of Defense Clark Clifford, seated at the far end of the table next to Senator Thomas Kuchel, the California Republican minority whip who had been comanager of the 1964 Civil Rights Act and 1965 Voting Rights Act.

"We will not unless called upon," said Clifford, adding that he knew and respected King and that "white leaders respected Dr. King."

Whitney Young challenged, "We need a dramatic demonstration of what Secretary Clifford said. We need funds for the cities."

Bayard Rustin agreed, "We must carry something to the people."

Walter Washington, the mayor of Washington, D.C., who had been up most of the night patrolling burning streets, told the president that "concrete and meaningful action" was needed to counteract the frustration expressed in the streets.

Gary, Indiana, mayor Dick Hatcher urged, "Congress must act so people can see something tangible."

As he sat in the meeting, Leon Higginbotham sensed that the president was afraid; memories of the Watts and Newark riots and the damning Kerner Commission report were fresh on the minds of everyone in the room.

The president predicted, "We will have marches and protests." He said to the lawmakers in the room, "We must organize in committee rooms to get things through. We need money for poverty. We need more money for housing."

He looked around and said, "I have made every opportunity to try to get through to the young people. How well I have gotten through remains to be seen. But also—how well have *you* gotten through?"

At noon, the president and the civil rights leaders adjourned the meeting to attend the memorial service for King at the National Cathedral. Only two weeks earlier, King had delivered an impassioned sermon from the pulpit of the cathedral, announcing his plans to bring the Poor People's Campaign to Washington and denouncing the Vietnam War once again.

The motorcade drove just blocks from looting and arson. The scenes they skirted on the way to the service belied the tranquil lyrics of the processional hymn "Victory":

The strife is o'er, the battle done
the victory of life is won
the song of triumph has begun . . .
The powers of death have done their worst
but Christ their legions hath dispersed
let shout of holy joy outburst
Alleluia!

As the organ played "We Shall Overcome," President Johnson and the other attendees of the morning meeting made their way into the sanctuary and sat in the front rows of the nave. More than four thousand people crowded into the cathedral; many, Nan Robertson noted in a report for the *New York Times*, were white, and most were young.

The thousands in the sanctuary sang "Take My Hand, Precious Lord." This song would be heard incessantly over the coming days. According to witnesses, King's last words before being shot were to musician Ben Branch, discussing the music planned for the scheduled rally. "Make sure you play 'Take My Hand, Precious Lord' in the meeting tonight. Play it real pretty."

The Reverend Walter Fauntroy, pastor of Washington's New Bethel Baptist Church and head of the Washington SCLC chapter, delivered a homily, saying, "Forgive us our individual and our corporate sins that have led us inevitably to this tragedy."

As the president and his entourage left, the cathedral's twenty-four-thousand-pound bell tolled. Johnson and the civil rights leaders returned to the White House and continued their talks. Just before 2 p.m., as Johnson was preparing to leave the White House, D.C. mayor Walter Washington left a message with the Oval Office. Rioting was so bad that troops needed to be called out. The mayor of the nation's capital city would have to ask Defense Secretary Clark Clifford for help.

Chicago City Council Chambers, midmorning

A large photograph of Martin Luther King was propped up on the rostrum at the front of the room. The picture was draped with purple and black bunting, and red roses surrounded the rostrum. The chamber could seat five hundred and was packed with people attending the special session called to honor King.

Mayor Daley sat with military representatives, including Major General John Chiles, deputy commander of the Fifth Army, and Major General Arthur Adams, reserve training commander of the Glenview Naval Air Station. Daley said that he would issue a proclamation calling the next day a citywide day of mourning. Visiting rabbis and priests made statements, and nine black aldermen delivered eulogies.

The biggest stir came from the visit by Jesse Jackson. He wore the same stained shirt and jacket he had on the night before. "I come here with a heavy heart because on my chest is the stain of blood from Dr. King's head," he said. Describing the bullet that tore off part of King's jaw, Jackson said, "He went through literally a crucifixion. I was there. And I'll be there for the resurrection."

Jackson told the mayor and city council that he would do all he could to help stop riots in Chicago. "I am going to challenge the youth here to be nonviolent. I'll tell them, 'Put your rocks down and put your bottles down.'" Looking at the mayor and the assembled military men, he added, "To those in power, I say, 'Beat your weapons into plowshares.'"

Howard University, early afternoon

Just a few hours after the service at the National Cathedral, Stokely Carmichael attended a memorial service on the campus of his alma mater, Howard University. The service started with elegiac eloquence. Students sang Brahms's "Requiem," followed by "Precious Lord."

After the music, university president James Nabrit Jr. delivered a memorial speech in which he said that, because of King's death, a "shadow has fallen on the land," but "his death shall not have been in vain if, from his blood, arise a thousand Martin Luther Kings."

Carmichael followed Nabrit to the podium. He startled attendees by waving a pistol and repeating, "Stay off the streets if you don't have a gun, because there's going to be shooting." Some cheers greeted Carmichael's appearance. Then an awkward silence followed. As Carmichael left the stage, students quickly and quietly filed out of the auditorium behind him.

Atlanta Municipal Airport, 1:30 p.m.

Marvin Mangham pulled up to the Atlanta airport in his mom's Buick Electra 225. The car was full; friends from Morehouse had begged for rides, and his girlfriend, Mary, tagged along as well; everyone was eager to see Mrs. King return from Memphis with the coffin. Marvin parked as close to the airfield as possible, and he and his friends walked out to the tarmac. In the crowd already gathered, they saw students from the Atlanta University Center; John Lewis, the former SNCC leader; and the Reverend Sam Williams, the lion of Friendship Baptist Church.

A convoy of police cruisers pulled up, and Mayor Ivan Allen, Vice Mayor Sam Massell, police captain Morris Redding, and Ann Moses, Allen's longtime executive assistant, got out. The mayor walked through the crowd, sympathetically shaking hands. Allen paused in front of the cluster of reporters and took a few questions. The mayor told the gathered press he had two concerns: helping the King family and preventing riots in Atlanta. He told reporters that he expected a number of black leaders, "including the militant ones," to start arriving in the city—by Monday at the latest.

When the chartered plane carrying Martin Luther King's body landed, the mayor, the Reverend Sam Williams, and the King children went on board. Mrs. King wanted her children to view the body in the relative privacy of the plane before they faced crowds outside. To Bernice it looked as though her father were asleep. She worried if he was hungry. He traveled a lot, and she was young, so she did not have many clear memories of him, but she vividly recalled his sitting at the table in the house on Sunset Avenue and eating long, green spring onions. *Can he eat those now?* she wondered.

After the coffin was sealed, the family and friends left the plane. As Bunny King walked down the steel steps leading from the plane to the tarmac, she heard a sound that reminded her of wind, but not quite.

"Daddy's breathing," she said to her mother.

"No, baby, that's the plane," said Coretta.

The family walked across the tarmac toward the waiting crowd while the coffin was unloaded. Yolanda King went over to her schoolmate Maria

Saporta, who had come with her parents to the airport. Yolanda looked at Maria and simply said, "He looked so peaceful."

At the same time that the chartered plane arrived, an Eastern Airlines flight landed in Atlanta. On board was Abigail McCarthy, whose husband, Eugene, was campaigning for the Democratic presidential nomination on an antiwar platform. Winston Johnson, an Eastern Airlines employee whose job was escorting VIPs, greeted Mrs. McCarthy, who asked him to take her to see Mrs. King. Winston Johnson drove a Town Car across the runway tarmac to where the coffin was being unloaded from the plane. Mrs. McCarthy walked over to Mrs. King and they embraced. Mrs. King invited the senator's wife to her home.

The coffin was carried to the waiting hearse, a black Cadillac. Onlookers surged toward the car, touching the windows, pressing close. Some in the crowd went back to their cars, ready to follow the Kings and the hearse to the next destination. Should we follow, too? Marvin and his friends debated. They weren't sure where the family was going and exactly what would happen. "No, let's not get into this," Marvin decided. He rounded up his friends and headed back to campus.

The hearse, flanked by police cars with bright lights and muted sirens, made its way to Hanley's Bell Street Funeral Home, followed by a convoy of fifty vehicles. The sidewalks were lined with people, and all along Auburn Avenue flags were flown upside down as a sign of protest about King's death.

Hanley's was surrounded by another cluster of gawkers. *Atlanta Daily World* reporter Marion Jackson called the scene outside the funeral home a "pulsating drama," exacerbated when reporters from "radio, television, and [print] media surged forward and jammed the seam-ruptured street." As a small group of family and friends went into Hanley's, Ralph Abernathy stopped at the door of the funeral home. "We have brought our leader home," he said, asking the crowd to give the family some privacy. "We're deeply honored by your presence and concern. For this is a dark day in the history of the nation and in the history of black people all over the world."

* * *

Winston Johnson, the Eastern Airlines VIP escort, drove Abigail McCarthy to the Kings' house on Sunset Avenue, arriving well before the family returned from the funeral home. He and the senator's wife walked in the house, and the first person they saw was Harry Belafonte. The singer stood in the middle of the kitchen, greeting well-wishers and overseeing the array of food and drink.

The house was crowded with visitors. *Washington Afro-American* writer Elizabeth Oliver described a domestic scene with "huge platters and trays" heaped with food, and "neighbors and crowds washing glasses, plates, and silver, hustling and bustling around to take that load off the family." Patricia Latimore, the Kings' babysitter, came by to offer her help, but the house was so crowded she could not find any family members. She decided to come back when the neighbors, celebrities, and reporters were gone.

When the family arrived back from the funeral home, Marty and Dexter ran out to the backyard to play with model airplanes, and Bunny took to the swing set. Over the next few days, other children would stop by to visit, especially their cousins, Isaac and Angela Farris, and the Abernathy children, Juandalynn, Ralph David III, and Donzaleigh. The younger Kings and their cousins were shuttled from house to house, spending a lot of time with their grandparents while their mothers planned the funeral and dealt with the myriad adult visitors. Yolanda, the oldest King child, seemed to emulate her mother's composure. Her classmates from Spring Street School came by with cards and flowers. Andrea Young, the daughter of Andrew Young, called Yolanda at her father's insistence. Both girls were twelve. Looking back decades later, Andrea described making that call as "one of the hardest things I've ever had to do in my life."

A photographer from *Life* magazine took pictures of the three younger children lounging on a green-velvet-covered window seat and playing Chinese checkers with Ralph David III. Bunny felt as though her eyes were burning from "flashbulbs going off all the time." Photographers were in the house at all hours. Shortly after King was killed, Coretta called photographer Bob Fitch and asked him to come to Atlanta and document the events. Fitch had known the Kings for several years. He took a leave from seminary to join the SCLC, photographing its efforts for internal publications and distribution to media. His photographs ran in publications ranging from small Southern papers to glossy magazines such as *Life*. The work took him along with King, Abernathy, and Andrew Young on marches and demonstrations throughout the rural South. In the King home, he moved easily from room to room, spending hours unobtrusively sitting in the corner of Coretta Scott King's bedroom, where most of the funeral planning took place. Andrew Young, Ralph Abernathy, Jesse Jackson, Christine King Farris, and others would walk in and out, barely noticing the man behind the camera, who had been "one of the only gringos" on many SCLC travels. Another *Life* photographer, Flip Schulke, with whom Fitch often worked, was there as well. The King children were relaxed around the photographers. "This is a household that was accustomed to a lot of activity," said Fitch, who was not surprised King's widow invited him to document the events. "There was a keen sense of the historical importance of what was happening."

It was impossible to avoid a keen sense of apprehension as well. No real progress had been made toward identifying and capturing King's killer, and the visitors entering and leaving the house passed Atlanta policemen on twenty-four-hour watch. Private security officers loaned by the Scripto company safeguarded the house as well.*

Peachtree Street, downtown Atlanta, late afternoon

While everyone gathered in the house, Xernona Clayton slipped out on a practical errand. Coretta asked her to select clothes for her and the children to wear over the next few days' events. Clayton's sense of style and her savvy about what wardrobe was effective in news photographs and on television would be a boon for the coming gauntlet of events, Coretta told her.

Clayton's first stop was Joseph's, a dress shop in downtown Atlanta. She selected a variety of dresses and told the owner she would be back with money.

---

*The Kings had bought the redbrick house with a drive-under garage and neatly fenced yard in 1965 for $10,000. It needed work, but could accommodate a family of six. According to biographer David Garrow, King fretted about the purchase to his friends and colleagues; he worried owning even a simple home in a modest neighborhood might be inappropriate for an antipoverty advocate.

Late in the day she went to Davison's, the department store at the heart of the Peachtree Street shopping and hotel district, to ask for help with creating a hat for the funeral. It was almost closing time, and the store manager asked Clayton to come to the back of the store. "I can find *that* entrance," she said with a wry chuckle, alluding to the recent past, when blacks had been restricted to using the back entrances of most department stores. Clayton recalled Coretta taking her to lunch at Davison's shortly after she and Ed moved to Atlanta, pleased that integration made it possible to treat a friend to a nice downtown luncheon. The lunchroom at Davison's did not have quite the cachet of the elegant Magnolia Tea Room at Rich's, but Rich's was where Martin Luther King had been arrested when he took part in the student sit-ins.

Clayton and the milliner discussed the hat; earlier, she and Coretta King had sketched some ideas. It needed to be veiled, but Coretta wanted to avoid having the headdress look too much like the long-veiled hat Jackie Kennedy wore at her husband's 1963 funeral. That hat was too memorable; Coretta did not want to seem as if she were copying. "Come back tomorrow," the milliner told Xernona. "We'll have something for you to look at."

Xernona Clayton drove back to Sunset Avenue. When she walked in the foyer of the Kings' house, she saw Harry Belafonte still acting as a greeter at the front door. He stood with the family's friend, attorney and activist Stanley Levison.

"I've just ordered a lot of clothes, but I'm not quite sure how to pay for them," Clayton told the two men.

"Don't worry." Levison pulled out a credit card and handed it to Clayton.*

"Take this one, too," said Belafonte, giving her another card. "Get whatever it is they need."

Clayton slipped the cards into her purse and went to the back room to check on Coretta and give her an update on the hat.

---

*Levison was a close friend and confidant of both Martin and Coretta King. He also, inadvertently, served as the excuse J. Edgar Hoover used to wiretap the phones of King and his associates. Levison had reportedly been a member of the Communist Party in the 1950s, and Hoover cited his close association with King as justification for the surveillance.

The White House Press Office, 4:42 p.m.

Press Secretary George Christian recapped the earlier meeting for reporters, telling them that the president told the leaders, "I need your help." Christian quoted some of their statements, including Justice Marshall's: it was "important to get the country out of the mood of depression"; and Judge Higginbotham's: "If we have resolve, we can turn this darkest moment into our finest hour." Christian then read a telegram Daddy King had sent to the White House: "Please know that I join in your pleas to American citizens to desist from violence and permit the cause of nonviolence for which my son died not be in vain."

Christian briefed the press corps on the riots in Washington. The president, mayor, chief of police, chief of army, and others had conferred and would use a plan similar to the response to violence in Detroit in 1967. Five hundred troops were en route. Also in transit was General Westmoreland, coming to talk with the president about the Vietnam situation because LBJ's planned trip to meet the general in Honolulu was canceled following King's death.

Newsroom, *Chicago Daily News,* late afternoon

Violence had already spread throughout Chicago, where dozens of fires burned. In the newsroom of the *Chicago Daily News,* reporters and editors worked late to cover the riots. Diane Monk, a new reporter confined to the "women's pages" of the features department, went to the city editor and offered to stay late to help; she would do anything that was needed, even if it meant going without pay to circumvent union rules about staying overtime.

"All right. You want a chance? Here's what you can do," the gruff night editor said. "Here's a list of people who have been reported killed in the riots. See if you can get some confirmation."

He handed Diane a police report that listed the addresses of people confirmed killed and a cross-address directory. "Start calling."

Diane dialed for hours. Finally, a woman who answered said, "I think I know who can help you. Hang on."

Diane heard the sounds of a crowded home in the background, then another woman came to the phone. Diane repeated the lines that had now become rote. "I'm calling from the *Daily News*. I'm looking for information about . . ."

"I'm his mother," the woman said.

"He was shot to death a few hours ago on Madison Street," Diane blurted out without thinking.

The woman on the other end of the phone began to scream, a keening wail that Diane had never before heard. "That's my son! He's been missing for hours. He was only fifteen."

No one told her, Diane thought. *If this had been a mother in another part of town, they would have sent someone right away to break the news to her as gently as possible. This woman's son has been in the morgue for hours, and no one tried to let her know because of the part of town she lives in.*

Diane went to her editor and told him about the woman. "Write up a couple hundred words; we'll try to get it in," he said. She wrote the story and filed it. Then she went to call her father, who worked in the Department of Veterans Affairs in Washington, D.C.

"You won't believe this," she said, telling him about the woman's son.

"You won't believe this," said her father. "I am watching Washington, D.C., burn." From his office at Vermont and H Street, two blocks from the White House, he could see dozens of fires blazing.

Diane went back to the newsroom and made more calls. At the end of the shift, she walked home with Rob Warden, a business reporter who had also pitched in to cover the riots. It was close to midnight, but the sky was light with an orange glow from the west, where fires blazed. As they walked, Diane felt something brush her skin. It was ash, falling from the sky and settling on the sidewalk. Soft, thick, and white, the ashes fell like snow.

A limousine traveling from the Boston airport, late afternoon

"James, James," councilor Tom Atkins pleaded with the Godfather of Soul as they were en route to the Boston Garden.

Brown was slated to play the fourteen-thousand-seat venue that night. Kevin White, the city's new, thirty-eight-year-old mayor faced a dilemma. So far Boston had seen isolated cases of rioting and violence. What would happen if a sellout crowd of riled-up teens came downtown for the concert? What would happen if the concert was canceled and all those teens came downtown anyway, now with another excuse to act out?

White and his aides* debated what to do. Worried that it was too late to cancel the show completely, they suggested Brown perform, but keep the crowd as small as possible. Finally they came up with a plan: broadcast the concert and urge kids to stay home and watch it. They would be out of the streets, and out of downtown.

As the limo drew closer to the Garden, the city councilor explained the plan. It's not a bad idea, said Brown, but I have a problem. He had taped a show that was supposed to air in New York and would face a steep penalty for violating the agreement by airing this show.

Eventually, Brown agreed to a deal. He would do the Boston show, allow it to be broadcast, and work out the details with the New York folks later. Mayor White would in turn come up with $60,000 to cover Brown's costs and the fine he faced for violating his deal.

The concert aired live, and the two-and-a-quarter-hour program was shown again immediately afterward. Only two thousand people attended the downtown show, but across the city, kids stayed home to watch or stood in front of appliance-shop windows gaping as Brown performed hits such as "It's a Man's Man's Man's World" and "Cold Sweat."

Office of Marvin Watson, White House Chief of Staff, Washington, D.C., 5:45 p.m.

The White House staff had anticipated a week preparing the president for his Honolulu trip to meet with commanders from Vietnam and hammer out peace talks. They had expected political strategy sessions as a result of LBJ's announcement that he would not seek the Democratic nomination. Now they unexpectedly faced a domestic crisis, a vast military mobilization, a shift in venue for the Vietnam talks, and political machinations in high gear.

King's funeral was obviously going to be a gambit in election-year

---

*Among them a young Barney Frank, who would go on to be elected to the U.S. Congress.

maneuvering; calls of all kinds came into the White House to discuss the politics of mourning. Don Kendall, president of Pepsi, left a message with Deke DeLoach, second-in-command at the FBI, and asked that it be passed on to Watson. "In view of the president's desire for a show of national unity, he should invite Nixon, Kennedy, and McCarthy to ride with him in the presidential plane to the funeral of Martin Luther King. Therefore not one individual could play politics with this situation," Kendall suggested. "I have discussed this with Nixon, who thinks it is a good idea. Nixon is agreeable, if the president agrees."*

Unsolicited advice about who should—or should not—go to the funeral, and how they should get to Atlanta, poured in. At 7 p.m., Watson received a memo from Johnson's legal counsel, Barefoot Sanders.† He had had a call from New York congressman Benjamin Rosenthal about efforts to get an air force plane to take members of Congress to the King funeral. "I hate to nitpick, but I have doubts about the legality of this." More important, Sanders stressed, "We cannot lose sight of the fact that the Rules Committee is still scheduled to take up Tuesday, April 9 at 10:30 a.m., the Resolution to concur in the Civil Rights Bill as passed by the Senate. We will need every member here for the Rules Committee and we will need every member here Wednesday—every Democrat, that is."

Five minutes later, former special assistant Jack Valenti, who had recently left the White House to become head of the Motion Picture Association of America, called. If there was a plane, he wanted a ride. "Go commercial—criticized," wrote Watson in neat cursive before checking the *no* box on the request form.

Any doubt that King's death was going to be a factor in presidential politics was erased a few minutes into the NBC evening newscast. The anchor turned to New York governor Nelson Rockefeller, then deep into

---

*The rivalry between Nixon and Johnson—or any of the contenders left in the race President Johnson had exited—was for serious stakes but bore more than a passing resemblance to the Coke-Pepsi feud of their respective corporate benefactors. "Coca-Cola was certainly the beverage of the LBJ White House," recalled one White House aide.

†Sanders's first name was Harold; Barefoot was a family name. He dropped the first name when running for head cheerleader in college and found it politically expedient—and memorable—to keep on using his middle name, Barefoot.

his third run for a Republican presidential nomination. Seated at a table in the studio, the governor looked at the camera head-on and said that on Monday he would address his state legislature and urge them to pass proposed laws "vitally affecting the lives of all our Negro citizens." The governor wore his trademark heavy-framed glasses and consulted his notes. "It is not enough for the American nation to ensure the enforcement of law. We must experience a renewal of love. For there will be fighting in the streets so long as there is fighting in our hearts."

Ebenezer Baptist Church, Atlanta, 7:30 p.m.

The Reverend Julius Hight opened the all-night vigil by saying, "Pray for the trigger-happy and those that don't think." The only decoration in the church was a carnation wreath in the lobby, decorated with a white ribbon bearing the words I HAD A DREAM. Black students at Emory University had sent the wreath. Earlier that day they organized a memorial in the campus center. Several hundred students came out, despite the ongoing bad weather, as the handful of minority students at the university led a quick service. Then the students walked through campus carrying the wreath on their way to Ebenezer.

A few miles away at the Atlanta Civic Center, more than five hundred people gathered for a meeting organized by the Metropolitan Atlanta Summit Leadership Congress (MASLC). The group was about equally divided between black and white attendees, and as reporters from the *Atlanta Constitution* noted, included "young and old of both races—from a bearded old white man wearing a black cloth band on his arm, to white 'hippie' youths in boots and jeans." The group had recently split off from the similarly acronymed Atlanta Summit Leadership Conference. Forming MASLC, its leaders issued a statement chastising the media for oversimplifying the contrast between King and his critics and underplaying King's effective strategies. Kicking off the meeting, MASLC executive committeeman Benny Smith said, "Let's demonstrate to the world that nonviolence will prevail in Atlanta."

The Reverend William Holmes Borders, the influential pastor of Wheat Street Baptist and a longtime civil rights crusader, who'd led the push to get black policemen hired in the 1940s and boycotted segregated transit in the 1950s, told attendees, "Let's show the people who believe in the sword that we can win."*

Joe Simmons, a white member of the MASLC executive committee, stood up and pointed at the other whites in the crowd. He asked them to support efforts to keep peace on the streets, instead of complaining about feared violence. "We need the help of the white leadership," he said. "Please join us."

Many white Atlantans stayed away from downtown during those turbulent days, shocked by the assassination, unsure of what might happen at home, and alarmed by news coverage from other cities. In Doraville, a northern suburb, Kathy and Norm Kohn spent most of Friday in shock watching reports on television and reading coverage in the newspapers. Norm was so upset by the death of King that he closed his art studio for the day; it just didn't seem possible to carry on with regular work, and he knew his clients would understand.

The White House, 10:58 p.m.

In the family quarters of the White House, the president sat down for a very late dinner. Judge Higginbotham, adviser Joe Califano, speechwriter Horace Busby, and aide Tom Johnson joined him. They talked intensely. How to prevent more violence, but also how to give people hope, were themes of the conversation, the longest one-on-one talk Higginbotham had had with the president. In the morning meeting he had sensed the president's worry and felt it escalate since the midday trip to the National Cathedral. During dinner, the president switched on the news to watch footage of the riots. Sitting at the dinner table, he commented to Busby that his planned speech to Congress on Monday would "make or break us." His speech declining the nomination a few days ago had been effective, "but the King thing has erased all that and we have to start again." The pressure was on Busby because counsel Harry McPherson's help

---

*Borders's granddaughter Lisa Borders was elected president of the Atlanta City Council in 2004. In 2009, she made an unsuccessful bid for mayor.

would be limited; his daughter Coco had fallen from a tree and hurt her arm and McPherson was at the little girl's bedside.

Dinner wrapped up just fifteen minutes before midnight, and the staff members were asked to stay in the White House to be close by in case of new developments. As he made his way to a guest room on the third floor, Tom Johnson worried about his wife, Edwina, and their two young children, not far away in an apartment in the Virginia suburbs. The fires and looting were only blocks from the White House; he wondered if the violence was spreading out of the city, too.

THREE

Saturday, April 6, 1968

More than twelve hundred buildings were destroyed in the arson and violence that erupted in Washington, D.C., after the King assassination. Army and National Guard troops were called in as rioting reached blocks from the White House. *Warren K. Leffler*, U.S. News & World Report *Magazine Photograph Collection, Library of Congress*

SCLC Headquarters, early morning

THE SCLC STAFF gathered for an emergency session. They knew they had to act quickly to officially name King's successor. Although Ralph Abernathy's ascension to the head of the organization was considered a given by most news outlets—as well as by most of the inner circle of the SCLC—the SCLC board had the final say. Whenever the fifty-three ministers, educators, and social crusaders gathered, debate, discussion, and a little hot wind were inevitable. The full board would not assemble until Tuesday, the day of the funeral, but the staff knew they needed to have a media statement ready.

Jesse Jackson, King's twenty-six-year-old protégé, who had already returned to Chicago, was a subject of discussion and watched carefully—by the SCLC insiders, the national press, and operatives working for J. Edgar Hoover. Everyone expected Jackson to make a power play. FBI sources on the ground in Atlanta sent bulletins back to D.C. reporting speculation that Jackson was pushing for the top spot. Hoover sent the president a memo that afternoon, saying the FBI had learned from an informant that "Ralph Abernathy is expected to be confirmed as the successor to Martin Luther King Jr., as head of the Southern Christian Leadership Conference," but "a power struggle for leadership led by Jessie [*sic*] Jackson of Chicago, Illinois, is possible."

One possible successor, King's widow, Coretta Scott King, was barely considered. Mrs. King had national celebrity, unparalleled poise, a track record as a fund-raiser, and charisma that could rival her husband's. But although the SCLC espoused radical social and economic philosophies for its time, it was no advocate of feminism, but deeply entrenched in the patriarchal views of its pastor founders.*

Although the men of the SCLC might not have been willing to elect a female leader, they did recognize the value of using King's widow as a spokeswoman. As they discussed strategies for quashing media rumors about dissent in the organization, they suggested that Coretta should present the decision about succession to the media. Impartial, sympathetic, and eloquent, she would be an effective messenger. Her participation would convey that the organization planned to carry on her husband's work. The person who ultimately persuaded her to take on the task was not one of the ministers, but Harry Belafonte, the media-savvy singer-actor.

Talk turned to details of the funeral. They agreed that Coretta King and Martin's sister, Christine, would organize the service inside the Ebenezer Baptist Church and the memorial event at Morehouse College.

---

*In late 2009, King's youngest child, Bernice, a minister and activist with a law degree from Emory University, was elected president of SCLC, the first female to be elected head of the organization.

The SCLC would work on the procession from the church to Morehouse. It would be a march, like those they'd participated in with King so many times. The one remaining question was how to transport King's coffin from the church to the college. Something formal, maybe a carriage, top hats. Stately. *Kingly*, thought Bernard LaFayette.

"No. No. No. No. No. No. No!" shouted Hosea Williams. "It has to reflect the Poor People's Campaign!"

Williams envisioned a mule wagon as hearse, with SCLC honorary pallbearers dressed in the uniform of the poor—denim overalls and work boots—a costume Williams had already taken to wearing practically full time.* This would emphasize King's commitment to fighting poverty—and promote the Poor People's Campaign, which had been delayed several times already. Williams's exuberance won out. All right, the group agreed. If you want a mule wagon, Hosea, you find one.

Williams went home after the meeting and got on the phone, calling people in every Georgia county where he had marched, been arrested, or led a voter-registration drive. His seventeen-year-old daughter, Elizabeth, home from her Colorado boarding school for the funeral, listened to her dad's calls with interest. It had to be just the *right* wagon, Williams insisted. Old. Weather-beaten. A perfect symbol for the television cameras and newspapers.

Khesanh, South Vietnam, early morning (local time)

As the helicopter landed, it stirred up clouds of red-clay dust. General Westmoreland climbed out. Lean, square-jawed, and with thick, dark eyebrows that gave him the look of a hawk, Westmoreland surveyed the mountain bunkers.

Reinforcements from Operation Pegasus were drawing closer. Close behind Westmoreland, a thousand troops arrived by helicopter in advance of the moving column of reinforcements.

Time magazine reported that the relieved marines "gamboled in makeshift showers" and even retrieved baseball mitts to play catch while

---

*Decades later, Williams would cohost a show on Atlanta public-access television and always appear in overalls, which he often paired with a jaunty red silk shirt.

"the roofs of bunkers blossomed with Marines who were not, for a change, either running or ducking."

After leaving Khesanh, Westmoreland continued on to D.C., where he arrived around 8 a.m. On the way from the helicopter landing to the White House, the general said in earshot of reporters, "I understand you had a little trouble yourself," referring to the riots.

Outside the White House, sidewalks were roped off to keep both tourists and rioters from getting any closer. LBJ had announced weeks earlier that Westmoreland was moving into a new role, army chief of staff, and speculation was rampant about who would succeed him.

Clinic, Central Presbyterian Church, downtown Atlanta, 9 a.m.

The Reverend Randy Taylor called an emergency meeting of church leaders. He wanted to discuss how the congregation would respond to King's death. A year earlier, when he'd left a church in Washington, D.C., to take the Central pastorate, the young minister caused a stir. Taylor was involved in the civil rights movement and had taken part in the Selma-to-Montgomery march. He was a vocal supporter of integration, a stance that had provoked some older members of the church, who left the congregation in protest when Taylor was installed.

At first the church leaders were taken aback at the early-morning meeting. Pastor Taylor knew he was infringing on "precious family time or golf time," but everyone had been watching the footage of the riots in other cities and highlights from King's historic life, and they turned out in force, "one of those moments of great emotional turnout," the pastor would later recall.

But the church deacons and leaders told Taylor they agreed that Central needed to do *something* to recognize King.

We can name one of the big rooms in our new wing after him, one suggested. Maybe this clinic?

That's a good move, said another, but no one but us will know we did that. Let's erect some kind of monument in front of the church.

On our front lawn—facing the capitol, suggested another. A public recognition of King.

The deacons agreed to do both, a room and a monument or marker.

How about right now, doing something practical? asked Taylor. We could help with the funeral; maybe host people coming in from out of town. I will find out what the SCLC needs.

The deacons looked at each other with some anxiety. All right, they said. We will help. Let us know when you hear from the SCLC.

They knew that they were authorizing a precedent-shattering project. Central was known for fund-raising and good deeds, but directly helping the SCLC to host mourners would mean inviting black people inside the historic sanctuary. This was a radical move. The bell of Central Presbyterian had sounded the alarm when Sherman's army approached Atlanta during the Civil War, and its pastor, Robert Mallard, was captured during the occupation. Sherman's forces had repurposed part of the church as a slaughterhouse, while Union troops set up camp around the state-capitol area.

"Grief and fear and guilt were at work," Pastor Taylor would conclude later.

Spelman College campus, Atlanta, early afternoon

Drivers from Hanley's funeral home transported King's casket to the campus of Spelman College. The body had been clothed in King's favorite suit and arranged in a silk-lined coffin that was sealed with a glass top to allow for viewing. When the drivers arrived at the campus, they realized a legal technicality required Coretta Scott King's approval before the remains could be transferred to a new location and public viewing could start. As they waited for her to arrive, the lines outside grew longer. Finally Mrs. King and a small group—including Harry Belafonte and his wife, Julie, King's parents, and Xernona Clayton—went into the chapel. Ron English, the assistant pastor at Ebenezer Baptist Church and a Morehouse College fraternity brother of King's, was one of the honor guards stationed at the chapel door.

Inside the chapel, the family circle eased back as the funeral director opened the casket. Xernona Clayton was startled by what seemed to be a big blob of makeup on King's face. His skin seemed reddish. "Is there anything we can do?" she asked the mortician. She recalled that when her husband, Ed, died a few years earlier, she persuaded an undertaker to carefully match his skin tone.

The mortician answered abruptly, "Miss, his jaw was blown off. This was the best we could do. We had to put clay on it."

Clayton recoiled. *So crass. So ugly,* she thought of the undertaker. Then she looked at the pale skin of Julie Belafonte, and Mama King's dark tan. "Do you have any face powder?" she asked each of them. She took their compacts and mixed the powders, then dabbed the new blend on King's face, dulling the redness of the clay that had been used to reconstruct his shattered jawline. Harry Belafonte leaned over and placed his handkerchief under King's chin, keeping the powder from soiling his collar.

After Clayton finished, Belafonte removed the handkerchief, put it in his pocket, and said, "This is a piece of history."

Then he looked down again and called, "Stop!" to the honor guard, about to open the chapel doors. He reached over and straightened King's tie.

"Now, let them come in," he said to Ron English. The coffin's glass top was lowered and sealed. In single file, people began to enter the church.

Over the next two days, an estimated sixty thousand people would come to see the body—moving through the chapel at a rate of close to twelve hundred an hour, with a mile-long queue winding through campus. Television crews captured the somber pace of mourners, most dressed in neat suits or dresses, many carrying Bibles, others carrying briefcases, as they waited on the tree-lined walks. Mothers clutched the hands of small children, and fathers carried toddlers on their shoulders. Dogwoods and azaleas bloomed, creating the vibrant backdrop typical of an Atlanta spring.

On entering the tall, white-columned building, mourners filed down a side aisle, passed the coffin at the altar area, and exited down the other side aisle. Few slipped in to sit in the pews; those who did sat with bowed heads. Bouquets and wreaths filled the front of the chapel—large clusters of yellow, pink, and white roses dominated.

On Saturday afternoon, Marvin Mangham waited in line for hours. When he finally reached the front of the dim chapel, he looked down at the glass-covered coffin, and all he could think was how obvious it was that morticians had reconstructed the lower part of King's face. *It's hard, just different-looking,* he thought.

Outside the chapel, students walked up and down the queues, handing out flyers that surprised some of the mourners. "The Black Tiger" read the headline on a flyer denouncing Stokely Carmichael. "He is going to blow your minds with black talk and fight talk. He has the power to move your souls, especially those whose emotions are more important than their reasons." Another Black Tiger flyer read, "Black power without black action is rhetoric." Flyers with the subtler but more direct statement "Riots hurt you and me" were designed by Robert Lee Webb of the Young Men's Civic League, a group from the Summerhill neighborhood, described by *Atlanta Constitution* reporter Duane Riner as "admitted former troublemakers."

FBI offices, Washington, D.C., 2:22 p.m.

J. Edgar Hoover sent a Teletype report to the president and carbon copied the heads of the CIA, army, and air force, the White House situation room, the secretary of state, and the director of the Defense Intelligence Agency. The memo recapped "selected racial developments and disturbances" around the country, including the reports:

In Washington, D.C., military troops in tanks were deployed throughout the city in response to "looting, robbing, window breaking, and shooting."

The mayor of Philadelphia banned groups of more than twelve people gathering for any reason other than "business or recreation" and closed liquor stores through April 10. Meanwhile, the city anticipated a 4.8-mile civil rights march from Camden, New Jersey, to Independence Hall in Philadelphia's historic heart to take place the next day and was putting in place plans for extra police protection.

In Flint, Michigan, NAACP representatives planned demonstrations that night and the next day. They had also "made numerous demands on city officials, including the appointment of Negroes to top positions in the school system and police department" and stated that they would "not be responsible for what happens if the demands are not met."

SNCC volunteers in Los Angeles issued a call for a general strike.

Fires, burglaries, and sniper fire plagued Detroit. Hartford, Connecticut, had seen fires and looting, and a curfew was implemented in

Savannah. Mobile, Alabama, also was under curfew from dusk until dawn. National Guard troops patrolled Memphis. In Albany, Georgia, a march by the Georgia Teachers Association was canceled, while Tallahassee, Florida's Agricultural and Mechanical University was in lockdown.

In Linden, New Jersey, someone fired a shot at Mayor John Gregorio's car, breaking a window.

The terse tone of the FBI memo did not capture the drama of what Americans read about on the front pages of their morning newspapers or saw, either on television or framed in the doors and windows of their own homes. Flames soared out of store windows in Chicago; grim soldiers marched down Washington, D.C., sidewalks; National Guard planes flew low over Memphis. In dozens of cities, empty shells of destroyed buildings were clouded with smoke from fires that still smoldered.

Sunset Avenue, afternoon

As he thought about the thousands of people coming to Atlanta for the funeral, Mayor Ivan Allen grew increasingly anxious about crowd control at Ebenezer, which could hold only 750 worshippers. He did not want to appear pushy, but did want to try for a change of venue, so he sent two women from his staff to Coretta King's house, hoping that they could persuade the widow to move the service to the new civic auditorium.

When Allen's emissaries, Ann Moses and Linda Mullá, walked into the home, Mullá's first reaction was how ordinary the setting seemed—"like any home in the South; ladies, friends, family members in the kitchen preparing food. Southern ladies in there making sure that they had everything ready for the groups coming in." Moses and Mullá were invited into King's study to meet with Coretta, Christine King Farris, and other family members. Books and papers were stacked on the desk. It looked as though King would return to pick up work on a speech or sermon at any moment.

Moses and Mullá passed along the mayor's offer of the auditorium.

Thanks, but no. We're staying with Ebenezer, said Coretta Scott King. There is no place in the city that is big enough to hold all the people who want to come.

She asked that her thanks be passed on to the mayor and dismissed the two women after a few pleasantries.

Then Coretta, Christine, and other friends went back to where the real planning was taking place: Mrs. King's bedroom. She balanced her public appearances with rest, swathed in a floral wrap and cocooned in a damask bedspread. Above the carved wood frame of her headboard hung a portrait of Mrs. King as a much younger woman, smiling, in a bare-shouldered gown, the scalloped bustline of her dress framed in white ruffles. A painting of Martin King and one of a biblical scene flanked that portrait. A long, low bench with delicately curved legs was placed along the foot of the bed; it seemed burdened with the teetering stack of photo albums and newspapers. The children came and went freely, sometimes getting into the bed and crawling under the covers with their mother. Ralph Abernathy, A. D. King, Bernard Lee, and others clustered around, discussing plans. Sometimes they sprawled in the armchair in the corner of the room or carried in cups of coffee and plates of food.

Atlanta Stadium, early afternoon

Coretta asked Kathryn Johnson for a favor. Could she take Daddy King to the Braves' stadium to watch the team practice? The senior King was a true baseball fan, and it would do him good to get out of the house. And would Kathryn take Dexter, too? The young AP reporter dropped King's father off at the stadium, promising she would be back to see him soon. He was so "wrapped in grief," she could not engage him in conversation. Dexter did not want to stay at the ballpark, so she brought him with her as she headed to her house to pick up a change of clothes before going back to collect Daddy King.

Dexter sat in the front seat. When Kathryn stopped at a traffic light, the little boy started to sob and would not stop. Kathryn looked up and saw that two police officers were looking into the car warily. She thought to herself, *No wonder they are suspicious. That's not something you see in Atlanta every day—a young white woman driving around with a little black boy in the front seat.* She was relieved when the light changed and she could drive on, although she checked the rearview mirror several times to see if the police were following her.

Over the next few days, Kathryn Johnson and photographers Bob Fitch and Flip Schulke would help out in all kinds of ways—driving the kids to playdates, running family members on errands. It was hardly the conventional way to report the news, but they were aware they were in the midst of the biggest story most of them would ever cover. "There was a sense we were seeing history," Fitch recalled.

Kathryn Johnson spent hours helping to sort telegrams, cards, and letters. They were stacked on every available surface in the King home; more than twelve thousand came in the first few days after King's death. The SCLC staff created a form letter for "Acknowledgment of Meaningful Letters of Condolences" to help streamline correspondence.* Some letters were simply addressed "Mrs. King, Atlanta GA" or "SCLC, Atlanta" or "Reverend Abernathy." Many were simple handwritten messages on torn sheets of notebook paper; others were formal missives on letterhead that told of proclamations issued by churches or civic groups in response to King's death. Some contained checks, others pledges to contribute funds either to the family directly or to SCLC. Many people sent poems or verses. In a letter dated April 6, Jane and Charles Kmosko of Plainfield, New Jersey, wrote to say they had "just written a letter to the House Rules Committee urging them to pass the Civil Rights Bill before them now."

Sister Ann Thaddeus of St. Thomas Aquinas School in the Bronx sent a package of more than thirty letters written by her second-grade students, including Socovo Santos, who wrote, "Do not be sad Mrs King be happy Mrs King." Students at the Wogaman School in Dayton, Ohio, sent a booklet bound with plastic spiral rings. The fourth graders addressed a poem to the King children.

> *Hush little Bernice, don't you cry,*
> *For love and freedom your daddy did die*
> *Hey little Dexter, be a big boy,*
> *For someday you're going to feel joy*

---

*The letter stated, "Dear Friend: Your recent letter has been received. While the volume of mail makes it impossible for us to respond in detail, we want to send you this note of thanks and appreciation. Your thoughts and comments are a source of comfort and strength to us in these difficult days."

Ebenezer Baptist Church, 5 p.m.

Around sixty reporters sat in the wooden pews, and another few dozen television cameramen and newspaper photographers adjusted lights around the pulpit area and fiddled with microphones. Everyone waited for Coretta Scott King.

She arrived along with Harry Belafonte, Bernard Lee, Ralph Abernathy, and Andrew Young. She sat behind a table with the three SCLC staffers while Belafonte stood to the side, watching intently. The television cameras captured her emotional strain. Poised and collected, in a fitted black sheath accented with a checked bow, her hair in immaculate waves, Coretta King looked strikingly beautiful but physically drained, her face wan, her voice flat, her anguish obvious. Lee told the reporters that Abernathy would be giving a statement the next day, but that for now the platform was Mrs. King's.

Barely glancing at her notes, Coretta addressed the cameras. Abernathy, she said, "could express and interpret [King's] views on nonviolence better than anyone else," and her husband "always said that if anything happened to him, he would like for Ralph Abernathy to take his place in the struggle and as the head of the Southern Christian Leadership Conference." Then she said:

> I would have preferred to be alone at this time with my children. We were always willing to share Martin Luther King with the world because he was a symbol of the finest man is capable of being. Yet to us he was a father and a husband. Our far-too-brief moments with him are cherished personal memories, too precious to be adequately described. . . . I have put aside traditional family considerations because my husband's work for his people and for all poor people transcends our wish for privacy.

Mrs. King, known to be as outspoken a critic of war as her husband, also stated, "Our concern now is that his work does not die. He gave his life for the poor of the world—the garbage workers of Memphis and the peasants of Vietnam. Nothing hurt him more than that man could attempt no way to solve problems except through violence."

She concluded, "The day that Negro people and others in bondage are truly free, on the day want is abolished, on the day wars are no more, on that day I know my husband will rest in a long-deserved peace."

Cameras clicked and bulbs flashed, but the end of her statement was followed by a subdued silence. Mrs. King's weariness and grief were palpable, and the press remained reserved, staying seated in the pews as she arose and walked out down the aisle.

Members of the SCLC realized that Abernathy would be compared to King—and that favorable assessments were unlikely. "Inside SCLC, members of Mr. Abernathy's inner circle, the same group that served Dr. King, realize that the greatest task now is to discourage comparison," noted Earl Caldwell in the *New York Times.* "'You have to let him be his own man,' they say of Mr. Abernathy. 'He is not Martin Luther King, and if he is going to be able to accomplish anything, he has to have the opportunity to be himself.'" Another *Times* article said of Abernathy's relationship with King, "In ways they complemented each other. Dr. King was the leader—eloquent and beloved by the crowds. Mr. Abernathy is calm, slow-talking and very polite." A photograph of Abernathy captioned "Dr. King's alter ego" accompanied the article. Media reports painted an image of Abernathy as self-deprecating and unassuming. The *Atlanta Constitution* reported that the "mantle of leadership" covered the "reluctant shoulders" of the companion who had been with King "since the Montgomery bus boycott."

Some media coverage underscored the less-than-flattering differences between Abernathy—always in the background despite his long-standing relationship with King—and the charismatic slain leader. The *New York Times* described the new SCLC head as a "stocky Baptist minister." *Jet* characterized him as a "quiet, expressionless man" and described him as "beefy shouldered." (Abernathy did, however, elicit sympathetic media coverage by telling reporters he had stopped eating after King's death. "He has taken liquid nourishment. He said he is trying to 'purify my soul' for the job ahead," reported Jack Nelson, Atlanta bureau chief for the *Los Angeles Times. Jet* noted that, in the time between King's death and the funeral, Abernathy lost fourteen pounds.)

Not only would Abernathy have to live up to the pressure of following one of the best-known orators of the century, he would have to rein in the strong-willed SCLC leaders and impose order on its upcoming campaign plans. "As an organizer, it is doubtful he has King's ability," noted the *Christian Science Monitor*, "and organization is what the SCLC will most need in the months ahead."

Most dauntingly, Abernathy would have to face critics claiming that the organization he would be helming was in danger of becoming irrelevant. As historian Lerone Bennett wrote in the May 1968 issue of *Ebony*, at the time of his death King "was involved just then in a struggle for his very existence as a national leader. Although he was still the foremost symbol of the struggle for racial justice, he was being pressed by a new breed of organizers and orators who stressed Black Power and militant self-defense." More ominously, a "new mood rising from the despair and determination of the very young and the very defiant" had eroded King's moral authority as a champion of nonviolence. The failed March 28 demonstration in Memphis had exacerbated debate over the effectiveness of King's nonviolent tactics.

On top of this, everyone was worried that King was not the only target of the sniper in Memphis. "I'm surprised they didn't take out at least another five of us," Bernard LaFayette said.

In preparing for the funeral, the SCLC leadership faced a daunting task. Not only did they have to assist in the logistics of what amounted to a state funeral (without state funding or support), but they also had to manage public opinion given that King's death occurred when the organization faced criticism on multiple fronts.

One criticism was that King and many of his colleagues came from the black middle class and did not relate to the poor people they claimed to represent. King's childhood on Auburn Avenue was infinitely more comfortable than that of most of his constituents, and Andrew Young, son of a New Orleans dentist, likewise came from a bourgeois background. Ralph Abernathy had grown up poor on an Alabama farm, but served in World War II and attended college on the G.I. Bill. Many of the younger SCLC staff had made their way through the student movement and came from working- or middle-class families that prized college.

The contrast between the King's advocacy for the poor and the rioting and looting happening in the poorest neighborhoods of America's cities hinted at the gap between the largely middle-class SCLC leaders and the rural and urban poor on whose behalf they worked. "There was an intensity and a fury of the rioters and looters that eluded the Negro middle class in the nation's capital," wrote Simeon Booker, D.C. bureau chief for Johnson Publishing, in *Jet*. Booker, the first black reporter for the *Washington Post* and acclaimed for his coverage of the Emmett Till murder and the Freedom Rides, quoted a rioter saying, "We don't believe in conciliation and negotiation. You can scrap the NAACP and the Urban League, keep their leaders busy talking on the radio about how great King is—dead."

Peachtree Street, downtown Atlanta, late afternoon

Xernona Clayton made her way back to Joseph's. "I'm here to pick up the clothes, and here's payment," she said, handing over the credit cards loaned by Harry Belafonte and Stan Levison.

"You don't have a bill with us. I'm a white American; I have to take some of this guilt and pain, and this is a way to assuage my grief. You have no debt here," said the store owner.

Clayton then went to the back door at Davison's and up to the millinery department. The store manager called in three people to work on the hat, and they stayed late translating the sketch into reality.

Clayton studied the hat, pleased with the results. The woven, rounded crown rose high in the front, which would flatter Mrs. King's strong features and elongate her face. The intricate woven detail of the headpiece was visible through a translucent veil that draped to collarbone level in the front and hung longer in the back. The veil was anchored by a thick border of solid black that would both hold the lightweight fabric steady and frame Mrs. King's face. The fine mesh of the veil would allow Mrs. King's expressions to be caught on camera, and she would be able to observe all that was going on around her. *She won't be veiled out of sight*, Xernona thought.

She thanked the Davison's staff for their help. "This looks wonderful, but it is not for me to decide. I have to take it to Mrs. King. She will have to approve."

Clayton left out of the back door of the department store once again.

Chicago, City Hall, 5:19 p.m.

"Mr. President. We're in trouble. We need some help," Richard Daley, mayor of Chicago, said as soon as the White House operator patched his call through to Lyndon Johnson. Daley, the consummate Chicago politico and Democratic Party stalwart, had been influential in gaining John Kennedy, a fellow Irish Catholic, the party nomination for president.

The president calmly reminded the Chicago mayor of the steps that were required before federal troops could be sent into a city. Calling the White House first disrupted protocol; the mayor needed to call the governor's office and have the situation officially assessed. "They have to make a finding," LBJ reminded Mayor Daley, who seemed dazed on the other end of the line.

The president talked about his own agony over the decision to push for federal troops to be sent into D.C. "I just cried. I ate my fingernails off," said Lyndon Johnson.

"How many troops do you think you'll want?" LBJ then asked.

"At least three thousand," said Daley.

"You had better say five."

A few minutes later, Attorney General Ramsey Clark called the Oval Office. As procedure dictated, he had heard from the Illinois lieutenant governor, Samuel Shapiro,* on behalf of Mayor Daley. "We are beginning the movement of troops right now," Clark told President Johnson.

The attorney general reminded the president that they could not rush to send troops to Chicago without following the proper steps. Trouble now flared in dozens of cities. Michigan governor George Romney was calling for federal help for Detroit. A plainclothes military team was on its way to scope out the situation, but it would be six or seven hours before troops arrived. When it came to Chicago, "we need to reconnoiter and make the judgment, like we did in Detroit," Clark told the president. This, he added, was needed "to keep Romney from saying 'he [Johnson]

---

*Shapiro would become governor a few weeks later when Governor Otto Kerner, who had headed the commission on riots, resigned to take a position on an appellate-court bench.

takes care of his buddies like Daley, but he doesn't take care of his political enemies like Romney.'"

Daley's urgency was fueled by escalating violence in Chicago. That morning snipers took to the roof of a housing project, firing at police and National Guard soldiers. A Molotov cocktail tossed into a window killed a ten-month-old. Newspapers reported that the mayor gave "shoot to kill" orders to police and National Guard.

By Saturday evening, United Press International (UPI) dispatches painted an even grimmer picture than the memo J. Edgar Hoover had sent earlier in the day. The UPI reported ten dead in Chicago, five in Washington, D.C., and two in Detroit. Violence seized more than twenty cities. Police arrested more than 800 people in Washington and 280 in Chicago, the two worst-hit cities.

In Atlanta, police encountered only a few scuffles and broken windows. On Ashby Street, teenage boys looted a supermarket. Others threw rocks at passing Atlanta Transit System buses. A would-be firebomber and Clark College student dropped an unlit bomb when police approached. He was promptly arrested by Eldrin Bell, a young detective, and his partner, W. J. Kleckley. The policemen also arrested three men who broke the windows of a liquor store at the corner of Vine and Magnolia streets and fled when the cops approached. Bell and other policemen would spend long hours over the next days patrolling on foot as part of Jenkins's riot prevention plan.*

Overall, Atlanta remained quiet. Mayor Allen and Police Chief Jenkins put the force on extended shifts. Still, the mayor was anxious. Later that night he called Jenkins: "Let's go out and look around." He picked up Jenkins and they drove from Summerhill to Mechanicsville to Vine City—and on to every other black neighborhood. At each stop they got out of the police car and walked around, talking to people on front porches and in businesses. "Here we were, two white middle-aged gray-haired men—the mayor and the police chief of the city—walking up and down the streets, standing on the corners, talking to people, trying to show them our concern," Allen would later write. As they strolled the

---

*Bell would rise through the Atlanta Police Department ranks, eventually becoming police chief. He later became chair of the Clayton County Commission.

neighborhoods, they could hear people talking about them; the mayor predicted that by midnight most of the city's black residents would have heard about their being out that night, and he hoped this would generate goodwill.

Before heading home, the mayor stopped at West Hunter Street Baptist Church, the church pastored by Ralph Abernathy. He was surprised to see the church basement packed with people taking phone calls.

One of the operators was Winifred Green, who had already been in the church basement for one day answering calls and would be there for two days more. Green, who had been working in Alabama for the American Friends Service Committee, had taken a temporary assignment with the SCLC in Atlanta to help work on the Poor People's Campaign. After she heard about King's death, Green went to see what she could do to help. "Help us with calls," she was told. Her task was logging calls from celebrities and dignitaries calling to request reserved seats during the private funeral at Ebenezer. At first the team struggled since the church office had only a few lines and calls to BellSouth for help went unheeded. As they were working, Earl Graves, an aide to the Kennedy campaign, stopped by.

"What do you need most?" he asked.

"More phone lines," Green said.

It seemed to her and the other volunteers like "this magic thing" when phone lines were installed in hours. *

Standing with Ralph Abernathy watching the phones ring, the mayor was dumbfounded.

"It's all long distance," Abernathy said.

"Long distance?" asked the mayor.

"Every one of them."

"Who the devil are they talking to?"

"People who're coming for the funeral."

The mayor watched the phone operators, stunned. He had been so preoccupied with safety for city residents, it had not dawned on him exactly how many outsiders would arrive in Atlanta for King's funeral. What would it be, a few thousand? Tens of thousands? A hundred thou-

---

*Graves went on to launch *Black Enterprise* magazine. He is the author of the bestseller *How to Succeed in Business Without Being White.*

sand? How would they keep the city safe with that many people? And where would everyone stay?

More anxious than ever, the mayor headed for home.

A few hours later, Green left West Hunter Street Baptist, too. She followed the code that had been suggested to her and other white volunteers who would be leaving the church in the dark after a twelve- or fourteen-hour shift: put a white cloth in the front window of your car as a signal of being friendly to the movement. Green affixed a white washcloth to the passenger window every night that week.

After only a few hours of sleep, the mayor was woken by a call from Attorney General Ramsey Clark that only increased his worry. Clark had several stakes in the Atlanta situation. He was overseeing the investigation into King's murder. As attorney general, he was in charge of civil rights compliance, and he worried about how Atlanta hotels and restaurants would accommodate the crowds arriving for the funeral.

Are facilities there *really* integrated? Clark asked the mayor. Are there even enough places for people to stay? Maybe they should set up shelters at nearby military bases. Finally, there was the really pressing issue. After a day of authorizing troops into cities across the country, Clark worried about safety in Atlanta. Would the city devolve into chaos like Chicago and D.C.? Did the mayor anticipate needing armed reinforcements?

The mayor found no point in trying to go back to sleep with his fears compounded by these questions. He was more anxious than he had been when he went to bed.

FOUR

Palm Sunday, April 7, 1968

Coretta Scott King's bedroom served as the command center
for the group planning the funeral. © *Bob Fitch Photo*

Pastor's office, Central Presbyterian Church, 9 a.m.

RANDY TAYLOR POLISHED his Palm Sunday sermon and pondered his announcement to the congregation about the church elders' decision to help the SCLC with the funeral in whatever way was needed. The phone rang. It was the SCLC: "There are so many people coming to town, we don't know what to do."

"We can take people at Central," Taylor said without hesitation.

Then he walked from his office into the dark-paneled sanctuary and welcomed the congregation to the Palm Sunday celebration. He told them that they would be hosting out-of-town arrivals for King's funeral and that the next few days would be busy. Startled gasps came from a few members, who quickly understood this would mean officially integrating the church. Others moved on to practical discussion about how to set up cots and meal lines. One of the church members had worked for Civil Defense and knew where to get cots in case of a natural disaster or fire. But what about blankets? Call the mayor, Taylor was told. You'll have to get them from Fort McPherson.

So after the service, Taylor called Allen at his home.

"Mr. Mayor, this is Randy Taylor. I have a problem."

You think you do? What about me? thought the mayor. *The city could break out in riots any minute.*

"I need six hundred blankets," explained Pastor Taylor. "Can you help?"

The mayor wanted to laugh. Compared to everything else going on, finding six hundred blankets was an easily solvable problem. As he assured the pastor that City Hall would help, the deeper implication of Taylor's call registered with Allen. Churches in Atlanta had remained segregated, by custom if not by law. An old-guard church such as Central opening its doors to welcome arriving mourners, most of them assuredly black, was not something he would have predicted.

Are you sure about your decision? he asked Taylor.

We're sure, the minister assured the mayor. And I think I will have other churches on my side.

Well, then, I can get you blankets, said Allen.

Within hours, representatives from the Shrine of the Immaculate Conception and Trinity Methodist, both, like Central, blocks from the capitol and City Hall, called the mayor's office to say they also would host out-of-town arrivals. By Monday, the list of white churches that had opened their doors to visitors grew and included Decatur Presbyterian, North Avenue Presbyterian in Midtown, and St. Anne's Episcopal in Buckhead. In a telex to the New York office, the Atlanta bureau of *Newsweek* noted that the "response of white churches in Atlanta was spectacular, suggesting a pent-up need to be involved."

Five years earlier, during a question-and-answer session at Western Michigan University, Martin Luther King had been asked about the role churches should—and did—play in integration. "At eleven on Sunday morning when we stand and sing, 'Christ has no east or west,' we stand at the most segregated hour in this nation," King had replied. "This is tragic. Nobody of honesty can overlook this."

Following the lead of the churches, a number of predominantly white colleges, including Emory, Georgia Tech, and Columbia Seminary, announced plans to open their dorms, dining rooms, and gyms to accommodate funeral guests.

Not everyone was happy with these moves. On Monday, student Robert Brown wrote a letter to Emory University president Sanford Atwood saying, "I strongly object to the use of the university facilities by agents of the SCLC." John McLaren, MD, who worked in the university-hospital radiation-therapy clinic, wrote a letter to Atwood decrying efforts to raise a scholarship in King's name, saying King associated with "known Communists," including "Bayard Rustin and Andrew Young." This was not McLaren's first protest to Atwood; in 1965, he sent a letter complaining about Atwood's involvement in the banquet honoring King's Nobel Prize win.

More discreetly than the churches and schools, businesses also helped. Honeywell, for example, used its corporate plane to bring nineteen pastors—black and white—to Atlanta. The company also chartered a bus to take the ministers on a tour of the city and to the funeral services.

U.S. embassy, South Vietnam, morning (local time)

The Stars and Stripes at the embassy hung at half-staff in honor of King, and inside, soldiers and diplomats listened to radio coverage of the riots at home. In recognition of Palm Sunday, the rock and pop that usually played on Armed Forces Radio was preempted for easy listening and news reports. Reporter Bernard Weinraub, interviewing G.I.'s for the *New York Times*, quoted twenty-one-year-old Specialist Reginald Daniels of New Orleans, "If I can come over here and try to liberate these people, I sure as hell can help liberate my own people."

Rondel Sinclair of Alabama said, "Somewhere, sometime, we all got to sit down together at a conference table like North Vietnam and South Vietnam and come to an agreement. Someday, like the man said, we will overcome."

NBC studios, Washington, 10 a.m.

Attorney General Ramsey Clark made a guest appearance on *Meet the Press* to talk about the search for King's killer. Clark said that the "trail had lengthened" in the search for the killer but offered few details. We might release a photo—after we have the man, he said. We have a name, but we do not know if it is the right one. A Remington rifle *might* have been used—we will tell you after the tests from the labs in D.C. are completed. Yes, a bundle was found. Yes, King was killed by a single shot. Yes, that bullet is being tested. No, I am not going to tell you anything else.

Ebenezer Baptist Church, 10:30 a.m.

Longtime congregants had grown used to the fuss that came with having a celebrity pastor. "Every time M.L. would be scheduled to speak and it was announced, there would be a crowd of tourists," recalled assistant pastor Ron English. But this morning was simply surreal. Television cameras pointed at the church from across the street, and reporters and onlookers clustered on the sidewalk outside. The sanctuary was so crowded that people stood up along the aisles and in the back of the church.

Daddy King delivered the opening remarks: "These are bewildering times in which we live. Sometimes I think that we have forgotten this is God's world."

His son—Martin Jr.'s brother—A. D. Williams King, a Baptist minister whose church was in Louisville, Kentucky, gave the sermon. He used a topic his brother had selected, "Why America May Go to Hell."

"America is a dying nation today. America is a sick nation," A. D. King said. "God is telling America, 'You've gone and spent it all, but I still love you, America. And I want you to come home. Come home, America, and make my world a better place.'"

Mahalia Jackson sang, and Dizzy Gillespie played the spiritual "Nobody Knows the Trouble I've Seen."

Pastors scrapped traditional Holy Week homilies in favor of sermons that addressed King's assassination. At West Hunter Street Baptist, Ralph Abernathy read a "letter" to King. Speaking of the rioters in other cities, he said, "I want you to know, Martin, we are going to point the way for them."

Abernathy ended with a challenge to City Hall, citing poverty, poor schools, and high unemployment in Atlanta's black neighborhoods. "I know you have great respect for Mayor Allen, as do I," he said to the congregation. "But we're going to tell him the Negro demands—not begs—for his God-given constitutional rights in Atlanta."

In Buckhead, a huge ecumenical service was held at the Episcopal Cathedral of St. Philip. Joseph Bernardin, Roman Catholic auxiliary bishop; Bevel Jones, president of the Christian Council of Metropolitan Atlanta; and A. S. Dickerson, pastor of Central Methodist, took part. Rabbi Jacob Rothschild of the Atlanta Temple,* one of King's staunch supporters, issued a challenge to "white America." The rabbi said of King, "His life is in our hands."

A few weeks earlier, Rothschild took the members of his own congregation to task on racism more sternly. On March 8, shortly after the release of the *Kerner Report*, the rabbi delivered a sermon in which he said, "The indictment against white America is a devastating one, and we do well to examine ourselves in the light of it." The racism described by the Kerner commission, he said, was "not the KKK" but "more genteel, less blatant racism that all of us are guilty of."

---

*Rabbi Jacob Rothschild coauthored the 1957 "Ministers Manifesto," published as a full-page ad in the *Atlanta Journal* and *Atlanta Constitution*. Viewed from today's perspective, portions of the document are disingenuously offensive (case in point: "To suggest that a recognition of the rights of Negroes to the full privileges of American citizenship, and to such necessary contacts as might follow, would inevitably result in intermarriage is to cast as serious and unjustified an aspersion upon the white race as upon the Negro race"). But the document was a bold step for Southern religious leaders and contained such assertions as "hatred and scorn for those of another race, or for those who hold a position different from our own, can never be justified" and "an expressed willingness on our part to recognize their needs, and to see that they are granted their full rights as American citizens, might lead to a cooperative approach to the problem which would provide equal rights and yet maintain the integrity of both races upon a basis of mutual esteem and of free choice rather than of force." Eighty ministers, including Bevel Jones, signed the manifesto. Rothschild did not sign it because the language was intentionally very Christian, to appeal to the broadest audience. But the rabbi supported the manifesto publicly. Rothschild's progressive stance on race relations was a key reason his temple was bombed by neo-Nazi extremists in 1958. After the bombing, a second manifesto was signed by three hundred ministers.

The gathering at the cathedral was almost exclusively white and included some of Atlanta's leading business, civic, and religious leaders. Some, like Rothschild, had supported King for years. Many had, if not actively resisted integration efforts in Atlanta, passively ignored them. "A glance at the names, even of some of those conducting memorial services for Dr. King, tells us this: some had stood up to be counted before; others had not," the editorial board of the *Atlanta Journal* noted the next day. At the cathedral service, "mourners read the lines from James Russell Lowell (who was often quoted by Dr. King) about the need to stand against injustices and for the solutions *before* it becomes popular to do so, not after it is in vogue. There was great irony."

Rabbi Rothschild did not hesitate to use the pulpit of St. Philips as a platform for speaking boldly: "White America, too, confronts a challenge. White America is run through with racism. It clings with determination and desperation to all the old shibboleths of entrenched white privilege and superiority. . . . It moves only when confronted by the threat of violence or violence itself. It passes laws and ignores them."

Wrote the editorial board of the *Journal*, "Atlanta must face the fact that many of its institutions are racist to the core. It has churches where an application for membership from Dr. King would have had to be 'carefully considered' by the church board; important clubs and other main gathering places of influential people which ratify bigotry by excluding Negroes; cemeteries where Dr. King could not be buried; and, of course, housing discrimination everywhere."

The white residents of King's hometown, the newspaper said, "need to convert sympathy into the hard stuff of action, lest those who are genuinely moved today retreat to an essentially racist position tomorrow."

Lester Maddox attended St. Stephen Methodist Church in Marietta and accepted the pastor's invitation to deliver a few words. The governor repeated his sympathy for King's family, but said that nonviolent civil disobedience such as practiced by King and his followers was "a sinful pastime."

* * *

The DeKalb Youth Coordinating Council held an outdoor memorial service in the park in Kirkwood, a working-class neighborhood on the southeastern edge of Atlanta's city limits. A few years earlier, Kirkwood had been a center of protests when the first black residents moved in. It was a headquarters of the White Citizens Council. On this Sunday, seventy-five teens from the youth council met in the park and heard from Maynard Jackson, a young lawyer, son of the late Maynard Jackson Sr. of Friendship Baptist Church, and grandson of civil rights pioneer John Wesley Dobbs. After speaking with the kids, Maynard Jackson raced home. His wife, Bunnie, was expecting their first child at any moment.

New Bethel Baptist Church, Washington, D.C.

The Reverend Walter Fauntroy, vice chair of the Washington City Council and the D.C. leader for SCLC, who spoke at the National Cathedral memorial service two days earlier, delivered a sermon in which he recalled talking with King a few days before his death. He remembered King saying, "I'm afraid, Walter, this country just isn't ready for nonviolence." The attendees included Robert Kennedy and Stokely Carmichael. After the service was over, Kennedy and his wife, Ethel, walked a twenty-two-block stretch of Washington, D.C., looking at the debris left from the riots.

Atlanta airport, late morning

June Dobbs Butts, a childhood friend of King's, finally landed at the main hangar. Her flight from New York was late. Planes circled the airport for up to forty-five minutes because the runways could not accommodate the glut of incoming flights—Eastern Airlines alone had thirty-three chartered flights booked for Monday on top of its regular flight schedule. Butts was picked up by her childhood friend Juanita Sellers Stone, but most of the people arriving had no idea where to go or what to do.

To handle the onslaught of arrivals, the Atlanta Transit System lined up buses in front of the terminal. Pete Kilgo, director of sales for Atlanta Transit, went to the terminal with a crew of drivers. Regular bus schedules were scrapped. Instead, when they spotted someone with a suitcase who'd come out of the terminal, they just asked, "Where are you going?" and put that person on a bus, thus determining that bus's route. "This one's headed for downtown!" they would call, once the first passenger took a seat. The ad hoc system meant that the buses were so crowded and busy that Atlanta Transit simply stopped charging fares.

Many people had no idea *where* they were going. Thanks to coordination by Xernona Clayton, SCLC staff, and City Hall, political dignitaries and celebrities had hotel rooms. For many others, the best option was to arrange a stay in a private home. For the rest, the only option was to head downtown and hope for a referral to a church basement or a school gym.

For those without a definite destination, Atlanta Transit set up a clearing center at the Atlanta Stadium parking lot. Buses dropped off loads of passengers who would wait until they were picked up by friends, family, or cars driven by volunteers.

Although volunteers hosted thousands of mourners for free, Atlanta certainly made a profit on the arrivals. Visitors to Atlanta spent $25 million over four days. One-way cab fares to town were $7.* Newsstands at the airport sold out of one hundred thousand copies of *Life* magazine's commemorative King issue—at $1.03 each compared with the regular price of thirty-five cents.

Jesse Jackson had gone back to Chicago after King's death, then flew to Atlanta. Arriving at the airport, he was struck by the amount of merchandise being peddled. *King paraphernalia*, he thought.

SCLC headquarters, midday

Requests for food and shelter flooded into the SCLC, jamming the organization's phone lines. Everyone needed help. Staff put together a hodgepodge fleet to collect arriving mourners. Staffers wrote SCLC COURTESY VEHICLE in fat Magic Marker on sheets of poster board and attached them to the sliding doors on VW buses with masking tape. The organization asked radio and television stations to broadcast a plea for donations.

After they heard one of the radio announcements, Kathy and Norm Kohn impulsively decided to help. They loaded their yellow Ford Falcon

*Nearly as much as a men's Hathaway shirt, advertised by Atlanta's Muse's clothing store for $9 that week.

station wagon with groceries and got ready to go downtown from their home in Doraville, at least a thirty-minute trek by car. They could not find a sitter for their young sons—Bryan, six, and Alan, three—so they put the boys in the backseat and headed out.

When they drew closer to Auburn Avenue, they felt apprehensive. Neither had really been in that neighborhood before, and they were aware of being the only whites around. *What have we done?* Kathy thought as she looked around. *Have we put our children in danger?* She and Norm had watched television coverage of riots in black neighborhoods in such cities as Chicago and Detroit. Would it be any different in the heart of black Atlanta? When they reached the SCLC offices, they agreed that Norm would stay in the car with the boys while Kathy went to find out where to drop off their donations.

"Take the stuff over to Central Presbyterian Church. It's going to be the clearinghouse," an SCLC staff member said.

Kathy felt relieved. Central Presbyterian was her church—she was a third-generation congregant; her grandfather joined in the early 1900s. When she and Norm got to Central, they hauled the grocery bags into the fellowship hall, feeling more at ease on familiar turf.

"Can you stay and help serve food for a while?" Pastor Taylor asked.

The couple debated for a few minutes, and agreed that Norm would stay. "I'll call you later to let you know how it's going," he told Kathy, and kissed her and the boys good-bye. Kathy drove back to Doraville, wondering when she would again see her husband. She was anxious but also a little jealous. She knew Norm risked being caught in violence, but she sensed that something big, something exciting, was happening. Norm would be in the middle of things, and she would be out in suburbia with two little children.

Norm Kohn ended up spending three days at the church. Cars and buses dropped off a constant stream of arrivals, and volunteers served whatever food was on hand. Restaurant trucks arrived with deliveries. Much of what they delivered was food prepped in anticipation of weekend diners. Fearful white Atlantans canceled restaurant reservations by the thousands, so restaurant owners dropped off whatever they had prepped in their kitchens and storerooms. (The driver for the Playboy Club restaurant pulled into a side alley when delivering food, not wanting to offend the church folk with the Bunny-emblazoned van—although plenty of congregants took notice.)

Don Robinson, Central Presbyterian's minister of music, worked with Norm and other volunteers. A new bus pulled up every few hours, dropping off hungry, tired mourners. The doors never closed. Sleeping bags and bed-rolls were strewn across the pews, and bodies stretched out on the floor of the choir loft. Three hundred people slept in the church at any given time, and more than four thousand people came by each day to be fed. Norm marveled at the people mingling in the church. He saw members of the Black Panther Party in leopard-skin suits and reporters from Europe, Asia, and Africa. Elegantly groomed women from Atlanta's wealthy northside neighborhoods helped dish up hot dogs and chips. Ginny Tuttle, a mother of five children, spent nineteen hours making sandwiches. At one point, flummoxed by a donated whole ham, she asked around for a knife. Reluc-tantly, one of the guests at the church handed her one. "It was the first time I'd ever carved with a switchblade," Mrs. Tuttle wryly commented later.

The Mangham home, Collier Heights, early afternoon

"I've got a gig for you, if you want it," James Wilborn, Marvin Mangham's friend, said. "There are televisions crews coming in town for the funeral and they need drivers and spotters. It's fifty bucks a day."

Marvin, always looking for ways to make extra cash, agreed right away. He had no television experience, but he had what the crews needed, a knowledge of Atlanta's black community and a local's sense of direction. He picked up the television crew early at their motel. He sensed that most of them had preconceptions about the South and Atlanta, and they were surprised by the tour he gave them. He drove them around his neighbor-hood, and they gawked and shot reels of film of the homes and streets of Collier Heights. No tour of the area was complete without cruising past Dr. McLendon's house with its indoor pool.* The television crew

---

*This pool became almost a clichéd shorthand for Atlanta's wealthy black class in the 1960s and early 1970s. Bus tours departed from the downtown Greyhound station for tours of famous landmarks of black Atlanta, including Collier Heights. Ivan Allen would bring visitors from overseas—or the states to the north—to tour Collier Heights, the doctor's home an inevitable showstopper.

was startled by the difference between this neighborhood and the Kings' home on Sunset, and the further contrast between the University Center and Auburn Avenue, the once "sweet" center of African-American business and culture and now a little shabby at best, sketchy for the most part. Marvin's dad would let him go to movies on Auburn Avenue (theaters in Atlanta were segregated until Marvin was in high school), but did not want him hanging out there after the show.

As Marvin took the television crew down Auburn Avenue, he was astonished to see so many people—so many white people—on the street. *It's like a holiday*, Marvin thought. *So much congestion.*

None of the NBC crew were people he recognized from watching the news. They were cameramen and producers sent to create the feed that would go to New York. They asked constant questions. They bought him lunch.

Even though he had known King and his family all his life, Marvin was taken aback at seeing the crowds. He knew King was famous, but the man on television did not seem the same as the old college friend of his dad's. King was like Andrew Young, who attended Marvin's family's church (First Congregational) and had a trio of young daughters. Marvin could not reconcile the man he saw in church on Sundays with the figure he saw on television or in the pages of *Ebony* and *Jet* and the *New York Times*.

Media from around the world came to Atlanta. A pressroom was set up in City Hall down the corridor from the mayor's office. Assistant Linda Mullá helped as much as she could, giving answers about funeral arrangements. The staff handed out cold bottles of Coca-Cola and gave directions to key locations in the city.

The SCLC offices were already overcrowded with the hospitality efforts, so media director Tom Offenberger set up a press center at the Samuel Archer gym at Morehouse College. He put together media kits with strict rules for the funeral coverage. Reporters would have to pick up press cards at the gym if they wanted access to events and press conferences. On the day of the funeral, only four photographers would be allowed inside Ebenezer during the services, and no flashes could be used. Two photographers would be in the balcony of the church and two at the front.

The funeral would change television programming, with most shows canceled or rescheduled. NBC's *Tonight Show Starring Johnny Carson* would, for instance, be preempted by a special documentary on King on Tuesday, the network announced. The Academy Awards ceremony, scheduled for Monday, was postponed to Wednesday.

All three networks sent anchors and crews to Atlanta and promised an uninterrupted full day of coverage on Tuesday, the day of the funeral. CBS, which had a thirty-person crew in Augusta, Georgia, to cover the Masters Golf Tournament, had rerouted them to Atlanta and sent Charles Kuralt to cover the services at Ebenezer with Walter Cronkite anchoring from New York.

While Marvin and the television crew scouted Auburn Avenue for background footage, in one building on the street—Ebenezer Baptist—federal agents were doing scouting of their own.

As they searched every corner of the church, FBI agents made a sketch—marking out the positions of pews, the choir loft, the altar, even the piano. Others agents were across town measuring and mapping the campus green at Morehouse, the 75-by-450-yard lawn ("open grassy area") where memorial-service attendees would be seated, the two-story house, the dorm buildings, and halls at the perimeter of the lawn, and the street at one side ("congested area"). They estimated the time it would take for vehicles to get between the key funeral locations, and from Ebenezer Baptist to Dobbins Air Force Base in Marietta (twenty to twenty-five minutes) or the municipal airport (thirteen minutes). "There are no suitable helicopter sites at any of the various locations," concluded the FBI scouts.

The Dale Creek Road home of Martin Luther King's parents, late afternoon

June Dobbs Butts and Juanita Sellers Stone drove to the elder Kings' home. June, who had grown up living around the corner from the Kings in Sweet Auburn, knew their old place "inside and out." This was her first visit to their home in Collier Heights, and she was struck by how spacious and airy it was—all the rooms with large glass windows opening off a huge living room.

"What can we do to help?" June asked Mrs. King.

"Sew veils on these hats," she was told.

June and Juanita made their way through the crowded main rooms and sat in a bedroom and quietly sewed for hours. They had both known the family for years. June and her five sisters grew up in a house on Houston Street, close to the King home, and June and her sister Mattiwilda spent hours with the King kids—Christine, Martin, and A.D. June, Christine, and Juanita were close friends, and Martin and Juanita had dated for a while as teenagers and later when both were in graduate school, she at Columbia and he at Boston University. Juanita was feisty and independent and took over the family business, Sellers Brothers Funeral Home, and proved to be a natural entrepreneur. June watched her friend sew and wondered how things would have turned out if fate had been different. *Would M.L.'s life have taken the same path? Would Juanita have been able to hold up to the pressure of living through a public tragedy like this?*

After they finished sewing, June and Juanita went to the kitchen, where they helped to greet arriving well-wishers and served food. Mrs. King told June that G. Mennen Williams, former governor of Minnesota, had given them money to help pay for the refreshments; they were overwhelmed by the number of guests streaming to the house.

As June greeted the visitors, she was surprised by how forward they were. "I'm your cousin. You didn't know about me, but we're cousins!" she heard people say to the Kings over and over. Having known the family since she, Martin, and A.D. played Monopoly together in elementary school, she was sure not all of the visitors were relatives; but she followed the Kings' lead and acted genially. Amid the pushy visitors, the gracious attitude of Aretha Franklin was striking. The twenty-six-year-old made the switch from church singer to superstar the year before with the hit "Respect," but June thought of her first as the daughter of influential Detroit minister C. L. Franklin. *She is sincerely distraught*, June thought. *What a humble young woman.*

South Lawn of the White House, 4:16 p.m.

After a quick press briefing on their meetings, the president, Defense Secretary Clifford, and other staff and senior officials accompanied General

Westmoreland in the helicopter that would take him back to Andrews Air Force Base.

Aide Tom Johnson rode in the helicopter with the president and looked at the burning city below as they flew across Washington, D.C. On the return to the White House, the president asked the pilot to fly lower, and they hovered over the path of fires along Fourteenth Street. "That image is seared into my brain," Tom Johnson said decades later.

King home on Sunset Avenue, 4:30 p.m.

When Xernona Clayton had taken the call from Richard Nixon and passed it on to Coretta, Clayton wondered what the response would be. The former vice president and 1968 presidential candidate had said that he wanted to pay his respects, but not make a show of it. He pulled up in a plain car, came in and chatted for a half hour, and quietly left. The visit did not completely escape the notice of reporters—the *Atlanta Constitution* covered it the next day—but it was a far lower key event than the house calls made by the other candidates, Clayton said.

Later on, Coretta King met with the team she'd enlisted to help organize the funeral. Wyatt Tee Walker, the former SCLC executive director, flew down from New York to oversee organization. Lonnie King managed the "outside" logistics and coordinated with police. SCLC veterans such as Bernard LaFayette and former student leaders such as Charles Black helped with training student marshals. Christine and Coretta planned the service at Ebenezer and burial at South-View, and Coretta and Abernathy planned the memorial at Morehouse.

They had started talking about the funeral service just hours after King's death was confirmed, and his sister, Christine, was inspired. "You know, M.L. has already preached his own eulogy," she said, reminding Coretta of the "Drum Major Instinct" sermon her brother gave at Ebenezer back on February 4. In that sermon he outlined what he would want said at his own funeral. They placed calls to William Stein, who produced the radio show *Martin Luther King Jr. Speaks* for the SCLC from New York, and tracked down a copy of the recording. The eulogy at Morehouse would, without doubt, be delivered by Benjamin Mays, president emeritus of the college and King's longtime mentor. Mays and King had made a pact that, whichever of them died first, the other would speak at his funeral.

Walker huddled with the widow, her sister-in-law, Harry Belafonte, Lonnie King, and others to go through the logistics, sketching out the route on paper and planning for eventualities. Walker sent political activist Allard Lowenstein to walk the procession route and time it. Walker had a car equipped with a phone, to stay in touch with organizers, paid for by Nelson Rockefeller.

It was after midnight before everyone had gone. Xernona Clayton urged Coretta to try on the hat for the funeral.

"I really can't bring myself to do it," the widow said. "I just can't think about it."

Xernona knew it had to be done. She tried joking around. She knew Coretta's reluctance came because of what the hat symbolized. *I have to get her to think about it as fashion, not what it represents—widowhood,* Xernona thought.

"Well, someone's gotta try it on," Xernona said. "If you don't, I will. And we can only imagine what *that* will look like."

Mrs. King looked up at her friend's head with its four-inch-high top-knot. At the thought of a hat balancing on that perch, the two women started laughing until they could not stop. The tension and exhaustion of the past few days was overwhelming, and they laughed until tears began to flow.

"Okay, I'll try it," said Coretta. She walked to her dresser and put on the hat. As Xernona knew it would, the hat framed her face perfectly. The veil hung smooth and sheer. Coretta faced the mirror for a long time before turning around.

"It's perfect," she said. There was no more laughter.

FIVE

Monday, April 8, 1968

Harry Belafonte, the three older King children, Coretta Scott King, Ralph David Abernathy,
SCLC leaders, and supporters join Memphis sanitation workers in a march King had been
scheduled to lead before his assassination. *AP Photo*

Downtown Memphis, midmorning

B LUE LIGHTS CUT through the fog as the police cruisers weaved
through downtown Memphis, escorting the latecomers to the
march. Coretta King and her group had been delayed by bad weather and
the tardiness of a few celebrity supporters. In a little bit of drama at the
Atlanta airport, a few students slated to join the trip to Memphis were
edged out by the arrival of actors Bill Cosby and Robert Culp, the biracial
duo who starred in the television show *I Spy*. The planes—one belonging
to Harry Belafonte, one chartered by Nelson Rockefeller—were packed.
Mrs. King flew in Belafonte's plane with her three oldest children, Ralph

Abernathy and his children, Rosa Parks, Andrew Young, and the photographer Bob Fitch.

The Atlanta group stopped at Beale and Main streets, and police surrounded the Kings and their supporters as they made their way to the front of the procession. The street was crowded with marchers, onlookers, and National Guard soldiers, whose bayonets bristled above the mass of people. Belafonte, tall and broad-chested, stood a head taller than most of the crowd, his face stern and his eyes shielded by big sunglasses. Mrs. King's face was barely visible, and the children were completely obscured by the crowd.

When they reached the head of the procession, the congestion eased, and the King family and their supporters walked at the head of an orderly and solemn column that moved eight or ten abreast through Memphis. It was another damp, misty spring day. The marchers, an estimated twenty thousand, walked in near silence, apprehensive and sad. Marshals had taken away umbrellas, saying that they could be construed as weapons. National Guard snipers crouched on rooftops of buildings along the route, and the hushed cadence of the marchers' footsteps was interrupted by the whirring of police helicopters above.

At the head of the procession were Coretta, Yolanda, Martin III, and Dexter King, flanked by Abernathy, Young, and Belafonte. Walking close to them were actor Ossie Davis and Benjamin Spock, the pediatrician famous for authoring *Dr. Spock's Baby and Child Care* and infamous for protesting the war.* Also joining the march (and later sitting on the speakers' platform with Mrs. King) were a number of labor representatives, including AFSCME (American Federation of State, County and Municipal Employees) president Jerry Wurf, United Automobile Workers (UAW) president Walter Reuther, a longtime supporter of King and the SCLC, and AFL-CIO civil rights director Don Slaiman. Cosby and Culp kept a low profile, marching toward the back.†

---

*Attorney General Ramsey Clark ordered the doctor's arrest in early 1968 because of Spock's antiwar protests. Interestingly, after Clark left the Johnson administration, he became heavily involved in the anti–Vietnam War movement.

†Their presence was noticed only by a few reporters and they were not included in the photographs of that day. Cosby's publicist confirmed that the actor and Culp had been at the Memphis march, but they deliberately underplayed their presence.

Bernard LaFayette and other SCLC tacticians, along with Bayard Rustin of the A. Philip Randolph Foundation, had spent the past few days organizing the march; there was no room for the chaos that marred the ill-fated event of March 28 that ended up with police shooting a black teenager. They trained five hundred volunteers to serve as marshals. The organizers of the march knew that the military force was there as much—perhaps even more—out of fear that the march would disintegrate into rioting as to protect the widow, children, and close colleagues of the man killed by a sniper's bullet in the city just four days earlier.

Whoever wanted King killed has already done their job, Jesse Jackson thought. But that did not lift his spirit. He felt dazed, angry, hurt. Bernard LaFayette marched warily, constantly on the lookout for potential trouble. Dexter King, then seven, was struck by how quiet and sad people were.

Many of the marchers wore sandwich-board signs that carried empathetic statements, such as HONOR KING: END RACISM! or familiar slogans such as I AM A MAN. Small pockets of white marchers carried banners proclaiming the names of their hometowns. When the procession reached the staging area at Civic Center Plaza in front of Memphis City Hall, white onlookers rushed the stage. They took pictures of King's widow and children, disrupting the end of the march in their eagerness to take souvenir snapshots.

The crowd eased back when Mrs. King stepped up to the microphone. She opened on a personal note, her children seated behind her serving as a reminder of the personal grief behind the national tragedy of King's assassination. "In spite of the times that he had to be away from his family, his children knew that Daddy loved them, and the time that he spent with them was well spent. And I always said that it's not the quantity of time that is important but the quality of time."

She spoke for almost fifteen minutes, without using notes or consulting the talking points Andrew Young had prepared on the flight up. "I challenge you today to see that his spirit never dies," she said. "His campaign for the poor must go on. We are very concerned not only about the Negro poor, we are concerned about all of the poor, in the United States and the world."

Reporting on the march in the April 25 issue of *Jet*, Simeon Booker described Coretta as "the Black Madonna of Grief" and said she "entered from the wings and demonstrated her mettle" as she "served as a symbol of valiant black womanhood." The magazine featured the widow and her children on its cover with the line "King's Widow: Bereavement to Battlefield." The *New York Times* depicted the widow, "wearing a simple black dress and with her face lifted up to the gray skies from which a few drops had begun to fall," telling the assembled crowd, "This experience . . . represents the Crucifixion, on toward the resurrection and redemption of his [King's] spirit." The *Times* reprinted the full text of Mrs. King's speech. *Life* magazine ran an excerpt in its April 19 King tribute issue.

The lovely and grieving widow overshadowed her husband's successor, although, as Vincent Burke and Ed Meagher of the *Los Angeles Times* noted, Abernathy delivered an "impassioned inaugural speech" in his debut as SCLC head. Building on the biblical reference to Moses and the mountaintop in King's final speech, Abernathy called himself "Joshua" and said, "We are bound for the Promised Land. I am not going to lead a short distance, I am going to lead all the way."*

After the end of the march, the King group and SCLC staff headed back to Atlanta as quickly as possible. The orderly planning had not been thorough enough. Dozens of the peacekeeping marshals were stranded near City Hall; buses that they had been promised would take them back to the procession's starting point never showed up, and the marshals were left to find their own way for the four-mile return trip.

While the march took place, the ongoing investigation into King's death continued. Thomas Powers of the *Chicago Tribune* reported that investigators had traced the gun found in the mysterious "bundle" near the Lor-

---

*Joshua figures prominently in the biblical story of the formerly enslaved Israelites' journey from Egypt to the Promised Land. He accompanies Moses part of the way up Mount Sinai when Moses receives the Ten Commandments and later leads the Israelites into Canaan when Moses is punished. Joshua is Moses' handpicked successor. Abernathy's selection of this reference shrewdly underscored his relationship to King and echoed King's "mountaintop" sermon of four days earlier. The title of Abernathy's memoir, *And the Walls Came Tumbling Down*, refers to one of Joshua's first victories after becoming leader. At God's instruction, he leads the Israelites in a march around the walled city of Jericho for six days; on the seventh day, the walls collapse, producing a victory without conventional warfare. (Joshua 6:1–25)

raine Motel to a shop in Birmingham, Alabama. The purchaser was a tall, slim, dark-haired white man. A report that a white man in a white Mustang was spotted near the Memphis procession sent police into high gear, worried that Abernathy, Mrs. King, or another high-profile marcher was being targeted for assassination. The driver of the car turned out to be oblivious of news reports that a white Mustang was suspected of being King's killer's getaway vehicle.

The White House, 10 a.m.

King's funeral was only a day away, and President Johnson had still not decided whether he was going. Concerns about safety mounted, and unsolicited advice continued to come to the White House.

Clerk Mike Manatos sent the president a memo with a message from Bill Helis, a New Orleans oilman, who had called and "asked that I relay to you his hope that the President will not attend the Martin Luther King funeral. He feels that this would be a dangerous undertaking for the President and that he ought not expose himself to any of the extremists who undoubtedly will be in the area." Buford Ellington, governor of Tennessee, called Chief of Staff Marvin Watson, saying, "The country knows the president has done enough for this man. His going very likely would cause serious white backlash." Ellington added, "More important is the terrible security problem it creates trying to protect the president." Later Watson sent LBJ another memo, based on a call from Georgia congressman Phil Landrum, who warned that the Atlanta papers were playing up the potential arrival of the president for the funeral and that "I frankly don't think it is safe in any respect" and that "the possibility of physical harm is there. Just like the possibility was in Memphis."

Despite advice that he remain in Washington, the president continued to agonize about attending the funeral. Marvin Watson reminded him that both Rufus Youngblood and James Rowley, the heads of the U.S. Secret Service, warned it would not be safe for either the president or vice president to attend the funeral. That said, if someone needed to go, it should be Vice President Humphrey, Youngblood and Rowley advised.

At 11:45, Joe Califano, the president's chief domestic adviser, sent a memo of his own, emphatically stating, "I still believe you should not go to the funeral, especially now that [Ellsworth] Bunker* is coming in" for talks about the war. Califano, a savvy political strategist, also reminded the president, "Like it or not, the vice president alone is still in many minds a candidate for office, and I think you should send others who are clearly not candidates, particularly in view of the fact that so many politicians are going to Atlanta." Califano suggested Thurgood Marshall, whom LBJ had appointed as the first black Supreme Court justice; Bob Weaver, the NAACP veteran whom Johnson had named as the first head of the Department of Housing and Urban Development; and Attorney General Ramsey Clark. Underscoring the political expediency of sending Clark, Califano noted, "It was the justice department that worked, through legal means, for civil rights, particularly in the South."

With the president still undecided, staff began to make contingency plans. At 1 p.m., Thomas Johns of the Secret Service sent a memo to Marvin Watson requesting a C-141 transport plane to take an armored car and "large number of secret service agents" to Dobbins Air Force Base outside of Atlanta "in the event one of the Principals attended the funeral." At 2:55, Watson sent a memo to the president relaying a call from Georgia congressman John Davis that a call had come in warning of danger in Atlanta. He passed along a folder from the FBI with security assessments and asked them to make considerations for either the president or Humphrey attending. "Give V.P. whatever he needs," says a handwritten note on the memo.

At 3 p.m., Barefoot Sanders sent a message to Appointments Secretary Jim Jones, also relaying a conversation with Davis, the Georgia congressman. Sanders said Davis had called saying that "a preacher friend of his— who is a fundamentalist, Ku Kluxer type" called Davis and said that going to Atlanta would put the president's life at risk.

Atlanta Municipal Airport, early afternoon

Vice Mayor Sam Massell was assigned VIP duty. For the next two days, he was stationed at the airport where a special hangar had been opened to handle the influx of charter flights. Massell greeted arriving politicians

---

*Ambassador to South Vietnam.

and celebrities. The young politician easily spotted elected officials. He felt less confident when it came to identifying movie stars and musicians. Massell would welcome announced VIPs effusively and later surreptitiously call his wife to figure out whom he'd just met.

Celebrities who arrived in Atlanta included actors Paul Newman and Peter Lawford; comedians Alan King and Dick Gregory; and performers Eartha Kitt and Dizzy Gillespie. Actress Diahann Carroll caused a stir when she strode hatless through the airport in a blue-and-orange minidress.*

The celebrities encamped in downtown Atlanta—and Atlantans came out to gawk. Paul Hemphill, columnist for the *Atlanta Journal*, felt a buzz in the newsroom. Atlanta rarely hosted Hollywood types—the last excitement Hemphill could recall had been an appearance by Frank Sinatra *Junior* at the old Imperial Hotel strip club.

Twelve-year-old Maria Saporta, Yolanda King's classmate, and her friends came downtown to hang out at the Marriott. With its groovy tropical pool and white glass lights, it had always seemed glamorous to them. Now, catching a glimpse of actors such as Sidney Poitier—the star of two movies up for Best Picture in that week's Academy Awards, *Guess Who's Coming to Dinner* and *In the Heat of the Night*—made it feel as if the hotel were the "center of the universe." Nearby at the Regency Hyatt House, the Kennedys had rented an entire floor. Richard Nixon booked a room at that hotel as well, as did Mahalia Jackson, Diana Ross and the Supremes, Sammy Davis Jr., and Marlon Brando.

Sam Massell went out on the tarmac to greet Mrs. King's plane when it returned from Memphis. As they left the plane, the Kings, Belafonte, and the SCLC inner circle were mobbed by camera crews and press photographers.

Later that afternoon, as the sky turned a dusky blue, Robert Kennedy and his wife, Ethel, flew in. After greeting Massell, Kennedy paused on the runway to respond to questions from reporters.

---

*Carroll would cause another stir in September 1968 when her show *Julia* debuted on NBC. It was the first television show starring a black actress in a "prestige" central role rather than as a domestic or a sidekick.

Wind whipped his hair and his usually boyish face was lined and haggard. Asked about the rioting in other cities, he said, "It's horrible, and unacceptable in our society." He then said, "We have to deal with the injustices that still exist for our poor within our country. Jobs are terribly important. It's also important that we have communication between whites and blacks—greater communication than perhaps has existed in the past so we can try to better understand one another."

While the candidate talked to reporters, Kennedy's staff went to the airport terminal to check on transportation and found that the mayor's office had arranged for cars—a Thunderbird and a Lincoln.

"That Thunderbird won't do," aides told the mayoral staff.

Almost every available rental had been taken, and it took City Hall and the Kennedy team some time to wrangle a politically suitable replacement, a Ford Galaxie 500. The candidate climbed into this car after giving his press comments. "When they come to mourn Dr. King, they must bring their politics with them," observed *Atlanta Constitution* political editor Remer Tyson. Along with Kennedy, every other major candidate for president was expected to be at the funeral. It would be the first time they were all in the same place at the same time during primary season.

Tallies of riot damages and deaths continued to rise. In Washington, D.C., an estimated six hundred homes and businesses were destroyed and more than four thousand people had been arrested, a quarter of them underage. The eventual tally would be more than a thousand destroyed buildings, and more than seven thousand arrests—about a third of the estimated twenty thousand rioters. Some twenty-five hundred jobs were lost as a result of the riots. In Chicago, more than a thousand people were left homeless because of fires. So far, more than two dozen deaths were attributed to rioting.

That morning, nineteen hundred federal troops had been sent to Baltimore to quash looting and arson. Ohio National Guard soldiers were sent to Cincinnati and Youngstown. Nationwide, the *Atlanta Constitution* reported, 57,500 soldiers and National Guard troops had been activated, more than at any other time in the country's history. It was the greatest military deployment on U.S. soil since the Civil War. In the *Los Angeles*

Times, reporter Max Lerner evoked an image of destruction: "The skyline of urban America in the past week has been a desolating one—not only the landscape but the manscape: fire-riddled blocks of houses and looted shops cordoned off in the Negro ghettos; at least a half dozen great cities turned into fortresses and watched over by guardsmen and soldiers; cities ravaged from within by their own dwellers and occupied by soldiers from without."

In Chicago, Jo Freeman, a former SCLC volunteer working as a low-level staffer at *Modern Hospital* magazine, was sent out on assignment. She had recently photographed an infant-health station on Chicago's west side. "Go see what condition it's in now that riots have started," her editor suggested. Jo tried to catch a cab, but no driver would to take her to that part of town. Finally she got someone to agree to drop her off several blocks from the clinic. She walked through streets where buildings still smoldered to reach the clinic, which had been destroyed. Most of the neighborhood around the clinic, where she had taken photographs just a few weeks earlier, was unrecognizable.

When she got back to the office, she found a memo from magazine management announcing that those who wanted to take time off the next day to attend services for Dr. King would be allowed to do so. *The unwritten message here is that this applies to "black people who want to go to their churches—here in Chicago," but I'm going to take it literally,* Freeman thought. She told her editor she was going to Atlanta for the service Tuesday; she would drive all night and be back at work Wednesday.

She had been using a darkroom in a west-side church, but because of the rioting she could not get there to process her photos of the destroyed neighborhood clinic. Instead she headed to the offices of the historic black newspaper the *Chicago Defender,* where she had a photographer friend.

"I want to go to the King funeral in Atlanta, but my editor won't send me," he told her.

"I'm going," she told him. "I'll take pictures for you."

"Here, take my camera."

Carrying her bags and the two cameras, Freeman then met up with her friend Karen Fuqua, a former SCOPE (Summer Community Organization and Political Education Project) volunteer. They had heard that a caravan of buses would be heading to Atlanta, organized by Jesse

Jackson's Operation Breadbasket team in Chicago. When they got to the Breadbasket/SCLC offices, they learned all the buses were filled. The two young women stood in the office lobby and debated whether they should hitchhike or take a Greyhound bus. An elderly couple overheard them and made an offer: "You drive our car, and you can ride with us." The four headed out in the evening to start the drive. They knew it would take all night to get to Atlanta; the hardest part would be getting through the burning streets of Chicago.

In Atlanta, police continued their extra patrols. All liquor stores in the city were closed. Mayor Allen issued a proclamation that no wine, beer, or "spirituous liquors" would be sold from 6 p.m. Monday through 8 a.m. Wednesday, April 10, the morning after the funeral.

In a second proclamation, the mayor announced that City Hall and all nonessential city services would be closed from ten the next morning through the remainder of the day in honor of King and to allow city staff to participate in the services. He asked that Atlanta businesses follow this example: "The executive heads of all businesses in the City of Atlanta are hereby requested, as a gesture of sympathy to his family and to the memory of Dr. Martin Luther King Jr., to declare their businesses closed for the period of Tuesday, April 9, 1968, or to make provisions for their employees to attend the funeral or the memorial services."

The mayor had also gone on the radio to ask Atlantans, black and white, to drive with their headlights turned on all day Tuesday as a sign of respect.

South Lawn of the White House, 6:48 p.m.

The president boarded a helicopter headed for Camp David. Earlier in the day, he had held a press conference announcing that he would be at Camp David for meetings with Ambassador Bunker, Secretary Clifford, and Dean Rusk, secretary of state. He read a statement from Hanoi and said he had notified U.S. allies and was attempting to negotiate plans for talks.

On the flight, he read letters from constituents—most were about his decision to step out of the presidential race. After reaching Aspen Lodge,

LBJ changed into casual clothes and went to the living room, joining Press Secretary George Christian and other staffers. The president and Walt Rostow, special assistant for national security affairs, talked awhile about the problems they would be discussing the next day. Johnson told his aides that he suspected most of the discussion would end up being about the "mood" of the country instead of the slated subject: military strategy in Southeast Asia.

Then the president fell asleep in his comfortable chair. Everyone else stayed in the room, talking in whispers. Johnson napped for close to two hours.

Sunset Avenue, evening

When Robert and Ethel Kennedy came to see Mrs. King, they were escorted back to her bedroom by Xernona Clayton. Robert sat in a floral-upholstered recliner tucked into the corner of the room, Ethel sat in a wooden dining chair, and Mrs. King perched on the edge of her bed, wearing the same black dress she had had on all day during the march in Memphis and on the flight home. The rumpled bedspread had been neatly straightened and the stacks of paper moved to the side.

Later the Kennedys went to the living room and talked awhile with the children. Robert Kennedy accepted a bottle of root beer and chatted with some of the other visitors in the home. People came and went constantly; a buffet of fried chicken and other Southern home cooking was set up in the kitchen. Earlier in the day Harry Belafonte, Bill Cosby, and Robert Culp had prepared hominy grits and eggs for people passing through. Later Cosby read books to the King boys and their cousin Isaac Farris.

Ebenezer Baptist Church, early evening

Hundreds of people stood in the two lines leading to the church doors. One line stretched east along Auburn Avenue toward Boulevard Avenue, the other went south along Jackson Street to Edgewood Avenue.

A hearse was parked outside the church, and when the doors opened and a blue casket was carried out, people looked at each other and wondered, "Who's that?" The answer: Mrs. Ruth Davis.

Ebenezer had just held a funeral for Davis, a longtime church member who had been Martin Luther King's Sunday-school teacher. She died on the same day as her former student. Daddy King officiated at the service, telling the Ebenezer congregation that he did not manage to go to Mrs. Davis's viewing. "I saw my son yesterday and it almost killed me," the pastor said. The day before, as he walked up to his son's glass-topped casket on display at Spelman, Daddy King had completely broken down, weeping and clutching the smooth glass surface, kissing it as he cried. Ushers had taken him to a pew in the chapel, where he tried to compose himself under the blinding flashes of news photographers. Coretta and her children had been calm as they made their way past the bier, although Yolanda's face portrayed her agony. Coretta and her sister-in-law Christine tried to prepare the younger children for what they would see, but they were still bewildered. For six-year-old Isaac Farris, this was a first viewing. He kept thinking that Uncle M.L. looked as though he were sleeping. *How strange it looks, that he is sleeping in a suit,* Isaac thought.

Today, as the senior pastor looked out over the pews of Ebenezer, talking about Mrs. Davis and his son, he said, "I'd rather remember them as they were the last time I saw them [alive]."

Auretha English, wife of deacon Jethro English and mother of associate pastor Ron English, stood to perform the solo, "Jesus Is Always There." She was an accomplished soloist and, like other members of her musical family, sought-after for special services. She began the hymn but could not finish and sat back down. While she tried to control her tears, the rest of the choir rose to finish the hymn.

Outside the church, the crowd chatter was drowned by the roar of police motorcycles moving up Auburn Avenue ahead of the hearse transporting King's coffin from the Spelman campus. A convoy of limousines and funeral-home vehicles followed. The crowd craned toward the door, watching as King's casket was unloaded and carried into the sanctuary. News photographers scanned the scene; when they spotted Aretha Franklin in line, they moved in to take her photograph and she quickly left.

After a while, the church doors opened and mourners filed in to see the body. King's casket sat on a platform in the baptismal well, surrounded by mounds of wreaths and floral arrangements that almost obscured the television cameras and tangle of lights and wires placed there in preparation for the next day's funeral service.

Jim Peppler, photo editor for the *Southern Courier*, a nonprofit newspaper that covered the civil rights movement in Alabama, had driven from Montgomery, arriving in Atlanta at dusk. He parked a few blocks from Ebenezer and made his way toward the church. Standing on a rise in the vacant lot across the street, he photographed people lined up to view King's body. Although it was growing dark, people still lined up for four or five blocks. While he concentrated on the technical details of night shooting, he thought back to a protest he had covered in Luverne, Alabama, a few years earlier. Waiting for SCLC demonstrators to arrive, he chatted with the police chief. A good old boy, seeing two white men talking, walked up and asked the officer, "Do you think Marty King is going to be here?"

"Nah," said the sheriff.

"Golly, that's too bad," the old boy said. "You know what we'd do to him if he got here. And I know just the place we'd go to dump the body in the creek."

Jim Peppler thought, *If somebody would go up to a police chief and feel comfortable discussing murder and disposing of the body, this is one of the tells for what is going on in the South. It's a matter of time before one of these yahoos pulls a trigger.*

So his reaction to the news of King's being killed felt like "the response you have when an aging relative you know will die actually does," Peppler said. "You dread the information and are shocked and taken aback when it comes, but not totally surprised."

Among those waiting in line was the Patterson family. That afternoon, they had driven from Lincolnton, Georgia, to Atlanta in their light blue Thunderbird, a sedan with "suicide doors" in the rear. William and Annie Patterson were high school teachers, both active in civil rights activities in their east Georgia town. Cynthia, seventeen, desperately wanted to get involved and fretted that she was not old enough to join SNCC or another college group. She waited for six hours with her parents and her younger sister, Sybil, fifteen, to get into the church. Cynthia and Sybil whispered to each other as they made their way up the aisle, wondering what Dr. King would look like, how a mortician would "fix his head" after a shotgun blast.

"Don't stare!" hissed their mother.

Cynthia tried to keep her eyes averted, scared of how she might react, but "morbid curiosity" prevailed, and she looked down into the casket. All she could think was how peaceful King looked.

After the viewing, the Pattersons drove to the home of friends. The house was crowded with guests from out of town coming to the funeral; every bed or couch held as many people as could be squeezed in. All four Pattersons crammed into a single bed. Cynthia barely slept, worried that if one person rolled over, they would all fall out.

Late that night, two sedans pulled up and parked in front of Ebenezer Baptist. Robert and Ethel Kennedy got out, followed by security guards and members of the campaign staff, including Earl Graves and John Lewis. The church was darkened and the doors closed, so Lewis led the group through a side building and down back passageways into the sanctuary, where an honor guard of SCLC staff and Ebenezer congregants stood near King's body.

Lewis lingered at the back of the church while the Kennedys went up to the casket. He watched as they each made the sign of the cross and knelt to pray. A few moments later, Lewis walked up to the casket as well and looked down at the corpse of his friend and mentor. *This is unreal,* he thought.

Outside the church, patrolmen walking the beat discovered that several thousand people were sleeping in a vacant lot across the street from Ebenezer. A few blocks away, photographer Jim Peppler slept in the backseat of his car.

Earlier, Earl Graves had arranged a meeting between Kennedy, Daddy King, and senior members of the SCLC staff, including Jesse Jackson, Andrew Young, Bernard LaFayette, Hosea Williams, Fred Bennett, and Dorothy Cotton, the SCLC education director. "Those of us who are left must carry on," the senator said, as he talked about his brother's assassination. "The struggle for freedom is as dangerous as the struggles against an external enemy."

During the meeting in Atlanta, Kennedy and his staff pledged their support for the Poor People's Campaign. Andrew Young would later write that this meeting changed his view of Kennedy, who had seemed to display a "rich-boy arrogance" and eschew working with black leaders, but in this conversation demonstrated a "passion for meaningful social change."

St. Joseph's Hospital, Atlanta

Maynard and Bunnie Jackson celebrated the birth of their first daughter, Brooke. Maynard had insisted on being present for the birth—unheard of back then—and the young couple searched to find a doctor who would accommodate their request. From the window of the hospital, Bunnie could see people on Auburn Avenue lining up outside Ebenezer for the viewing.

Hosea Williams's Home, Atlanta, late evening

As soon as they arrived in Atlanta, Peter Geffen and Mickey Shur went to see their old boss, Hosea Williams. They had worked with him as SCOPE voter-registration volunteers in rural South Carolina during the summer of 1965.*

"I've got two jobs for you," Williams told the students. "Both involve pickups. Today you can pick up Rabbi Abraham Heschel. Tomorrow you are going to help me with a couple mules."

Peter and Mickey headed to the Atlanta airport to collect Heschel, the forceful antiwar advocate who'd marched with King in the antiwar rally in New York in 1967. They took Heschel to where they were staying, the home of Peter's grandfather Rabbi Tobias Geffen.† Tomorrow morning, they were instructed, you will get the mules, bring them to Ebenezer, then escort the rabbi in the funeral procession.

Williams had struggled to find the right wagon; the task had proved

---

*Peter Geffen decided to work with SCOPE after the death of his college classmate Andrew Goodman, who had been killed in Mississippi in 1964.

†Rabbi Tobias Geffen was head of Atlanta's orthodox Congregation Shearith Israel for sixty years. He occupies a particularly vaunted spot in Atlanta lore: it was he who was summoned to certify that the ingredients of Coca-Cola were kosher. "He's one of the only people in the world to know the ingredients, although they did not show him the proportions, so it wasn't technically the real secret recipe," notes Peter Geffen.

harder than he'd imagined. Finally he called Ralph Abernathy. I have it. It's perfect.

Where did you find it?

I stole it, said Williams blithely.

You had better pay for it, Abernathy said. Williams assured him that he would.

Williams and SCLC staffers hunting for the wagon gave up on obtaining a working one from a rural county when they found one outside Cook's Antiques & Stuff, a shop on Gordon Road in the West End area of Atlanta. They stopped by the store several times, never seeing the owner, so finally hauled the wagon to the yard of Ebenezer, where it was painted green.

Mexico City, late night

United Press International reporters filed a dispatch saying Mexican police had been brought into the search for King's killer. Copies of the FBI sketch of the suspect—young, white, dark-haired, and long-nosed—had been circulated on the Mexico-U.S. border. Rolando Veloz Canales, the Mexican consul in Memphis, saw a copy of the sketch and told police he remembered a similar long-nosed young man applying for a travel permit to Mazatlán.

FBI agents also expanded their search to Chicago and Birmingham based on evidence that included handprints in the room they believed the killer stood in to fire the shot at King, a rifle, and a piece of luggage. "Police said they had never seen a case where there was so much evidence left behind," wrote Martin Waldron in an article published by the *New York Times* on April 10.

Not yet reported was that the search was moving to Atlanta as well. Investigators were following leads that a white Mustang like the one linked to the shooter in Memphis had been seen in Atlanta.

Central Presbyterian Church, around midnight

Norm Kohn and pastor Randy Taylor were talking in the church study when the phone rang.

"What was that?" Norm asked when the minister hung up.

"Someone calling to pass on a report. There have been reports of riots in East Point."

"What are we going to do?" Norm asked, mentally calculating how quickly violence might spread from East Point, nine miles south of Atlanta.

"The same thing we're doing. Take care of people," said Taylor.

He and Norm walked down to the sanctuary, careful not to wake people sleeping in the pews and on the cots that had been crammed into the aisles.

SIX

Tuesday, April 9, 1968

Coretta Scott King; her mother-in-law, Alberta Williams King; and sister-in-law,
Christine King Farris, on the morning of the funeral. © *Bob Fitch Photo*

Clayton County, before dawn

M ICKEY SHUR AND Peter Geffen, following Hosea Williams's
instructions, made their way to Auburn Avenue while it was
still dark. At the SCLC offices, they met Stoney Cooks, an SCLC officer working in the Poor People's Campaign. Also waiting was farmer Ed
Peek. The foursome headed over to the farmer's flatbed truck. Cooks and
Peek climbed in the cab up front, and Mickey and Peter got into the back.
It was a twenty-mile ride to the farm in Clayton County, and the students
were jostled as they drove.

At the farm, it took all four of them to shove the mules—Ada and Bell—onto the flatbed. The two students each used one arm to hold on to the neck of a mule and the other arm to clutch the side of the truck. They were nervous as the farmer navigated his way back to the city. The mules seemed calm.

Sunset Avenue, before 8 a.m.

The Associated Press office called Kathryn Johnson to say that Jackie Kennedy was scheduled to visit the King home, so Johnson raced over to get there early and file her report. Arriving when most of the household was still asleep, Johnson went into the kitchen, put on an apron, and started making breakfast for Coretta's parents, Obadiah and Bernice Scott. The eggs were sizzling, the toast was ready, and Johnson stood in the door of the dining room, a kitchen towel over her arm, when Jackie Kennedy arrived. The former first lady walked over and shook Johnson's hand firmly. *Could she possibly think that the Kings have a white maid—and it's me?* Johnson wondered.

As Johnson continued her breakfast preparations, Xernona Clayton walked Jackie Kennedy back to Coretta King's bedroom. Clayton watched from the hall as the widows greeted each other with a long embrace. *They are communicating in spirit*, she thought. In the back bedroom, Mrs. Kennedy sat and talked with Juanita Abernathy, Christine King Farris, and Coretta.

People continued to stream through the house. June Dobbs Butts and Juanita Sellers Stone arrived to deliver condolences and passed Jackie Kennedy in transition. *How poignant*, thought June, thinking of the widows' shared experience.

When Kathryn Johnson returned to the Associated Press office to file her brief on Jackie Kennedy's arrival at the King home, her editor thanked her for her the diligent work, then handed her a gas mask. As a precaution, masks were being issued to every reporter in the bureau. *I can't carry everything I need, the tablet and the pens and all, and a gas mask*, she thought. *This isn't worth worrying about.* So after she finished her report, she left the gas mask on her desk, grabbed her things, and headed to Ebenezer Baptist.

Camp David, 8:15 a.m.

President Johnson sat down to breakfast with Ellsworth Bunker, the ambassador to South Vietnam; Dean Rusk; Robert McNamara, recently resigned secretary of defense; General Earle Wheeler; and top aides. Meetings would go on all day, with Averell Harriman and the current defense secretary Clark Clifford joining the group.

The president sent a message to the troops in Vietnam about the lifting of the long siege at Khesanh:

> The enemy intended to overrun the base at Khesanh. For this purpose he emplaced around that base at least two divisions of North Vietnamese regulars. Less than 6,000 United States marines and South Vietnamese rangers—backed by our tremendous air capacity—pinned them down, kept them away from the populated areas at the peak of the winter-spring offensive, and imposed heavy casualties.
>
> Now the siege of Khesanh is lifted. But clearing the fighting in South Vietnam is not yet at an end. The enemy may throw new forces into the battle. You, I know, intend to continue to move forward.

Atlanta City Hall, 9:00 a.m.

From the second-story window, Ivan Allen and Sam Massell watched uniformed men march up to the capitol, which sat diagonally across the street. Lester Maddox had called up 160 troopers to surround the building.* Several thousand National Guard soldiers were on standby at Dobbins Air Force Base in Marietta—just a short drive from downtown. There was no sign of Maddox, but Allen and Massell knew he was inside the capitol.

"A small fortress" is how Tom Greene and Steve Ball of the *Atlanta Journal* described the capitol, surrounded by soldiers "armed with rifles,

---

*A few months later, a book about Maddox would claim that on the day of the funeral he had told the troopers that if marchers tried to enter the capitol property, orders were to "shoot them down and stack them up."

shotguns and riot guns, carrying big nightsticks and wearing helmets." The *Washington Afro-American* referred to the capitol as an "armed camp" presided over by a "segregationist hashslinger-turned-governor." *New York Times* reporter Homer Bigart depicted Maddox "sitting in his office under heavy guard," and *Time* magazine described "helmeted, machine-gun-armed cops of Governor Lester Maddox at the Georgia Statehouse."

Maddox's wife, Virginia, stood by his desk as the governor signed documents and talked with reporters. Maddox told journalists that Atlanta businesses and banks had been coerced into closing for the day, pressured as much by Mayor Allen as by fear of violence. Tension was so high, the governor said, he would go ahead and close the capitol by early afternoon. Productivity was at a standstill anyway, he said; all the state employees were distracted, looking out of the capitol windows toward the procession route.

Across from the capitol, Central Presbyterian Church music director Don Carl Robinson, who had been there for days staffing the church's makeshift hospitality center, went outside to pick up paper plates and napkins that had been discarded on the church lawn. Mourners, virtually all of them black, continued to come and go from the sanctuary. A trooper strode over to Robinson.

"What are you doing at this nigger church?" the soldier asked.

"This is my church," Robinson replied. "These are our guests."

The soldier scowled and went back to his post.

Robinson looked over at City Hall. Ivan Allen had ordered the neo-Gothic facade of the building draped with black bunting, and mourning wreaths hung on the massive doors. The outward display of respect presented a marked difference from the scene at the capitol.

Inside City Hall, Allen and Massell looked over at the church. They knew that in just a few hours the thousands of mourners clustered on the lawn of Central Presbyterian would be joined by many more; Police Chief Jenkins predicted today's crowd would reach 150,000 by noon. That mass of grieving humanity would move down Central Avenue—right between the church and the capitol. Jenkins ordered every police officer in Atlanta on duty; the "morning watch" stayed on duty and the "evening watch" had been called in early, the only time in Atlanta's history the full force was on the clock simultaneously. For extra measure, more than a hundred firefighters were also stationed in key positions along the procession route.

The mayor turned from the window and walked out of his office. In the anteroom a few staff members manned phone lines. Atlanta schools were closed for the funeral, so Marie Dodd brought her nine-year-old daughter, Sandra, to City Hall; there was nowhere else for her to go. As the adults turned back to the phones, Sandra went over to the window and climbed on the sill. She aimed her Polaroid camera out the window, capturing Central Avenue in her viewfinder. Something big would happen today, and she was ready to witness it.

The Marriott Motor Hotel, downtown Atlanta, early morning

Before heading out to the church, a cluster of celebrities gathered to listen to Harry Belafonte's plans for a tribute performance to Martin Luther King. Initially they had hoped to stage a concert after the funeral tonight, but that was canceled because of security concerns. Terry Kay, the *Atlanta Journal* entertainment editor, reported that a "hushed room" listened to Harry Belafonte's "soft melodic voice" as he urged the entertainers to get involved. "The nation is going up in smoke and it is the souls of men that is at stake," Belafonte said.

Some of the entertainers gathered for the funeral already had long records of supporting the civil rights movement. In 1967, according to *Jet*, Belafonte, Sidney Poitier, Aretha Franklin, and Joan Baez raised more than $250,000 for King and SCLC with a seven-city concert series (Atlanta was not on the tour). Mahalia Jackson, scheduled to sing at the service, consistently raised money for King. Giving an interview from her bed in the Regency Hyatt, she told reporters she collected $40,000 for King at a single concert in Chicago the year before. Her first fund-raiser had been during the Montgomery bus boycott, where she staged a concert and donated the proceeds to cover cab fare and private cars for participants in the boycott.*

Pete Kilgo, the head of sales for the Atlanta Transit System, considered

---

*Xernona Clayton, as an SCLC communications assistant, had helped enlist celebrity support for King and his efforts. She said it was hard not to be skeptical about some of the celebrity outpouring at the time of the funeral. "I couldn't help think, a few weeks ago, I'd call to ask if you could help, and you'd say, 'I'm busy,' and I'd say, 'Wait, I haven't even told you the date,' and now here you are."

staying home; his wife pleaded with him to do so. Many Atlanta Transit workers called in sick, worried that they would be caught in the kinds of riots seen in Chicago, Detroit, and D.C. But Kilgo went to work anyway and, when he got in, was ordered to duty, not in his role as sales director, but to his old job—driving a bus. He was assigned a special route, picking up celebrities from the hotels downtown and taking them to Ebenezer. He got in the bus and headed to the Marriott.

Auburn Avenue, 10:15 a.m.

For hours, people waited outside Ebenezer Baptist Church, climbing up on a hill across the street, pressing up against the church walls, lining the sidewalks. On the rooftop of Holland Cleaners, just a block away, people stood five deep. A young white man in a clerical collar climbed up a utility pole and held a small home-movie camera. People crowded onto the tops of cars parked near the church. Reporter Kathryn Johnson stood on a car trunk, silently praying that she could keep her balance in high heels. A quintet of nuns huddled under an umbrella next to a group of hipsters in slick, tailored suits. Preteens clustered near the church door, joking with the police officers, whose dress-uniform caps stayed crisp in the rain. Delivery men walked into the church carrying heavy floral wreaths; when the doors would open to let them in, the kids would try to peek inside. Each car that passed brought a craning of necks and calls of "Who's there?" and "Is it them?" Kids moved into the street to get a look through windshields. A photographer climbed onto the church marquee to get a better angle.

As he hurried down Auburn Avenue toward the church, Bernard LaFayette passed the SCLC offices and saw people coming out of the door with armloads of papers and books. He went into the office and saw people taking memorabilia from desks and shelves. He pulled the door closed behind him to prevent anyone else from getting in, then told the curiosity seekers to leave right away.

"You can't take those things!" he shouted. "Put them back!"

As he shooed would-be looters out the door, he noticed one man running down the street carrying a pair of shoes and yelling, "I've got Dr. King's shoes!" LaFayette could not help laughing. The shoes were Abernathy's, not King's. (The "movement twins" wore shoes with lifts inside to make them appear taller; both King and Abernathy were well under five foot ten.)

Jo Freeman, her friend Karen Fuqua, and the elderly couple they had shared a car with on the drive from Chicago pulled up to the SCLC offices just as dawn broke. Seeing no one around, they walked over to Ebenezer and joined the crowd in the vacant lot. On the drive down, Jo had imagined she would get to the church and walk up to Mrs. King and offer condolences. In the late summer of 1966, she had worked as an assistant to Mrs. King, after volunteering with SCLC voter-registration efforts in Mississippi. *That's obviously a fantasy!* she realized as she looked at the press of people so deep that getting near the church door was impossible. She started taking pictures, alternating between her camera and the one belonging to the *Chicago Defender* photographer. She quickly lost track of her friend Karen and the elderly couple.*

Also outside the church was Winifred Green, who had been manning phones at West Hunter Street Baptist for the past few days. She had walked over with her friends American Friends Service Committee community relations director Barbara Moffett;† Connie Curry, AFSC southern field representative; and Jean Fairfax of the NAACP Legal Defense Fund.‡ Andrew Young, on his way into the church, stopped and said hello, kissing Jean Fairfax on the cheek. But other than recognizing Young, Green had a hard time making out faces in the crowd, even though she knew she should have been able to. The whole day felt "like a daze—like

---

*That evening, Jo Freeman and Karen Fuqua made their way back to the SCLC offices, hoping to find out about buses headed for Chicago. A man there told them he expected riots to break out in Atlanta now that the funeral was over, and that he was leaving as soon as he could and would drive them as far north as he was going. They left town before dark fell. After he dropped them off, they hitchhiked the rest of the way back to Chicago, getting in around noon. Jo went right to work. She was fired for missing more than the day allotted for attending services.

†Barbara Moffett was instrumental in the dissemination of one of the most pivotal documents of the civil rights movement, Martin Luther King's 1963 "Letter from Birmingham Jail." She helped to copy and distribute the letter while King was in jail, according to her *New York Times* obituary.

‡Jean Fairfax and her sister, Betty, an educator, became noted philanthropists, creating such programs as the Dan and Inez Wood Fairfax Memorial Fund, which provides college scholarships for black students.

being underwater or in humid weather; you're aware of the moment but not aware fully of all that is around you." She stood there with a "sense of horror and loss and disappointment." Later she recognized a few people from back in Alabama—Albert Turner, head of the Alabama SCLC, took the reins and led the mule wagon, and Ben "Sunshine" Owens walked alongside him.

Charles Black drove over to the church in his new convertible and parked as close as possible. He had made a sign out of poster board—LEAD MARSHAL—and taped it to the driver's side door. He had a walkie-talkie to radio to the marshals ahead. Even though he had been anticipating a crowd, he was staggered by its size. Police officers estimated that thirty thousand people crammed into the few blocks in front of the church. It was nearly impossible to move, and people were already tired and getting frustrated. Charles Black saw Ralph Abernathy come out of the church and try to rouse the crowd's spirits. The new SCLC president clambered up onto the roof of a black hearse.

"My friends, this is Ralph Abernathy," the minister called.

What is he doing? Charles Black wondered.

Abernathy called again. "My friends, my friends—"

"Hey, get off my hearse!" yelled a funeral-home employee.

"Who's your leader now? I am!" Abernathy shouted again, "Who's your leader now? I am!"

He tried several times to get a cheer going, but the crowd mostly ignored him. Reporter Paul Hemphill, standing nearby, watched as the hearse's driver grabbed at Abernathy's calves and ankles, attempting to pull him from the top of the car.

Charles Black stared at the scene. *I can't believe this. Why is he doing this? Why right now?*

After a while, Abernathy went back inside and the onlookers moved a little closer to the church. When a fleet of black limousines pulled closer, the kids surged from the church steps into the street, and adults followed close, too, making it hard for anyone to exit the cars.

"Move back! Hear?" called a police officer.

"Move back, move back, please," pleaded lanky young men in dark suits with gray flannel armbands indicating they were marshals. "Move away please."

Eventually, the student marshals and Atlanta police officers created a sort of receiving line, grabbing hands to form two human chains that served as barricades on either side of a makeshift aisle. Celebrities and dignitaries made their way between the cops and marshals, past the gauntlet of gawkers, and toward the church door.*

"Clear the way for Wilt!" came a shout as Wilt Chamberlain worked his way toward the door, towering over Republican presidential contender Richard Nixon. Sammy Davis Jr. flashed a grin and waved. Heavyweight champ Floyd Patterson and Jim Brown, the Cleveland Browns star turned actor, used their size to move through the crowd.

"Hello, Jackie!" came calls as Jacqueline Kennedy arrived, along with her brothers-in-law Robert and Ted Kennedy. Sargent Shriver—the ambassador to France, former Peace Corps head, and husband of Eunice Kennedy—was there also. As the Kennedys approached, onlookers broke from their somewhat orderly ranks, reaching in to try to touch a shoulder or grab a hand for a quick shake.

New York governor and presidential contender Nelson Rockefeller and his wife, Happy, headed into the church, along with Supreme Court Justice Thurgood Marshall, Vice President Hubert Humphrey, and Senator Eugene McCarthy. Governor George Romney of Michigan, a previous contender for the Republican nomination for president, was present. Attorney General Ramsey Clark, Labor Secretary Willard Wirtz, Housing Secretary Robert Weaver, and Under Secretary of State Nicholas Katzenbach attended. FBI and Secret Service agents were scattered around the area, and some positioned themselves strategically inside the church.†

---

*"With a good deal of firmness and shoving, the police could have pushed the people back and cleared the street, but had they done so there was the possibility of creating an unpleasant incident, and this was not the time or place for that," Police Chief Herbert Jenkins would write later of the on-the-fly crowd-control tactic.

†Reports in the *Atlanta Constitution*, *Atlanta Daily World*, *New York Times*, *Washington Post*, and *Washington Afro-American* reported dozens of well-known attendees in addition to those mentioned above. A sampling follows. Governors: Otto Kerner, Illinois; Harold LeVander, Minnesota; Raymond Shafer, Pennsylvania. Mayors: Richard Hatch, Gary, Indiana; Carl Stokes, Cleveland; Jerome Cavanagh, Detroit; and Henry Maier, Milwaukee. Congressmen: Paul Findley (R.-Ill.), John Dellenback (R.-Oreg.), Marvin Esch (R.-Mich.), Fred Schwengel (R.-Ia.), Charles Whalen (R.-Ohio), and Charles Goodell (R.-N.Y.). Celebrities: Henry Fonda, Nina Simone, Eartha Kitt,

John Lindsay, mayor of New York City, and Walter Washington, mayor of Washington, D.C., attended. John Daley of Chicago sent his administrative assistant Erwin France. Ralph Bunche, undersecretary general of the United Nations, and Bill Moyers, the former White House press secretary, were spotted. More than twenty ambassadors were there, representing such countries as Britain, Nicaragua, Morocco, Norway, Jamaica, Guyana, Liberia, the Netherlands, Chad, and New Zealand.

Carl Sanders, the former governor, and Attorney General Arthur Bolton were the only Georgia elected officials representing statewide office who attended. Supporting King might have been good for presidential contenders and politicians from the Northeast, but for Georgia's politicos, participation in the funeral would guarantee white-voter backlash.

Other attendees included Floyd McKissick of CORE; James Farmer, the former CORE head; John Johnson, publisher of *Jet*, *Ebony*, and *Tan* magazines; Berry Gordy of Motown Records; and Walter Reuther of the United Auto Workers.

Charles Black scanned the crowd for trouble as he watched the politicians and celebrities file in. Jackie Kennedy walked so close to him that he could see the fine hairs on her face.

"Stokely, baby!" came cries from the onlookers as Stokely Carmichael arrived with six bodyguards and his fiancée, South African singer Miriam Makeba. He flashed a Black Power salute. Reporters noted that Carmichael, unlike the denim-clad SCLC supporters and somber-suited politicians, was dressed modishly. *Time* magazine described his "zippered suede diddybop boots" and the *New York Times* dubbed Carmichael "the black power apostle . . . wearing a light blue turtleneck sweater under a dark sports coat."

Lonnie King, stationed at the front door, consulted the list given to him by Coretta King and the SCLC staff. He made some snap judgments, too. Wilt Chamberlain and Richard Nixon, not on the list, were allowed in. Later on, when he saw Whitney Young of the Urban League, King

---

Nipsey Russell, Dizzy Gillespie, and Ray Charles. Clergy: Gardner Taylor, president of the Progressive National Baptist Convention, and the Reverend John Wright, bishop of Pittsburgh.

decided to avoid a scene—"there were so many people who would have to be turned away"—and asked Young to wait. A few minutes later, he led Young through the basement of the church, and up behind the pulpit.*

June Dobbs Butts arrived in one of the cars driven in a convoy from the King home. Years later she would recall, *People lined up like a human carpet; it got thicker as we got toward the church.* When she got out of the car, she saw Ron Karenga and Stokely Carmichael with a large pole, hammering at the church door.

"This is an outrage! You won't let us in but you're seating white dignitaries!" they called.

They are right, but they shouldn't behave like that, June thought. The whole scene seemed "surreal, unreal."

June, Juanita Sellers Stone, and others from their group were escorted via the back route Whitney Young had just taken. Once inside Ebenezer, June Dobbs Butts saw Carmichael making his way to the front of the church, where he knelt beside Coretta Scott King and talked. *How can he be that obtrusive?* she thought. From his assigned spot at the front of the church, photographer Bob Fitch captured the conversation between Coretta and Stokely; the photograph would run in the next issue of *Life* magazine.

As he stood in the front of the church watching the pews fill, Ralph Abernathy kept feeling something was "wrong with the scene." Later, he would write in his memoir, "I realized: This was Ebenezer Church, yet most of the people jamming the pews were white. So many politicians and celebrities had come for the funeral that there wasn't room for all of Martin's friends and relatives, the people who came to this very church to hear him preach on Sundays." He was relieved that the march to Morehouse would allow more people to take part.

---

*Jenkins wrote later that he deliberately decided to keep police away from the church door and perimeter so as to avoid hostile feelings that could trigger outbreaks of violence. This strategy was not clear to observers, especially those watching television coverage. "When the King family and others had to fight their way into the church on national television, you have been indited [*sic*] by the world as prize slobs, along with pig face Maddox who had some 'previous' business. World history was made today and you and your 'nigger shooters' identified yourselves with your lack of planning and effort toward control," wrote C. R. Fairall, identifying himself as white, in a note to the police chief.

Outside Ebenezer, where he had been set up since dawn, photographer Jim Peppler stood as close to the church as he could. Many faces were familiar from years of covering the movement. Watching Andrew Young and Jesse Jackson, he knew what a difficult event this was for them personally. Jackson and Young were movement figures, but in his years of covering King and SCLC, Peppler noticed a "strange level of celebrity" associated with their efforts. "You would see Marlon Brando or actors and actresses showing up—in the middle of rural Mississippi."

In the midst of it all, his camera caught a startlingly familiar face— Sheyann Webb, the girl who had at eight signed up as King's "youngest freedom fighter," volunteering for the Selma-to-Montgomery voter-registration march. All day, Peppler worked with a photographer's detachment, getting the right shot, focusing on camera angles and technical details, thinking ahead to the newspaper pages that needed to be filled. But he was overwhelmed by the poignancy of seeing the young girl wearing her good Sunday dress and standing among the mourners. *Sheyann in some ways represents the loss of all those generations of people who are not going to have Dr. King,* he thought.

The sheer number of people astounded Jim Peppler. "I'd always felt the inspiration of King to be speaking to me directly as an American, that what he said was an extension and affirmation of the Declaration of Independence." Looking at the tens of thousands of people crammed into the confines of Auburn Avenue, he thought how many people had the same feeling that King's universal message spoke to them directly.

The Patterson family, tired after the fidgety night spent sharing a bed in their friends' home, waited in the crowd. Annie had packed snacks, and her daughters, Cynthia and Sybil, became anxious when their mother started to share their lunch with people around them.

"We're not going to get in the church; let's go on to Morehouse," said their father, and the family started walking the four miles toward the campus. Cynthia and Sybil wore traditional mourning outfits of eggshell and beige; for once they appreciated their mother's insistence that they find comfortable dress shoes. Around them, people moved ahead, knowing that the "real" procession would not be starting for a while. "There was no urgency. People just went up the street," Cynthia recalled years later.

Students from the colleges waved them along the route, making sure the out-of-town guests found their bearings.*

Pete Kilgo and his busload of celebrities did not make it through the crowds to get anywhere near the church, so they waited a few blocks up Auburn Avenue, ready to join the procession later. Alan King, the comedian, stood in front of the bus next to Kilgo. "Who's in there?" bystanders asked, and King sent in scraps of paper for autographs. A limousine hired by Diana Ross and the Supremes trailed the bus. While they all waited outside the church, passengers from the bus hopped back to the limo to get drinks.

The clouds lifted and the day got hot. "Do you want to see a fat man disappear?" Godfrey Cambridge asked Kilgo. "Point me in the direction of the Regency Hyatt." And the stocky comedian vanished.

Kilgo looked over to see Peter Lawford, the British actor who had been married to Patricia Kennedy, sister of John and Bobby, digging through an ice chest filled with bottles of Coca-Cola.

"How did you get those?" Kilgo asked.

"I found a pay phone and called room service at the Marriott and had them deliver it," Lawford said.

The actor tossed bottles of icy Coke to people in the crowd.

The swarms in the street created an almost carnival-like atmosphere. Someone had attached a sign to a small dog that read, I HAD A DREAM. AMEN. AMEN. The dog trotted along Auburn Avenue attracting charmed smiles from people waiting in line—and the attention of photographers and television cameramen.

Inside Ebenezer Baptist, 10:30 a.m.

The church was stifling. More than 1,000 people crowded into the tiny sanctuary that could just hold 750. The rain exacerbated the humidity of a warm Georgia spring, and the church felt airless. Many people fanned themselves with the sixteen-page funeral program, the front

---

*Years later, Cynthia Patterson would marry one of those marshals, Loncy Lewis, who had been a student at Morehouse at the time of the funeral.

of which was labeled OBSEQUIES MARTIN LUTHER KING JR. and the back of which carried credits for the Hanley Bell Street Funeral Home and Thornton Mortuary in tiny type.* The pages were outlined by a thick black border and included a three-page biography that opened, "Martin Luther King Jr. is like the great Yggdrasil tree, 'whose roots,' a poet said, 'are deep in earth but in whose upper branches the stars of heaven are glowing and astir.' His roots went deeply into the inferno of slavery, this black baby born January 15, 1929 to Alberta Williams King and Martin Luther King Sr." Some of the senators, congressmen, and candidates might have been taken aback by the accompanying time line, which started with the 1955 Montgomery bus boycott and ended with the Poor People's Campaign and Memphis, incorporating the entry "1967—the war in Vietnam and the call for peace." The two pages of quotations included the line King had honed while making his forceful antiwar statements: "There comes a time when one must take a position that is neither safe, nor politic, nor popular, but he must take it because conscience tells him it is right."

The program outlined the themes of the first three parts of the services: Ebenezer, "Family and Faith"; Memorial March, "Commitment and Movement"; and the Morehouse College Campus, "Knowledge and Wisdom." The fourth scheduled event, Interment, was accompanied by an italicized quote: *Free at last, free at last! Thank God Almighty, I'm free at last!*"

Associate pastor Ron English walked to the podium to deliver the opening prayer. He'd put a great deal of thought into how the prayer could address the violence in other cities, and to use it as a means of thwarting potential violence in Atlanta. The barrel-chested pastor barely needed the microphone to transmit his deep baritone.

"O God, our leader is dead. And so now the question that he posed during his life finds us in all its glaring proportions: 'Where do we go from here? Chaos or community?' We pray, o merciful Father, that the removal of this man will not nullify the revelation given through him."

English went on to pray, "Deepen our commitment to nonviolence

---

*The program was later reprinted. The reprint version carries the tagline "Copyright Coretta Scott King" on the back cover.

so that this country will not be run asunder by a frustrated segment of the black masses who would blaspheme the name of Martin Luther King by committing violence in that name."

As he listened to the prayer, Ivan Allen, seated next to his wife, Louise, in a front-row pew just behind Vice President Humphrey, anxiously looked around. The mayor wished he could be out on the street, checking on policing efforts. Inside, the church was oppressive; outside, he knew, along with the crowds listening to the service played on loudspeakers, were more than fifty members of Congress who had not been able to get in the sanctuary, busloads of celebrities, and hundreds of SCLC veterans. He knew that Chief Jenkins and his officers were doing all they could to prevent a riot from starting in the crowded streets and that APD specialists, along with FBI and Secret Service agents, were looking out for would-be assassins. Looking around the church, Allen saw a disheveled white man acting as an usher; in a yellow jacket, the man looked out of place among the dark-suited and well-groomed black ushers of Ebenezer. Earlier, the mayor had overheard the man arguing with one of the photographers in the church, and the photographer had said something about the yellow-jacketed man being a member of the KKK. Allen asked police captain Morris Redding to try to find out more; the captain sat next to the man during the service and watched him carefully.

After English's prayer, Harold DeWolf, King's professor at Boston University, walked up to the pulpit to deliver a tribute. DeWolf, the only white person scheduled to speak at the service, reiterated King's philosophy of nonviolence and urged listeners to adhere to that credo, saying: "Martin Luther King spoke with the tongues of men and of angels. Now those eloquent lips are stilled. His knowledge ranged widely and his prophetic wisdom penetrated deeply into human affairs. Now that knowledge and that wisdom have been transcended as he shares in the divine wisdom of eternity. The apostle Paul has told us that when all other experiences and virtues of humanity have been left behind, faith, hope, and love remain. But the greatest of these is love."

As attendees sweated, the service continued with several songs (including "Softly and Tenderly" and "Where He Leads Me") performed by the 160-member Ebenezer choir. Jethro English, a longtime church deacon, sat in the choir loft as he had for decades of services, weddings, and funerals. He found it hard to sing because he was overcome with emotion.*

Mary Gurley, one of the most well-known soloists in the Ebenezer choir, and a former leader of the Scripto Pen strike, sang "My Heavenly Father Watches over Me." After listing her performance, the next line on the funeral program stated simply, "Sermon Excerpts." Ralph Abernathy came to the pulpit and said, "Mrs. King has requested we play a recording of his last sermon."†

A moment of silence, then a few crackles of static and King's unmistakable voice echoed through the church: "Every now and then I think about my own death, and I think about my own funeral. And I don't think of it in a morbid sense. Every now and then I ask myself, 'What is it that I would want said?'"

As the audience listened, King's rich tones resonated through the small church: "I'd like somebody to mention that day, that Martin Luther King Jr. tried to give his life serving others. I'd like for somebody to say that day, that Martin Luther King Jr. tried to love somebody. Yes, if you want to say that I was a drum major, say that I was a drum major for justice. Say that I was a drum major for peace. I was a drum major for righteousness. And all the other shallow things will not matter."‡

Hearing her father's voice, Bernice King was startled. She jerked her head around, expecting to see him. She stared at the casket intently. The little girl was not the only one shaken; Andrew Young wept visibly.§

---

*Jethro English and his wife, Auretha, would perform a duet at the funeral six years later for Martin Luther King's mother, who was killed when a gunman opened fire in the church as she sat at the organ.

†This was not technically King's last sermon at Ebenezer. According to Ron English, King had preached a sermon about love on the Sunday before he went to Memphis.

‡King's notes for the sermon and the manila folder in which they were stored are in the King Collection at the Robert Woodruff Library at Morehouse College. The folder is stamped with the logo of the Ivan Allen Company, Atlanta's leading office-supply firm.

§The decision to use the "Drum Major Instinct" recording had been announced to the media before the funeral, and the text of the sermon ran as an op-ed in the *New York Times* the day of the funeral ("Drum Major for Justice"). That King seemed to prophetically prepare his own eulogy proved fascinating to the press, with headlines such as *Jet*'s "Rev. King Preached Own Funeral Before Death" or the *Washington Post*'s "King Gave Outline for Eulogy."

Crouched at the corner of the church with the other members of the press corps, Bob Fitch, who'd chronicled beatings and protests, found that for the first time his camera did not serve as a shield for his emotions. The photographers and reporters near him were a "tough and crusty bunch," and in years of covering the SCLC he had never before seen them weep. At several points throughout the service he was so overwhelmed it was a challenge to focus and frame a shot. But as he listened to King's voice and glanced over, he saw Bernice crawl into her mother's lap and peer up at Coretta, who looked down at the girl with a hint of a smile. At that instant, Fitch felt an almost mystical experience, seeing captured in that image their personal loss and the universal nature of grief.* He took a photograph of the mother and daughter and kept on taking pictures, the camera serving its trusted role of emotional stabilizer once again.

The morbid foreshadowing of King's delivering his own eulogy was underscored by other quotes selected for inclusion in the program that seemed to indicate he knew he would die early and violently. A 1962 statement included the lines "It may get me crucified, I may even die. But I want it said even if I die in the struggle that 'He died to make men free,'" and an excerpt from the "Mountaintop" speech given in Memphis the night before King died stated, "Longevity has its place. But I'm not concerned about that now."

The sermon was followed by the spiritual "Balm in Gilead."

There is a balm in Gilead
To make the wounded whole
There is a balm in Gilead
To heal the sin-sick soul.

---

*Fitch's photograph of the mother and child ran in the April 19 issue of *Life* magazine. Moments later, when Bernice slid down in Coretta's lap and looked directly at the camera, another photographer, Moneta Sleet, on assignment for *Ebony* and *Jet*, took an image that would be widely reproduced in newspapers, earning Sleet a Pulitzer Prize for news photography, the first awarded to an African-American. "I was a little jealous," Fitch said. "But Moneta worked for many years and got little credit but produced stunning work, and the recognition was great."

As the recessional played, pallbearers Jethro English, C. K. Steele, and Fred Bennette slowly carried the coffin down the center aisle and to the church foyer. The church doors swung open onto a chaotic scene. Farmer Peeks maneuvered the wagon as close to the sanctuary as possible, but so many people crushed around, it became impossible for the mules or the wagon to move. Denim-clad members of the SCLC pushed forward to lift the coffin above the heads of the crowd and hoist it into the wagon bed.

There still was no way for the mules to move out and lead the procession as planned. Finally, someone grabbed a megaphone and yelled, "If you don't move back, I think that mule will move *you* back!"

The crowd began walking up the street, creating enough space for the church-service attendees to exit and the march to begin. Everyone gathered behind the mule-drawn wagon, its hastily applied new coat of green paint already flaking off.

Funeral organizers had planned an orderly progression for VIPs, who were designated "honorary pallbearers." This should have been, in order, SCLC board and staff; clergy, the New York delegation, the Pennsylvania delegation, and the Michigan delegation; governors, senators, and congressmen; other elected officers; actors, singers, and performers; and labor officials. The "general procession" was slated to take up the rear, but in actuality, many of the regular people who'd waited all morning ended up leading the procession, starting out as the funeral service ended in order to ease congestion on Auburn Avenue.

Clearly the sole activity in downtown Atlanta that day was the funeral. Businesses were closed; the only people around either took part in the procession or lined twenty deep on the sidewalks to watch. People sat on high walls, stood on building rooftops, hung from office windows, and even perched on top of the portable toilets installed along the procession route.

The thousand student marshals were spread out along the parade course. Some stood at street corners, ready to signal to their counterparts up or down the route if trouble flared. Others were assigned to accompany dignitaries, ready to flag other marshals for help if needed. Peter Geffen and Mickey Shur, recovered from their predrawn trip to fetch the mules, stuck close to Rabbi Abraham Heschel, as Hosea Williams had instructed them to do.

As the procession made its way through downtown Atlanta, bystanders joined in and the number of people marching grew; reports estimate at least one hundred thousand paraded that day with observers bringing the crowds in the city to a quarter million. Later, describing the scale of the funeral, Andrew Young wrote that the assembly was "frighteningly enormous."

To further underscore the Poor People's Campaign initiative, members of the SCLC wore overalls, work shirts, jeans, or denim jackets, signifying their solidarity with the working class. Abernathy wore the same scuffed boots that he wore when marching with King; they peeked out from under his robes when he presided over the Ebenezer service. Jesse Jackson appeared to have on the same blood-spotted turtleneck and jacket he wore the night King was killed.

The mules created one of the most memorable impressions for participants in the procession as well as television viewers. "Today, there was only the clop, clop, clop of two mules pulling Dr. King's body through the streets of the city," wrote John Goldman in the *Los Angeles Times*. Sam Williams, an intern in Ivan Allen's office who took part in the march, recalled, "Everybody was crying. Everybody. Adults, grandmothers, children. It was a mosaic of people. I remember the distinct sound of the mules' hooves on the street. That sound lingers with me to this day." The dominance of the mules' hooves was noticed by a number of reporters. Interestingly, that detail—made possible by the relative stillness of the march—resulted from a practical matter. Experienced protest organizers knew that keeping the crowd quiet would allow marshals to hear any scuffles and be alert to potential security breaches. "We kept it quiet, so all you could hear was the mules, so that way we could hear if anyone tried anything," Bernard LaFayette said.

The melancholy tenor of the procession was mitigated by the presence of politicians and celebrities, who distracted participants—and the reporters, photographers, and camera operators covering the funeral. Television crews captured the somber pace of the mules and the endless refrains of "We Shall Overcome," but also the casual conversation and banter as marchers walked for hours through an increasingly sunny Atlanta day.

"Sammy Davis is back here!" Ethel Kennedy remarked to the man next to her.

"Sammy Davis!" he exclaimed. "Really?"

Geffen, Shur, and Heschel walked near the Kennedy group for a while, and Shur saw passersby break into the procession to shake Kennedy's hand or shout good wishes.

Many of the celebrities skipped the procession, but a few walked the entire route. Marshals and fellow marchers helped blind singer Ray Charles. Eartha Kitt took off her shoes and walked in stockinged feet.

As Jesse Jackson marched behind the wagon and looked out over the crowd, he thought, *How many of these people were with us April 3, fighting for the garbage workers, and the Poor People's Campaign? It's cheap grace to admire a great sacrificial person. There were many who admired him but few who followed him.*

As the procession passed the Shrine of the Immaculate Conception, the bell tolled every twelve seconds. A huge floral wreath hung on the door of Rich's department store.

The march wound along the four-mile route from Ebenezer to the campus of Morehouse College, King's alma mater. June Dobbs Butts was happy that she brought a pair of walking shoes to wear instead of high heels ("the only time I've done that in my life"). Patricia Latimore, the Kings' babysitter, had assumed the cars that brought the family to the church would take them to Morehouse and wore heels. After walking part of the route, she was in pain. Eventually she caught a cab back to the house on Sunset Avenue and watched the funeral on television.

The morning rain stopped and the April sky grew bright and clear, and like so many Atlanta spring days, it began to grow hot. By noon, it was well over eighty degrees. Neva Bethel, an Emory University employee, walked to the church from her apartment on Ponce de Leon Avenue a few miles away. She wanted to join the march but was so overcome by heat she sat down and leaned against the side of a building. A marshal called for help and two African-American policemen assisted the middle-aged white woman into a car, where she rested while the crowd moved past. Then they took her to a bus station to get a ride home.*

---

*"Even if we grant that they were at their highest point of courtesy and efficiency because of the particular occasion, I felt their earnest willingness and sincere desire to take care of me," Mrs. Bethel wrote to Police Chief Jenkins on April 11. "I wish I had the presence of mind to ask for their names, or their badge numbers or both. . . . I am happy to go on record with my appreciation for these two policemen."

As the march made its way to the Hunter Street viaduct, a burst water main created a six-foot stream across the hot pavement. Some marchers splashed through. Others paused, removed their shoes, and cooled their feet in the water. That afternoon, hundreds of people collapsed in the heat. The six first-aid stations along the processional route were put to the test.

As the procession drew close to the capitol, marchers grew even quieter. *Atlanta Journal* columnist Paul Hemphill imagined the governor "scared to death, peering out at us through the Venetian blinds." As they passed the front of the capitol, the marchers sang "Swing Low, Sweet Chariot." It was solemn and calm, but fear was also palpable. Sam Massell recalled, "We were the center of liberal America at that moment, white and black, Jew and gentile, Northerner and Southerner. [The procession] had the leadership that thought progressively, and it had the opponents, like [those] across the street from City Hall standing in the door."

The marchers rounded the corner where the Red Cross had set up a station near City Hall, handing out ice water. Kathy Kohn and other volunteers at Central Presbyterian took a break from cleaning up and stood on the church lawn watching the mourners pass by.

When the procession reached Morehouse, so many people crowded around the mule wagon that the coffin could not easily be removed.

"Stay back!" marshals called out.

People pressed closer and closer, towering over the King children, who were shoved up toward the back of the wagon. Dexter and Bunny held hands, staring straight ahead at the back of the wooden mule wagon as the adults shouted back and forth in the space over their heads.

The quadrangle at Morehouse College, early afternoon

Marvin Mangham watched through the viewfinder of the television camera as thousands of people moved up Fair Street and into the quadrangle at Morehouse. He was astounded by the number of people; in all his years of attending college events—brought to alumni affairs by his dad, and attending as a student—he had never imagined so many people could fit into the campus.

The quadrangle filled with people hours before the procession reached Morehouse. People sat on the grassy field near Harkness Hall, on roofs and balconies of the buildings nearby, even in tall trees that shaded the field. Rows of chairs were arranged in the center of the grassy area and near the stage at the front of Harkness, but these were roped off and assigned to dignitaries. Secret Service agents walked the perimeter of the quadrangle and peered up into trees, asking people to climb down.

Morehouse students from the Black Action Committee walked up and down the rows of waiting mourners and poured water into paper cups and empty soft-drink bottles.

Cynthia Patterson and her family were at the front of the quadrangle, right below the stage. Because they started walking before the end of the funeral, they had a prime view for the memorial service. The procession reached the campus around two, and marchers began finding their way to places to sit—claiming reserved spots or squeezing besides spectators already waiting.

So many people crowded into the grassy square that the Pattersons were buoyed up by the force of the crowd. Cynthia was flipped up and onto her back, supported by the heads and shoulders of dozens of people surging toward the stage. It was terrifying.

"Get back! Get back!" student marshals called. As the crowd eased back, the Pattersons and others in the front row were lowered to the ground, shaking as they attempted to stand upright again.

At 2:17, members of the Morehouse Glee Club started proceedings by singing a selection of hymns. James Wilborn, who had skipped practice to work for the television crews as a driver, tried to work his way onstage to sing. No, he was told. You were not here to practice, you don't sing. So he went with the television crew to South-View Cemetery, losing a chance to be in front of the cameras.

Around 3 p.m., Ralph Abernathy made his way to the stage and took the microphone, asking people to "make way for Senator Robert Kennedy of New York to come to the platform."

It was so crowded it was hard to move. Mickey Shur and Peter Geffen were still near Rabbi Heschel and Kennedy. Shur took it on himself to shout, "Please move! Get out of the way!" to help the rabbi and the senator make their way to the stage. Shur was swept onto the platform himself. He edged as far to the back as he could get. The sun beat down and Ethel

Kennedy looked over and asked the fair-skinned Shur if he was getting too much sun. *It's like my mother is here,* he thought.

Kennedy moved up to the platform, seeming chagrined by the attention. Abernathy again came to the microphone, asking the crowd to move back a little from the platform; people were fainting in the heat.

"Everyone take ten steps backward!" Andrew Young called out. "This is a near emergency!"

When everyone was settled, the program started with Mahalia Jackson's rendition of "Take My Hand, Precious Lord." Tears rolled down the faces of observers as her rich voice filled the vast space. Many remembered her singing "I Been 'Buked and I Been Scorned" at the 1963 March on Washington right before King delivered his "Dream" speech. The crowd broke into massive applause.

Events were running behind schedule, so Abernathy announced that six planned speeches were canceled and simply introduced the speakers instead: Mayor Ivan Allen; the SCLC board chairman, the Reverend Joseph Lowery; Robert Collier, head of the board of deacons at Ebenezer; Rosa Parks; Bishop John Wright of Pittsburgh; and Andrew Young.*

The program moved into the eulogy by Benjamin Mays, president emeritus of Morehouse, and King's mentor. He and King had had an agreement, he said, that whoever died first would be eulogized by the other. When he made that pact, the elderly educator said, he had not expected King would be first to die.

Like Ron English's prayer earlier that day, Mays's eulogy referenced the political situation as he issued a challenge to the audience: "It is now for us, all the millions of the living who care, to take up his torch of love. It is for us to finish his work, to end the awful destruction in Vietnam, to

---

*"I regretted very much that I didn't get to speak," Lowery recalled later. "They cut me out—and they cut the mayor out, too. They apologized later, and I cussed them out. But it was a long funeral and there was a lot said. People were rejoicing at the opportunity to hear Mahalia, and Dr. Mays was eloquent. It was a long, hot day, but people were respectful—they endured the lengthy program. We were all still in a state of shock." Lowery was featured on a far larger stage four decades later when he delivered a show-stealing prayer at the January 2009 inauguration of President Barack Obama: "Help us work for that day when black will not be asked to get in back, when brown can stick around, when yellow will be mellow, when the red man can get ahead, man, and when white will embrace what is right. Let all those who do justice and love mercy say amen."

root out every trace of race prejudice from our lives, to bring the massive powers of this nation to aid the oppressed and to heal the hate-scarred world."

Interestingly, while Mays delivered the most classic formal eulogy of the day, it did not receive as much media coverage as other elements of the funeral, perhaps because his words were overpowered by the size of the crowd. King biographer David Lewis suggested, "On another day, perhaps a cooler one, and assuredly at an earlier hour, Dr. Mays's eulogy would have registered with great impact."*

As the ceremony went on, Xernona Clayton stood to the side at the back of the quadrangle with her friend Lillian Miles.† John Lewis, the former SNCC head, came and stood with them. Lewis looked around at the crowds and the dogwood trees. The beauty of the Atlanta spring day reinforced his overwhelming sense of loss.

More than 120 million people watched the funeral on television that day—over half the total U.S. population. Across the country, shops and schools were closed. People gathered in homes and churches, even stood on the street in front of appliance showrooms to watch. Cars and taxis idled in the streets while drivers listened to the sermons and hymns broadcast on radio. Police in cities that had been wracked with violence reported a ceasefire. Reports sent to the Secret Service officer at Camp David stated that in Washington, D.C., "the entire city appears to be quiet during this funeral period," although "military have sent additional troops to the northeast section of the city, in the event there is trouble after the funeral."

Among the millions of television viewers were White House staffers with the president at Camp David. That afternoon, when LBJ returned to

---

*Copies of the Mays eulogy were distributed in April 1968 by the AFL-CIO to its supporters. "The AFL-CIO mourns the death of Dr. King and renews its determination to help achieve the goals for which he died," wrote Don Slaiman, director of the union group's department of civil rights in a note accompanying copies of the eulogy text.

†John Lewis and Lillian Miles would get married in December of that year, with Daddy King performing the service in the sanctuary of Ebenezer Baptist Church.

the lodge after escorting Ambassador Bunker and others to the helipad, he found people clustered around the television in the living room.

At 4:07 that afternoon, Clint Hill, the Secret Service officer at Camp David with LBJ, would get a report from Secret Service agents who attended the funeral: ". . . church was very much over-crowded. After the sermon, one of Dr. King's speeches was played to those in the church; at this time persons became very emotional and tension was felt among those in the church."

The Secret Service agents also dutifully reported, "No incidents of concern to this service were reported," and noted, "Stokely Carmichael attended the church services."

In newspaper and magazine coverage, Hosea Williams's efforts to find a photogenic wagon had clearly paid off. An aerial photo of the wagon and mourners dominated the *New York Times* April 10 front page, and similar photographs ran in prominent positions in other major newspapers. Television cameramen zoomed in for close-ups of the wagon's rusted wheels and the weary mules.

Reporters outdid themselves trying to lyrically describe the wagon. In the *Washington Afro-American*, George Collins profiled "Ada and Bell— the epitome of poverty that afflicts the nation's poor and oppressed," describing them as "unshod, unsheared . . . their bones pressed tightly against their hides." He speculated that "malnutrition had become a way of life with them just as it has for Dr. King's millions of followers." Collins described the wagon that Williams "borrowed" from the antiques store: "It bore marks of wear and tear to the extent that a disciple of the poor kept watch over the rear wheel to assure it did not fall."

In *Ebony*, Lerone Bennett Jr. wrote, "One has to go back more than ten decades, to the traveling Lincoln bier, to find an analogue to the marching King casket and the rivers of people following his body in misery," adding, "hundreds of thousands followed the plain wagon and the two Georgia mules which bore him."

Moved by what they saw on television, people from around the United States wrote to the King family. In neat blue ballpoint on lined paper, fourteen-year-old Leslie Harper wrote to Coretta King, "I just thought

I'd like you to know I am a Negro girl and am very proud of my heritage."
Mrs. Lawrence Greene of St. Albans, New York, wrote, "You have today
made yourself a woman among women. In your time of grief, you thought
not of yourself but of us that cry in the night." Sister Mary Bonaventure of Wadsworth, Ohio, wrote, "My class and I watched the funeral
services of Reverend Dr. Luther King [*sic*] on T.V. and we were all deeply
impressed."

Not everyone was positive. In an unsigned letter from San Diego
dated April 9, a writer asked, "Just who did you think you were? Another
Mrs. J.F. Kennedy?"

Central Presbyterian Church, 5 p.m.

In the morning, Kathy Kohn drove to downtown from Doraville to relieve
Norm. They talked briefly in front of the church, then he drove home to
stay with the boys and take a much-needed nap. For the first few hours,
Kathy barely had time to look up. Central served more than five thousand
people breakfast before the funeral started (included in the menu: 150
dozen doughnuts donated by Krispy Kreme). Throughout the morning,
she helped serve food to people who stopped in from the parade route.
The afternoon was spent straightening and going through the provisions.
Absolutely nothing was left. All the donations were gone.

An older man came in, returning from the procession, and asked if
there was anything to eat.

"I am so sorry, I don't have anything I can give you," Kathy said. "All I
have is water."

"That would be fine," he said.

Kathy poured a glass of water and handed it to him.

He drank the whole glass in almost one gulp.

"I think that is the best thing I have ever tasted," he said.

Kathy looked around the church, where cots and army blankets were
crowded into every empty corner, and debris from the thousands of meals
served was still evident. She looked back at the man, tired and drained.
Three generations of her family had gone to this church; she doubted any
one of her relatives had shared a meal or a drink with a black person.

South-View Cemetery, Atlanta, evening

The crowd thinned and only close friends, family, and supporters followed the casket—now transferred to a hearse—to South-View Cemetery, the graveyard built by freed slaves in 1886. Christine King Farris and her husband shared a limousine with Andrew Young and other SCLC staff; as they drove from Morehouse to the cemetery, Young fell asleep. *He must not have slept more than a few hours in the past five days*, Christine thought. Xernona Clayton drove with her friend Lillian and John Lewis.

Roberts Marble Company of Atlanta, a family-run business founded in 1898 that had made the crypts for both the demagogic former governor Eugene Talmadge and black legal pioneer A. T. Walden, had crafted a two-crypt mausoleum in Georgia marble in less than a week. The phrase FREE AT LAST! FREE AT LAST! THANK GOD ALMIGHTY, I'M FREE AT LAST! had been stenciled on the marble; the actual engraving would be completed later.

Abernathy delivered the final homily. He said that God created King as "a leader to heal the white man's sickness and the black man's slavery," a visionary "willing to die but not willing to kill." As he spoke, Mrs. King, who had remained stoically calm all day, started to cry softly. Harry Belafonte, seated next to her, placed his fist inside his mouth as though to hold back sobs. Standing with her friend Juanita, June Dobbs Butts, in sight of her own parents' graves, was overcome with grief. The rest of the inner circle, composed for the long day of public mourning, let go with "weeping and wailing."

Saying that the ground of this historic cemetery was "too small for his spirit," Abernathy ended his prayer, then also started crying. Abernathy reached out and dropped flower petals over the casket. Looking through his lens, Jim Peppler saw the blur of petals and behind it a cluster of news photographers standing on top of a nearby mausoleum.

A member of a television crew came over to remove a microphone cord from around Abernathy's neck. Other SCLC ministers who were nearby put their arms around him. Abernathy left the cemetery while the King family were still there. As the coffin was eased into the crypt, photographers moved closer, most holding their cameras up overhead and clicking rapidly. A *Newsweek* reporter at the scene noted that all the cam-

eras deployed at once were "clicking grotesquely, like teeth." Some photographers shot from a platform that dangled from a crane; they had paid
$100 apiece to use it; the crane operator, however, asked for checks to be
made out to Mrs. King or the SCLC.

Tom Houck, as he watched the coffin being placed into the crypt, listened to Abernathy, and saw the weariness of the King children, thought,
*I now know Martin Luther King is dead. For five days, we knew he was assas-
sinated, but we knew he was still with us.*

The rain, which had stopped for the day, returned in a downpour, and
the mourners rushed to their cars.

Jim Peppler, a young photographer, served as the photo editor of the *Southern Courier,* a short-lived Alabama-based newspaper that supported the civil rights movement. He had frequently photographed King and members of the SCLC, and when he learned of the assassination, he drove to Atlanta to document the funeral. This portfolio highlights the more than five hundred images he captured that day, most of them never before published.

Ralph David Abernathy presides over the final service at South-View Cemetery.

Andrew Young comforts King's parents at the cemetery.

Crowd scene looking west on Auburn Avenue the morning of King's funeral.

Harry Belafonte at South-View.

Coretta Scott King leans on the arm of her brother-in-law A. D. King and holds the hand of her daughter Bernice during the funeral procession.

Ralph Abernathy, A. D. King, and others closely follow the mule wagon that carried King's casket.

Photographers paid $100 each
to go up in a crane that offered a
bird's-eye view of King's tomb
at South-View.

Thousands of people camped out overnight to be near Ebenezer Baptist Church
the morning of the funeral.

Daddy King and Coretta Scott King at the cemetery.

Jacqueline Kennedy, escorted by Atlanta police officers outside Ebenezer Baptist Church.

Robert and Ethel Kennedy arrive at the church.

Pallbearers, including Jesse Jackson and Hosea Williams, at South-View.

The crowd on the campus of Morehouse College before the afternoon memorial service.

I HAD A DREAM. AMEN. AMEN, reads the sign attached to this dog, who distracted the waiting mourners along the funeral procession route.

Presidential candidate Richard Nixon and Wilt Chamberlain wait along with others for entrance to the service at Ebenezer.

Mourners looked for any possible vantage point to get a view of the procession.

Sheyann Webb, whom King called the "smallest freedom fighter," took part in the Selma-to-Montgomery march.

Sammy Davis Jr. was one of the celebrity attendees.

Stokely Carmichael and Miriam Makeba make their way through the crowd on Auburn Avenue.

The crowd outside Ebenezer was so thick that cars carrying dignitaries and family members could not easily reach the church.

SEVEN

Wednesday, April 10, 1968

FREE AT LAST was stenciled on the marble of the hastily completed monument at South-View Cemetery for the funeral and would be engraved later. *Jim Peppler*, Southern Courier *Collection, Alabama Department of Archives and History, Montgomery, Alabama*

South-View Cemetery, Atlanta, early morning.

IT WAS STILL raining and the plainclothes detective assigned to guard King's tomb sat in his car to stay dry. A reporter from the *New York Times* watched the scene and saw seven white women approach the tomb as the rain eased up. They looked at the crypt and adjusted the flower arrangements piled up around the edges of the mausoleum. A few extra guards stood watch; they had been sent and paid for by the head of Scripto, the pen company whose workers Martin Luther King had supported in a strike.*

---

*According to the memoir by Christine King Farris, her brother's body would be transferred several times before ending up where it is today, on the Auburn Avenue grounds

Throughout the day, more than one thousand people came to see the crypt, about half of them white, Detective J. M. Mulliford told the *Atlanta Journal.* Most would walk over, look at the site quietly, and head back to their cars. There were no signs of vandalism. Many more people simply drove by slowly, pausing on Jonesboro Road to look over at the burial site.

Mary Bentley, who worked in the South-View offices, tried to console a news photographer who stood near the crypt and cried. He had followed King since the 1955 Montgomery bus boycott and was forlorn to realize this would be his "last assignment."

Atlanta Transit System offices, 9 a.m.

Shortly after he got to work, Pete Kilgo got a call from Robert Sommerville, the company president. "You need to fix me a bill," Sommerville told Kilgo. "All the rides given for free over the past few days need to be accounted for."

"You told me to do it; nobody said anything about charter orders," protested Kilgo.

"I need a bill."

So Kilgo improvised. He dug through records and looked for staff time sheets. Every hour booked outside of regular service over the preceding three days he allocated to the funeral. The total came to around $50,000.* He pulled together a bill and presented it to his boss, who accepted it silently.

Weeks later, wondering what had happened to the bill, Kilgo went to the accounts receivable department and flipped through the files. He

---

of the Martin Luther King Jr. Center for Nonviolent Social Change. "I orchestrated a series of early-morning, quiet, dignified transfers of M.L.'s body, under the cover of predawn darkness," she wrote. First, the body was moved to a vacant lot near Ebenezer. Then it was transferred to a spot farther up Auburn Avenue. When the King Center was under construction, the body was moved again, to a spot near the intersection of Auburn Avenue and Boulevard. Ralph Abernathy would write about taking part in one of these transfers, and seeing King's body under the coffin's glass top, which had been lifted off so undertakers could remove green mold from his suit and the casket lining, then replaced with a seal they claimed would last for centuries. After her death in 2006, Coretta Scott King's body was placed in the other side of the marble crypt.

*About $314,000 in 2010 dollars, according to the Bureau of Labor Statistics.

found his jerry-rigged statement marked PAID. The payer was Robert Woodruff, former president of the Coca-Cola Company.

Over at the Atlanta Police Department, as each shift changed, Herbert Jenkins called the officers on duty in for a special meeting and thanked them for their efforts over the past week. During the entire funeral period, only forty arrests occurred, according to Chief Jenkins. In total, 875 policemen and 250 firefighters were on duty the day of King's funeral. With all the overtime hours over the funeral week, the city owed at least $100,000 just in extra pay for police, controller Charles Davis told reporters.* In addition were a host of other charges, ranging from security details at the King family homes and added airport capacity to more prosaic matters such as installing portable restrooms along the procession route.

The next week, at the Board of Aldermen meeting on April 15, the city finance committee proposed that, if favorably voted on, the city comptroller "pay expenses incurred by the city related to the funeral of Dr Martin Luther King Jr. not to exceed the sum of $9,000."

At the capitol, Lester Maddox met with reporters and praised Allen, Jenkins, and even the SCLC for the success of the day before, saying a city had never faced "such a tense situation and such an influx of visitors" as Atlanta. His congratulations, however, came with implied criticism: "If any of our Negro leaders, college students, or people who had been involved in violence before had called for anything other than peace, there would have been something other than peace."

Police Chief Jenkins began to receive mail over the next few days from Atlanta leaders who had a stake in the successful outcome of the funeral, ranging from heads of businesses to powerhouses of black leadership. "It is this kind of high performance that makes one happy to be a citizen of the city of Atlanta," wrote the Reverend Sam Williams in his capacity as head of the Community Relations Commission. "Please know that the

---

*The annual report of the Atlanta Police Department lists salaries for 1968 at $6.9 million, an increase over the $6.2 million spent in 1967. A large percentage of the $700,000 difference is presumably due to funeral-related expenses, as nothing in the 1968 annual report indicates budgeted staffing increases on the force. The 1968 report does not contain a summary of the funeral events, but it does include a photograph of a crowd scene.

Commission stands ready to cooperate in any way it can with the Police Department to help keep Atlanta the fine city it is endeavoring to be." Narvie Harris, president of the Georgia Congress of Colored Parents and Teachers, thanked the chief and his force for "services rendered beyond the call of duty during our hour of distress." John Middleton, president of Morris Brown College, wrote to express appreciation on behalf of the college and "others of goodwill."

"You have done yourselves proud and have presented to the world an image of Atlanta that should speak something to all mankind regarding race relations as well as international affairs," wrote F. Burt Vardeman, administrator for the Presbyterian Center of Atlanta. "I had a great feeling of pride in knowing that our police department was so helpful, warm and 'on top of it,'" wrote Dr. Tom Leland of the Atlanta Psychiatric Clinic, a lecturer at police training sessions. "Chief: you did a magnificent job throughout the week! Congratulations," wrote former congressman Charles Weltner.

Enthusiastic thanks came from leaders of Atlanta businesses. "The possibilities which loomed before you and your associates were mountainous—probably more than any of us can imagine," wrote Theta Miller, president of the Women's Chamber of Commerce of Atlanta. "We are grateful for your wisdom and courage which gave to all of us under the influence the needed assurance that capable and conscientious leaders were directing our path." Robert Bivens, executive director of Central Atlanta Progress, the downtown-Atlanta business alliance, extended thanks for a "superb performance during the recent time of human tragedy and concern in our city." Similar words of gratitude came from dozens of names on the roster of Atlanta movers and shakers, including George M. Erwin, president of the American Agency Life Insurance Company; J. W. Pinkston, executive director of Grady Memorial Hospital; W. O. Duvall, chairman of the board of Atlanta Federal Savings and Loan Association; Harold Brockey, president and general manager of Rich's department store; Marvin Goldstein, president of the Atlanta Americana Motor Hotel; and George Manners, dean of Georgia State College.*

---

*Now Georgia State University.

Some of the writers were candid about their fears that riots could have happened. "I shudder to think what could have happened to and in Atlanta during these sensitive times," wrote Lieutenant Governor George Smith—who had been conspicuously absent during the funeral.

"Everybody was busily congratulating everybody else yesterday for Atlanta's response to the funeral of Dr. Martin Luther King Jr. And it is true; Atlantans did meet the logistical challenge and they did keep the faith," the editorial board of the *Atlanta Constitution* would write the next day. But of everyone who pitched in, from the mayor to the church volunteers, those who earned praise the most were two groups of young people, the students at the Atlanta University Center who mounted Operation Respect to prevent violence, and the Young Men's Civic League of Summerhill, who distributed flyers stating, "Riots hurt me and you, baby." Their response, the editorial board commented, "merits the gratitude of the entire community."

Helen Bullard, the longtime political adviser to Mayors Hartsfield and Allen, wrote to Ivan Allen the evening of the funeral, urging him to keep up the momentum of goodwill from the past week, perhaps by starting a scholarship fund or erecting a shrine to nonviolence. "I know you are utterly exhausted and only the urgency of the situation makes me intrude now, but it seems to me that after the funeral is the dangerous time and that you have no choice but to continue this course of leadership."

Amid the praise and goodwill, conspiracy theories abounded. Robert Noble of Newark sent a handwritten letter to Ivan Allen asking that the mayor get Atlanta's police chief to investigate King's death as a "put up job," citing a *New York Times Magazine* interview in which King's staff, referring to the Poor People's Campaign, said that a big event was needed to raise funds. "It would appear that the whole affair was set up by the so called Afro Americans. . . . A good conviction of this sort would possibly end the 'desecration' of my country," wrote Noble, who added that he had previously lived in Laurel, Mississippi. "Remember, the BIBLE states that these people are 'Brother Killers.'" Noble attached with his letter a clipping from the *New York Daily News* with a statement from Harry Belafonte: "In response to numberless inquiries that have come to me as a close friend of Dr. King and his family asking how to perpetuate his teachings, I suggest that contributions be sent to the Martin Luther King Memorial Fund."

It was pouring rain as members of the Wednesday Morning Study Club, the Atlanta women's social club founded in 1907, arrived for their monthly meeting, this time hosted by Ruth Smith. Despite the rain, the club members paused to admire Ruth's garden, which bloomed in full spring glory.

Jean Beatty delivered the report for the program committee. She discussed the next program, which was to be a historical look at the club's record on civil rights. This had been in the works for a while, but the club members voted unanimously to proceed. "Jean articulated for all of us the appropriateness of the committee's decision. The funeral for Martin Luther King, Jr. had been held on the preceding day," noted recording secretary Florence Harris in the minutes. "Even though the committee's plans had been completed prior to the assassination of Dr. King, it could not have been more timely."

Atlanta airport, midmorning

Departures were almost as chaotic as the arrivals had been. Buses lined up outside the terminal dropping off passengers; planes lined up for hours on the tarmac waiting to take off.

The scene was just as crowded in the parking lot of the Atlanta Stadium, which still served as a clearing center. Travelers were dropped off by host families or in church buses and sat on their bags waiting to see what bus charters were scheduled.

Even for those who came by private car, the congestion was heavy. As they left Atlanta to drive home, Cynthia Patterson looked out of the window of the family car, amazed to see police helicopters hovering over the city. *They must have been there the day before, too,* she thought, *but I didn't notice in all the crowds.* Police cars were everywhere.

House of Representatives, Washington, D.C., late morning.

After hours of final arguments, the Civil Rights Law of 1968 passed by a vote of 250 to 171. It was pushed through a reluctant Congress with the help of Oklahoma's Carl Albert, who attended the White House meeting with civil rights leaders a few days earlier, and Louisiana's Hale Boggs, who had opposed the Civil Rights Act of 1964, but then supported the Voting Rights Act the following year.* Gerald Ford, Republican, opposed the bill and attempted to hold it up, pushing for it at least to be postponed until Congress returned from an Easter break scheduled to start that evening. By a 229 to 195 margin, his delay measures were thwarted. Every member of the Georgia congressional delegation, including Fletcher Thompson, the representative who had voted for a House version of the act the previous summer, opposed the bill. "Eighty-two percent of the people in my district are opposed to this legislation," Thompson told the *Atlanta Constitution*, explaining his about-face.

The 1968 bill, called the Open Housing Law, would mean that by year end all owners or landlords of multiunit buildings would be forbidden to discriminate against potential buyers or renters on the basis of ethnicity, age, or religion. An exception allowed owner-occupants of small buildings with four or fewer units to discriminate.† By 1970, the law would be extended to cover all single-family homes sold or rented through agents, which government estimates put at 80 percent of all property.

Additional measures tacked onto the bill outlined federal penalties for intimidating civil rights workers or preventing black Americans from accessing schools, registering to vote, serving on juries, or using public facilities. The bill also included some protections for Native Americans.

---

*Today, most Americans know of him as the father of television journalist and National Public Radio commentator Cokie Roberts. In 1972, a plane in which Boggs was traveling disappeared over Alaska, leaving no trace of him or the aircraft. His wife, Lindy, won his seat in Congress and served for more than two decades. In 2001, she was appointed ambassador to the Vatican.

†This provision has long been dubbed the Mrs. Murphy Clause, in honor of a hypothetical prejudiced operator of a rooming house. Mrs. Murphy should not, lawmakers argue, be obligated to share a duplex with someone with whom she would not associate socially.

To appease conservatives, the law contained antiriot measures, such as making it illegal to manufacture a firebomb to be used in a riot, a direct response to the widespread use of Molotov cocktails by rioters in the previous summer's unrest in Detroit and Los Angeles, as well as in the still-smoldering upheaval following King's death.

In the Senate, efforts to squash a House bill authorizing funding for Head Start and jobs programs were defeated. "Nothing could be a greater memorial to Martin Luther King than rejection of the bill excluding money for summer jobs and Head Start," said Senator Jacob Javits.

Later that day, President Johnson held a news conference announcing the passage of the Civil Rights Law of 1968. "We have passed many civil rights pieces of legislation, but none more important than this," he said. "It has been a long, tortuous, and difficult road. There have been days of sunshine and sorrow."

West Hunter Street Baptist Church, early afternoon

Ralph Abernathy called yet another press conference. The new president of the SCLC looked haggard and worn, his eyes sunken and surrounded by dark circles, his cheeks sagging. He consulted his notes frequently. "I come this afternoon with Dr. Martin Luther King being absent from my side," he said. "Most of the time, I have come before you at *his* side." He thanked the SCLC board for elevating him to its presidency but quickly stressed that he wanted to express "deep regret for having to assume this position." He told reporters that every member of the SCLC's executive staff had agreed to remain in his or her present position through the Poor People's Campaign.

Abernathy also announced that the board's members had voted to name Coretta Scott King and Harry Belafonte to the SCLC board of directors. Mrs. King would, Abernathy noted, return to Memphis as the strike there was resolved and would participate in the Poor People's Campaign events in Washington, D.C.

Discussing the events of the funeral, he said, "We are particularly thankful to Mayor Ivan Allen Jr. and the city of Atlanta for their tireless help in arrangements," and said he thought the whole city "moved forward with nonviolent military precision." He claimed that a half million people participated in one way or another—"thousands upon thousands of poor people, black and white," as well as dignitaries. "I call now for the black people, and all of the poverty-stricken, and Christians of goodwill in this nation to channel our energies and constructive efforts to fight poverty and injustice."

In response to a question from a reporter, he said the Poor People's Campaign would be delayed but it would happen, that SCLC staff were planning a session to work out the details.

Asked about the passage of the Open Housing bill, he said, "I have not heard from the president at all." He added, "This is a great stride toward freedom for white America, but it is barely a step in the right direction for black America." He turned to Andrew Young for commentary.

Young, immaculate in a dark suit and crisp shirt, said, "Until the question of jobs for the jobless and a guaranteed income for those people who are unable to work is dealt with by Congress, there won't be any serious dealing with the question of poverty." The campaign against poverty would, Young said, be taken "to the seat of government" by the SCLC in the coming months.

Bone-weary and emotionally drained, the SCLC board members and senior staff had met the night before to officially appoint King's successor. Since Abernathy's anointment as heir had publicly been stated several times over the past few days, and King's loyal friend had assumed the main role in the day's ceremonies, there was little debate. Each plausible contender for the position had drawbacks. SCLC board chairman Joseph Lowery was not ready to move into the role. Andrew Young, the brilliant spokesperson and political strategist, could have handled the job ably, but did not particularly want it. He would move into national politics with a history-making bid for the U.S. Congress in just a few years. Jesse Jackson, fiery and charismatic, had the personality to pull off the role and the naked ambition to be a national leader, but lacked the support of the SCLC elders and faithful and the trust of the white media and power structure.*

---

*Jackson's intelligence, charisma, and natural political ability did result in two presidential bids in the 1980s, garnering breakthrough primary bids and victories in several

Joseph Lowery recalled the decision's being clear and easy. "There was never any debate or question. Martin had already placed Ralph in the position to be his successor. Ralph inherited a tough task." Bernard LaFayette agreed. He listened to the debate but knew it was a useless exercise. Abernathy would move up; after all, everyone in SCLC referred to King and Abernathy as the "movement twins."

Santa Monica Civic Auditorium, 8 p.m. EST

Bob Hope's opening monologue left the celebrities in the audience for the fortieth annual Academy Awards ceremony aghast.

"About the delay of two days, it didn't affect me," he said of the unprecedented decision to delay the broadcast in honor of the King funeral. "But it's been tough on the nominees," Hope continued. "How would you like to spend two days in a crouch?" But for a few awkward giggles, the room was mostly hushed. "We also voted a special Oscar to the ABC programming department. They just committed hara-kiri."

Gregory Peck, the Academy president, eased the tension with a statement paying homage to King. "The lasting memorial that we of the motion picture community can build to Dr. King is to continue making films which celebrate the dignity of man, whatever his race or creed." Peck, Oscar winner for his role as *To Kill a Mockingbird*'s Atticus Finch, the Southern lawyer who defends a black man accused of rape, noted that two of the evening's Best Picture nominees (*In the Heat of the Night* and *Guess Who's Coming to Dinner*) "dealt with the subject of the understanding between the races."

A star of those two films, Sidney Poitier, earned huge applause from the celebrity audience when he came onstage. Poitier, not nominated as an actor for either film, presented the award for best actress to his *Dinner* costar Katharine Hepburn. Later on, his *Heat* costar and Best Actor winner, Rod Steiger, thanked him.

---

states. In the thought-provoking book *April 4, 1968*, Michael Eric Dyson dubs Jackson King's "heir apparent" and writes, "In the forty years since King's death, it is Jackson who has best captured his mentor's spirit, extended his work, and interpreted his vision as the most prominent and powerful black leader in the post-King era." (This was published in early 2008 before Barack Obama's presidential victory.)

"We shall overcome," Steiger said at the end of his acceptance speech.

The Kohn home in Doraville, evening

Kathy and Norm spent most of the day resting, completely drained from their time at the church. They watched some coverage of the funeral on television; it was strange to see it from the perspective of aerial shots of the large crowds walking through the streets, of the services at Ebenezer and at Morehouse. They had been immersed in the funeral from the perspective of the fellowship hall at Central Presbyterian, but still aware of the crowds and the risk and the convergence of people from all over the country.

They realized this was the biggest thing they had ever been part of, and it would probably be the biggest event of their lives.

The King home on Sunset Avenue, night

Everyone was gone, the house was calmer, and babysitter Patricia Latimore came over to help. The children were wiped out and Mrs. King was completely drained. Cards and letters still covered every counter and table. Patricia went to work straightening the kitchen. The house was quiet; everyone was asleep.

January 15, 1969

Coretta Scott King, Harry Belafonte, and members of the King family attend a memorial service held at Ebenezer Baptist Church on January 15, 1969, what would have been King's fortieth birthday. *AP Photo.*

Atlanta University Center, early morning

WEARING A BLACK-VEILED hat, Mrs. King held a press conference at the Interdenominational Theological Center to announce plans for memorials to her husband. "Today my husband would have been forty years old," read Mrs. King from her statement. "Under ordinary circumstances this might be considered an occasion for nothing more than sentimentality and tears. But Martin Luther King Jr. was no ordinary man, and these are not ordinary experiences."

The memorials would be clustered around two physical locations. On Auburn Avenue, the Victorian home where King was born and raised would be restored and—along with a park and a planned Freedom Hall—

would become a place for people to visit and pay their respects while learning about King's life and work. King's crypt would be moved from South-View Cemetery to the park. The other cluster of memorials would be located near Atlanta University Center and include the Institute for Nonviolent Social Change, a center for Afro-American studies, a museum of Afro-American life and culture, and a library housing documents relating to King and the civil rights movement. The center, Mrs. King stated, would "emerge out of the black experience" but "be for all people."

During the press conference that followed the announcement, Mrs. King had to field questions about her book deal. Were the rumors true, reporters wanted to know, that she'd nabbed half a million dollars and had twelve assistants helping her with the book? The advance, she said, was a "private arrangement" between her and Holt, Rinehart and Winston, the publishing firm, which had assigned *one* editor to the project.* The book would be released that summer.

Over the eight months following King's death, Harry Belafonte and Stanley Levison advised Mrs. King as she navigated the rush of publishing deals and interview requests. According to informants reporting to J. Edgar Hoover, Belafonte and Levison helped the widow land her memoir deal. After King's death, Hoover assigned operatives in Atlanta and elsewhere to trail Coretta King, using the same rationale he had invoked for spying on her husband—friendship with Levison, a white lawyer who reportedly had links to the Communist Party. In a memo dated April 23, 1968, just two weeks after the funeral, Hoover said an informant "advised recently that Stanley Levison, long-time secret Communist Party member, has been in contact with Coretta King . . . twice and counseled her relative to public appearances and finances." In light of this news Hoover wrote, "The Atlanta Office should immediately open a case on Mrs. King and conduct a discreet investigation to follow her activities through established informants and sources. You should furnish the Bureau with the results of a file review concerning Mrs. King's background and activities in a form suitable for dissemination."

It did not take covert action to see that after King's death tension fermented between Mrs. King and her husband's successor and friend, Ralph

---

*According to an FBI informant, the deal was for at least $750,000.

Abernathy, over money, the future of SCLC, and King's legacy. Abernathy and some SCLC leaders wanted the widow to help them raise funds for SCLC projects; she wanted to continue King's work in the broader area of nonviolence and to focus on the memorials. The widow started work on the library and King Center immediately; by late April 1968, she was working with Harding and others on plans for the library, institutes, and memorial center, and those plans included fund-raising.

While Mrs. King worked on the memorial project, King's followers pushed through with the Poor People's Campaign, which took place in the late spring and early summer of 1968. Chaos plagued the Washington, D.C., encampment, which literally sunk in mire as early-summer rains turned "Resurrection City" into a boggy mess. The emotional impact of King's death and funeral services turned out to be both a blessing and a curse for the campaign. "Millions of dollars came into SCLC after King died; it would have been hard to fund the Poor People's Campaign without all those donations," said SCLC staffer Tom Houck. But the poignantly dramatic mule wagon used in the funeral turned out to have publicized the Poor People's Campaign too well; rather than having to comb the rural South looking for people to bring to Washington, SCLC was deluged with volunteers.*

Unlike the most successful SCLC-led campaigns, which had definite goals—ending segregation of public facilities in Birmingham, for example—the Poor People's Campaign was nebulous in its focus and broad in its reach. Problems at the tent city included embarrassing racial polarization within the ranks of the poor people, defying the harmonious image SCLC intended to project. By June 1, the *New York Times* reported on "friction" within the SCLC, with Abernathy "reacting to criticism of his leadership with uncertainty and snappishness." Critics also included

---

*Although the publicity helped build volunteer forces for the campaign, finding enough mule teams proved to be as challenging as it had been to find the perfect wagon for the services in Atlanta. Winifred Green, who had manned phone banks at West Hunter Baptist before the funeral, was sent to buy mules by Albert Turner, who had marched at the head of the mule wagon in King's funeral procession. Turner said, "You know they won't sell mules to black people." He told Green to "stand there and look a long time, and then walk up to the man and say, 'Open his mouth'—and then look for a long time and ask, 'Is he broke to the wagon?' If the answer is yes, buy it." Green bought about a half dozen mules on behalf of SCLC.

officials in the White House, which shared many of the antipoverty goals of the campaign, but worried about what one official called its "unpromising circumstances."

The June 5 shooting of Robert Kennedy and his death on June 6 overshadowed the campaign, and underscored King's absence.* The dramatic arrest of King's accused assassin, James Earl Ray, in London on June 8—the same day as Robert Kennedy's funeral—only intensified media attention on King's death and away from the efforts of his successors.

Although they pledged to stick together, the members of the SCLC inner circle drifted apart, and dissension continued after the end of the Poor People's Campaign. In January 1969, Abernathy and SCLC struggled to raise funds. In a letter dated January 2, 1969, Abernathy said, "I cannot turn to white America, I must turn to you.† If SCLC lives, so lives Martin Luther King Jr. If SCLC dies, so will Martin Luther King Jr. have died in vain."

Senate Chambers, Georgia State Capitol, early morning

State senator Leroy Johnson's bill proposing that January 15, King's birthday, be celebrated as a state holiday met with interested murmurs. Other proposals had already been made at the state and national level. A "man on the street" poll published in the *Atlanta Journal* the day before was headlined "Most Agree on Honor for King." Janet Butler, one of those surveyed, called it "a good idea" and told reporters, "He was a fine man and did a lot for the black cause."

But what really surprised the gathering of Georgia lawmakers were the guests that Johnson brought to the capitol, including Daddy King; Rosa Parks; the Reverend Walter Fauntroy; George Olumagin, representative from Nigeria; Andre Kumuamba, the first secretary of the Republic of Congo. Leroy Johnson, the first black elected to the Georgia General Assembly since Reconstruction, was joined by his fellow representative

---

*Kennedy had been scheduled to speak to the residents of Resurrection City at a major rally on June 19.

†Interestingly, I found that letter in the correspondence files of the (very white) Rabbi Rothschild.

Horace Ward, an attorney and former classmate of King's.* "His life and work will stand as testimony of his endeavors to make America a better place for all Americans to live," Ward told the assembled legislators, going on to quote from King's "Dream" speech, "I have a dream that one day on the red hills of Georgia the sons of former slaves and the sons of slaveowners will be able sit down together at the table of brotherhood."

Reporting on descendants of slaves and slaveowners meeting in the capitol, *Atlanta Constitution* political editor Remer Tyson described encountering a good-old-boy state senator from a rural south Georgia district after the event. Standing in the hallway of the capitol, the senator told Tyson, "I wouldn't want to see this in the paper, but it don't hurt me to come up here and learn something." Tyson ran the quote in the paper the next day.

Across the street from the capitol, a bronze plaque had been mounted in front of Central Presbyterian Church. Unveiled August 28, 1968 (the fifth anniversary of King's "Dream" speech), the plaque listed King's birth and death dates and stated, "In reaffirmation of those principles of love, justice, and reconciliation for which he stood."

At the unveiling ceremony, attended by Kings' parents and brother, Central Presbyterian pastor Randy Taylor said, "Let it be sufficient to say that by the grace of God in the critical year of 1968, men and women in a predominantly white church in the heart of this Southern city sensed and saw that the dream shall not have died in vain."

Daddy King prayed, "We thank thee God for those who are determined to see that his cause shall not die but that the cause shall continue to live and that dream come true."

Norm Kohn, who was on the planning committee for the memorial, was particularly pleased with its placement. The plaque at Central directly faces a statue of Tom Watson, the segregationist Georgia politician who influenced some of the strongest Jim Crow laws in the state and was instru-

---

*In 1950, Ward was denied admission to the University of Georgia Law School on the basis of his race. He earned a law degree from Northwestern and was part of the legal team that in 1961 successfully desegregated UGA, gaining admission for Hamilton Holmes and Charlayne Hunter (today known to many Americans as Charlayne Hunter-Gault, the noted television journalist). Ward later became the first African-American judge on a federal court in Georgia.

mental in disenfranchising black voters in the early 1900s. The statue of Watson shows the orator shaking his face in the air, seemingly right at the church. The plaque honoring King seems to echo with a quiet response.

The White House, early morning

Calls came in all morning congratulating LBJ on the speech that the president had delivered the night before—a final address to Congress that served as a State of the Union and formal farewell.

"To achieve the goals of the Housing Act of 1968 that you've just passed, we should build this year more than five hundred thousand homes for needy families in the coming fiscal year." He talked about Model Cities, the passage of civil rights laws; "the doors of public service are open at last to all Americans, regardless of their color."

He said, "The antipoverty program has had many achievements," quickly conceding, "it also has had some failures. But we must not cripple it after only three years of trying to solve the human problems that have been with us and have been building up among us for generations.

"I regret more than any of you know that it has not been possible to restore peace to South Vietnam," he said, adding a note of tribute to the troops.

"I hope it may be said a hundred years from now that by working together we helped to make our country more just—more just for all of its people as well as to insure the blessings of liberty for all of our posterity. That's what I hope. But I believe that at least it will be said that we tried."

A reporter observed that the president, while bidding farewell to Congress after three decades of serving in the House, Senate, and White House, spoke with a voice infused with "a richness and timbre it has often lacked." He "appeared to have trouble controlling his emotions . . . he blinked his eyes and pursed his lips." As LBJ left the chamber, lawmakers sang "Auld Lang Syne."

In five days, Richard Nixon would be sworn in as the new president. Johnson's efforts to step out of presidential politics had been an effort to gain a year to work on the country's problems and adjust his legacy before leaving office. The death of King—and the violence that followed—set back the gains in civil rights laws and urban economic development. The subsequent assassination of Kennedy changed the outcome of the election.

Earlier in the week, Nixon had met with a group of civil rights leaders. After the meeting, he was criticized by Matthew Wright of the Black Power Conference as well as Ralph Abernathy. Wright said that Nixon's selection of Daniel Patrick Moynihan, the author of studies critical of urban social structures, as the assistant for urban affairs, demonstrated a "white mind-set" and "has added to the possibility of disorder in the streets." Abernathy told the Associated Press, "Nixon put the black people and the nation a step backward by failing to name a Negro to his cabinet."

Ebenezer Baptist Church, 10 a.m.

More than a thousand people crowded into the small sanctuary, and another thirty-five hundred waited on the cold streets outside, to hear a memorial service that included a lengthy musical program and appearances by notables ranging from Rosa Parks to John Conyers, the congressman from Michigan who founded the Congressional Black Caucus. Randy Taylor, pastor of Central Presbyterian Church, and Father J. J. Mulroy of Sacred Heart Roman Catholic Church, were among local attendees.

Ralph Abernathy delivered a sermon that, like the one he gave on the Palm Sunday before King's funeral, was constructed as a "letter to Martin." Abernathy concluded the sermon by talking about James Earl Ray, the man charged with King's assassination: "We call on good people everywhere to spare the life of the man who killed you. It was the system that took you from us, Martin, and it would be wrong to put one man to death because of it. . . . In remaining true to the principles of non-violence, I call upon the forces of goodwill throughout the land to exert their total influence in seeing to it that the life of James Earl Ray—or whoever pulled the trigger that felled our sainted and beloved leader—is spared."

Mrs. King nodded at Abernathy's words, and many in the church clapped.

After the service, Mrs. King and Abernathy led another march through Atlanta, this one described by local papers as more of a "parade" celebrating King's life than a mourning of his death. The two-thousand-person procession wound two and a half miles to the eight-acre construction site for Martin Luther King Village, a planned low-income-housing development not far from the Atlanta Stadium.

Mrs. King was joined at the groundbreaking by Mayor Ivan Allen and Lieutenant Governor George Smith. Smith, absent during King's funeral, said he was "honored to be here" to recognize King, who "dedicated his life to bettering the living conditions of people."

During the groundbreaking ceremony, Abernathy led the crowd in a liturgy:

Leader: O Lord, we dedicate this hallowed ground in fulfillment of a dream about a "City of Hope."

People: Build me more stately mansions, O my Lord.

Leader: May this "City of Hope" be the beginning of the ending of poor housing in the richest and most affluent nation in the history of mankind.

People: For this earth is the Lord's and the fullness thereof and they that dwell therein.

Leader: As I break this hallowed ground, may the spiritual unity of the Southern Christian Leadership Conference and the Ebenezer Baptist Church in constructing the Martin Luther King, Jr. Village be a reality to humanity that "spires will always outlast spears and altars are more lasting than armaments."

Unison: *Bless this house, O Lord, we pray*
Keep it safe by night and day
Bless the windows firm and stout
Keeping want and trouble out
Bless the roof and chimneys tall
Let thy peace lie over all
Bless the folk who dwell therein
Keep them pure and free from sin
Bless them all that one day we may dwell,
O Lord, with thee. Amen.

On the day of the memorial events, Economic Opportunity Atlanta announced its "Start Atlanta Now!" tours, which promised to take concerned citizens on sightseeing trips through low-income sections of town to help them understand the need to assist Atlanta's poorest residents. On the day the tours were launched, three hundred people signed up for the experience.

Nine days earlier, Ivan Allen announced he would not be running for reelection in the mayor's race that fall. On January 6, a television crew followed the mayor through a busy day of speaking. Panning around his office, the camera caught the gleaming wooden desk, the rows of ceremonial groundbreaking shovels, the neat piles of paperwork. Allen walked out below the MAYOR'S OFFICE sign and down to a waiting car. In his immaculate camel-hair coat and neat tie, he looked at the camera face on. "Being mayor of a city is a grave responsibility," he said.

Allen strode down Peachtree Street, as lean and confident as ever, into the Dinkler Plaza hotel. He made his way to the blue-silk-draped dais at the front of the room and stood behind the podium carved with the Rotary Club symbol.

"I am speaking now as a private Atlanta citizen with complete candor on what I consider to be the most grievous problems that the American city is confronted with today," said the mayor. "There are matters I wish to speak of to the Atlanta Rotary Club and to the people of Atlanta on what I consider to be the most difficult era in which we go into and the most difficult problem that we have—and that is the problem of race as it confronts almost every American city today."

The mayor looked out over the room. Almost every face was white and male. Most of these men belonged to the same clubs he did, cheered on their children at the same school functions, and played on the same golf courses. They lived in the hilly seclusion of Buckhead or left the city proper for outlying suburbs after school integration. They listened with well-bred attention as the mayor's voice rose and his face grew stern.

"I'm anxious to have the privilege to speak to the white community of Atlanta with the complete freedom that goes where no one says that what you are saying is being said because you are seeking the Negro vote. I want to talk about a problem every right-thinking American citizen today acknowledges. The right-thinking person knows the biggest problem is the twenty million Negro citizens who have been denied—and all of us are part of the guilt of denying them—equal rights and equal opportunities in this great democracy."

Other cities, he said, worried about racial tension and inequality. Boston, for example, had a 10 percent black population and New York a 20 percent ratio. Atlanta, he noted, "is a city with a forty-six percent Negro population and growing." Many of the city's black residents, he said, were as ingrained into the community as the white Rotarians, being "an established population that has been here a long time. It's the Alexanders, the William Holmes Borders, the Martin Luther King Seniors, the Bill Calloways, Dr. McLendon . . . a conservative, constructive group that acquired a substance in this city and were part of this community." But too many of Atlanta's black residents did not have opportunities. "Atlanta has used all the major programs available, but the bottom level has got to be raised if you are going to build a foundation." The mayor said emphatically, "The Negro citizen has got to be raised to a decent standard of economics and social position."

Allen's speech was greeted with loud applause, and after the meeting adjourned, the Rotarians lined up to shake his hand and thank him for his decades of service. The mayor was leaving office with an impressive legacy: a rapidly rising skyline; expanded air service; new corporate citizens; a stadium (and pro sports team to play in it); new highways, parks, and schools; a civic center; and arts complex. The man who, as head of the Chamber of Commerce, launched the Forward Atlanta campaign promoting the city as mayor ended up being its chief promoter, largely through influencing peaceful integration efforts—in contrast to neighborhoods like Birmingham. He put action behind the city's "too busy to hate" slogan and along the way personally evolved from a genteel segretationist to a sincere supporter of civil rights.

Of all the eventful episodes in his time in city hall, the King funeral symbolized this transformation more than any other. Allen—and most Atlantans—behaved beautifully in the crisis of hosting the funeral. Atlanta's inherent energetic spirit and innate sense of crisis aversion once again helped its black and white communities come together in a time of emergency. While more than a hundred other cities dealt with chaos and destruction, Atlanta appeared an oasis of peace.

As Atlanta's African-Americans mourned the assassination of a home-grown leader, they witnessed national attention focused on their community. Their churches, schools, colleges, politicians, and political activists were under a stronger spotlight than ever before during the marathon media coverage of the funeral. The central role that black leaders, both old activists and young students, played in the city's successful hosting of the funeral underscored the growing political power African-Americans wielded in Atlanta and the important place that Atlanta held in national racial politics. A few months after King's death, Maynard Jackson, the young lawyer whose daughter was born the night before the funeral, would impulsively announce a run for U.S. Senate. Although he lost the race, he won a third of the statewide vote and all of Atlanta. In 1969, vice mayor Sam Massell was elected to replace Allen, and Jackson in turn replaced Massell. In 1973, Jackson would defeat Massell and become Atlanta's first black mayor, the first step in a more than three-decade dominance of city hall by African-American officials.

For white Atlanta, the funeral was another proof that racial harmony resulted in good press for the city. But would the five days of harmony result in lasting transformation? Many pitched in to help, but was this, like the PR push for integrating schools, more about saving face than deeply changing? The Rotary Club members shook Allen's hand, clapped him on the back, and praised him, but statistically, it was likely that many of the men in that room would ignore the mayor's challenge to create opportunities for their black fellow Atlantans. Just a month after the King funeral, the Civil Aggression Study Team at Emory University's Center for Research in Social Change surveyed Atlantans about their reaction to the assassination and the way the funeral was handled. The researchers found that 90 percent of the city's black residents approved of how Ivan Allen had acted, while only 59 percent of whites did. More tellingly, 41 percent of whites said they agreed with Lester Maddox's actions (a view held by just 5 percent of blacks).*

---

*Contemporary surveys conducted in other parts of the country provide a contrast to Atlanta's experience. Most black Atlantans felt that King's death would result in social change, an opinion shared by fewer whites. Surveys of African-American political opinion conducted by the *Miami Herald* a few weeks before the assassination and a few weeks after revealed "more militancy." A survey in Columbus, Ohio, conducted in the same time frame showed an uptick in "political disengagement" after King's death. Positive

Furthermore, the researchers found that 84 percent of white Atlantans said King's death would have no impact on their personal attitudes about racial problems. "These proportions demonstrate once again that white Atlantans simply did not identify with Dr. King; his death to them was simply an event which would not affect the individual lives of white people," the researchers concluded.

There would, of course, be cases of individual change, starting with the more than half of white Atlanta that did approve of Allen's actions during the funeral. Some transformation would be quietly private, like Norm and Kathy Kohn, who emerged after three days of intense service during the funeral as committed advocates of social and racial justice. Some changes would be more dramatic, like the press conference held a few weeks after King's death by Calvin Craig, the KKK Grand Dragon. Craig announced that he was renouncing his Klan membership, citing as his influence his relationship with Xernona Clayton. The two of them would give speeches and seminars together, and Clayton became known as the Dragon Slayer.

South-View Cemetery, 4 p.m.

The gathering in honor of Martin Luther King Jr. was far smaller than it had been eight months earlier. About three hundred people carried on from the groundbreaking ceremony to South-View Cemetery, shivering under a wintry sky.

They watched as Martin Luther King III slowly walked toward his father's crypt and placed a wreath at its base. Above, the epitaph that had been stenciled on the Georgia marble eight months earlier was engraved into the stone.

FREE AT LAST!

---

views about police, for example, decreased from 89 percent to 57 percent among African-Americans who were surveyed, while positive views about whites decreased from 70 percent to 52 percent. Among the Ohio respondents, the assassination "had little impact on whites but produced some strong alterations in Negroes affective ties to the political system."

ACKNOWLEDGMENTS

THIS BOOK'S GENESIS was an oral history I produced as part of a special issue of *Atlanta* magazine. Editing that issue, which examined Martin Luther King's legacy in his hometown, was the most rewarding creative experience I had during my seven years as editor in chief of the magazine, and I am lucky to have worked with a wonderful team on that effort, in particular Eric Capossela, Michele Cohen Marill, Hector Sanchez, Chandra Thomas, Ciara Walker, and Paige Williams. I am indebted to Deborah Paul, Emmis Publishing editorial director, for championing that particular issue and for being a friend and mentor for more than a decade. The *Atlanta* magazine and Emmis family have been—and continue to be—wonderfully supportive, and I am a richer person for knowing them, especially Susan Bogle, Steve Fennessy, Kit Rachlis, Betsy Riley, Evan Smith, Deborah Way, and David Zivan. Sean McGinnis, Gary Thoe, and Greg Loewen supported my transition from print to digital and gave me the flexibility I needed to work on books. I owe everything to Lee Walburn, who took a chance and hired me back in 1998.

The vision for expanding that article into this book came from my amazing agent, Robert Guinsler of Sterling Lord Literistic. Thank you, Robert, for your advice, support, and genuine good cheer. Thank you, Doug Crandell, for introducing me to Robert.

I could not have asked for a more ideal editor than the brilliant Alexis Gargagliano, whose insight, patience, and deft suggestions helped me write a far better book than I could have ever done on my own. Kelsey Smith at Scribner offered invaluable assistance as the book made its way from rough manuscript to finished product.

The beginning of the book project overlapped with the end of my graduate program at Georgia State University, and a number of professors made me a better writer, researcher, and critical thinker. My thesis adviser, Michael Bruner, helped me place this narrow sliver of history in a broader context. David Cheshier and James Darsey taught me to think about rhetoric more precisely. Leonard Teel helped me cultivate a passion for archival research. Cliff Kuhn's class on oral history transformed the way I approach interviewing.

During the research for this project, I was assisted by many talented archivists and librarians. I am especially grateful to Cynthia Patterson-Lewis at the King Center; Wesley Chenault of the Auburn Avenue Research Library; Andrea Jackson of the Robert W. Woodruff Library at Atlanta University Center; Kathleen Shoemaker and Randy Gue at Emory University's Manuscript and Rare Book Library; and Sue Verhoef at the Kenan Research Center at the Atlanta History Center. Claudia Anderson of the Lyndon Baines Johnson Presidential Library helped with long-distance requests.

Tom Johnson, a professional mentor and personal inspiration, shared his insights as a member of the Johnson administration. June Dobbs Butts, a woman who inspires me more than she can know, generously shared her memories of growing up in Atlanta as a friend of M.L.'s.

Friends and family provided much-needed encouragement at key points along the way. Big thanks to J. C. Burns, Robert Burns, Kim Taylor Cloud, Linda Guthrie, Melissa Poynor, Susan Poynor, Sarah Satola, Paula Schwed, and Sammy Smith.

Finally, if I were a better writer, I would be able to adequately articulate how much I appreciate my wonderful husband, James Burns, and incredible daughter, Brigid Rose. I am not eloquent enough to express how much your faith, patience, and support mean to me, so I must resort to my characteristic terse prose: I love you.

SOURCES

Firsthand Accounts

Interviews. I interviewed in person and by phone dozens of people who participated in the events. Some twenty-five of these interviews appeared in my oral history article, "Funeral," that was originally published in the April 2008 issue of *Atlanta* magazine.

Oral histories. Interview transcripts at the Lyndon Johnson Presidential Library offered insight into the events at the White House, background on the relationship between King and the administration, the riots of 1965–67, the rioting that following King's death, the early days of the investigation into the King assassination, and the Poor People's Campaign. Those cited or referenced directly are listed in the selected bibliography. I also reviewed transcripts of oral-history interviews gathered as part of the *Eyes on the Prize* documentary, the companion transcripts published online by Washington University in St. Louis as part of the Henry Hampton Papers collection, and edited transcripts in the Hampton coedited book *Voices of Freedom.* The Voices Across the Color Line collection at the Atlanta History Center offered insight into the Atlanta student movement and racial dynamics in the city in the 1940s through 1970s.

Memoirs. Personal accounts of the funeral events as well as background on other crucial periods (such as King's 1960 arrest in Georgia and the Memphis sanitation workers' strike in 1968) added additional perspective. Memoirs referenced include those by Ralph David Abernathy, Ivan Allen, Xernona Clayton, Christine King Farris, Coretta Scott King, Dexter King, John Lewis, Benjamin Mays, and Andrew Young.

Funeral Planning and Logistics

The subject and correspondence files at the King Center Archives of the Martin Luther King Jr. Center in Atlanta, and the King Papers Collection at the Robert W. Woodruff Memorial Library at the Atlanta University Center, contain documents such as funeral programs and memos outlining plans. In addition, these files hold letters, cards, and telegrams that are representative of the thousands sent to the King family and SCLC in response to the assassination and funeral.

Public Safety in Atlanta

Details on public safety efforts in Atlanta during the funeral period come from the King funeral subject file in the Herbert Jenkins Papers collection at the Atlanta History Center, which includes arrest reports, police schedules, memos, agenda, and other primary sources. I also referenced Jenkins's memoir, *Keeping the Peace*, and his white paper, "Forty Years on the Force." In addition, I reviewed accounts from the three daily Atlanta newspapers and minutes from the city's Board of Aldermen meetings.

Visual Details

I reviewed thousands of still photographs of the aftermath of the assassination, the riots, the April 8 march in Memphis, and events before, after, and during the April 9 funeral in Atlanta. In addition to news images from the Associated Press, Getty, and Corbis archives, the following collections were particularly valuable. From Memphis: *Life* magazine images from April 4, 1968, by Henry Groskinsky, and the King assassination collection from the *Memphis Commercial Appeal*. Of behind-the-scenes planning in Atlanta and the April 8 Memphis march: Bob Fitch's personal collection and the Hosea Williams Photographic Collection at Auburn Avenue Research Library. Of the April 9 funeral in Atlanta and related events: the Jim Peppler photograph collection at the Alabama State Archives, and the Floyd Jillson and Bill Wilson photographic collections at the Kenan Research Center of the Atlanta History Center. I also reviewed hundreds of published images in contemporary newspapers and magazines in addition to smaller archival sources, such as the campus-life images from Emory University, that showed memorial services on campus.

The WSB Newsfilm collection, much of it raw footage, at the University of Georgia Libraries, provided rich background on the funeral and was the source for much of the visual description of the April 9 events. Snatches of dialogue that are not attributed to specific print or interview sources in the notes are from this WSB film. I also referred to archival footage from CBS, ABC, the BBC, and from the *Eyes on the Prize* series.

Events at the White House

All times and locations for events in the White House come from the White House Daily Diary records for April 4–10, 1968, obtained from the Lyndon Baines Johnson Presidential Library and Museum. Details of meetings, memos, and phone messages from the period are from the subject file on the King funeral from the LBJ library and selected correspondence files and phone-conversation recordings. I also referred to the extensive oral history collection at the library, in particular interviews with Cartha "Deke" DeLoach, Ramsey Clark, Harry McPherson, and Clark Clifford.

King Assassination and Investigation

I accessed details on the King assassination through the "Report of the Select Committee on Assassinations of the U.S. House of Representatives: Findings in the Assassination of Dr. Martin Luther King, Jr." This is published online and can be can accessed through the National Archives or the FBI's Freedom of Information Act (FOIA) online reading room. Another useful source was the digital archive of evidence, photographs, and other materials maintained by Shelby County, Tennessee. For background, I also reviewed the FBI files available for Coretta Scott King, Stokely Carmichael, and Stanley Levison.

General Background and Context

For context and background on King and the SCLC, I consulted the excellent biographical histories by David Garrow and Taylor Branch. King's autobiography, edited by Carson Clayborne, was a useful resource, while *King: A Critical Biography*, by David L. Lewis, provided a different perspective.

For background on the interracial and intraracial dynamics of Atlanta in the 1960s, I referred to Harold Martin's *Atlanta and Environs*, vol. 3; Gary Pomerantz's *Where Peachtree Meets Sweet Auburn*; Kevin Kruse's *White Flight*; Winston Grady-Willis's *Challenging U.S. Apartheid*; and the Ralph McGill and Jacob Rothschild papers at Emory University's Manuscript and Rare Book Library (MARBL). Context on historical Jim Crow regulations in Atlanta and the impact of the 1906 Atlanta race riot on the older generation of black activists and white segregationists came from my own research for the book *Rage in the Gate City*, as well as Allison Dorsey's terrific history of Atlanta's black community, *To Build Our Lives Together*.

For an overview of the broader national and international context of 1968, I referred to *1968* from Time Books and Robert Dallek's biographies *Flawed Giant* and *Lyndon Johnson: Portrait of a President*.

Other Archival Sources

The end notes contain details on a range of archival sources that were cited, of which the following are particularly noteworthy. The *Newsweek* Atlanta Bureau Collection at Emory University's MARBL is a trove of material on Atlanta from the 1950s through 1980s, with subject files that contain clippings, press releases, bureau telexes, reporters' notes, and a host of other documents assembled by the bureau's reporters. Likewise, the Southern Regional Council files at the Auburn Avenue Research Library contain a wealth of materials from disparate sources. The files of Vincent Harding, also at Emory's MARBL, contain documents relating to the founding of the King Center in Atlanta, offering insight into the dynamics between the family and the SCLC, in particular during the year following the funeral.

Media Coverage and Analysis

Public relations efforts by the SCLC, King family, and Atlanta leaders and the resulting media coverage of the funeral was the focus of my master's thesis ("Mourning and Message," Georgia State University, 2008). I drew on my analysis of primary and secondary sources for that research in this book. In addition, the work of two academics, Michael Eric Dyson and

Richard Lentz, was particularly helpful for framing the context of King's media image pre- and postassassination. Scott Hoffman's "Holy Martin" essay also provides a thought-provoking look at "canonization" of the slain leader through a media lens.

NOTES

Abbreviations for Frequently Cited Sources

AARL—Auburn Avenue Research Library

AC—*Atlanta Constitution*

ADW—*Atlanta Daily World*

AHC—Atlanta History Center's Kenan Archives

AJ—*Atlanta Journal*

AJC—*Atlanta Journal-Constitution*

AM—*Atlanta* magazine

CSM—*Christian Science Monitor*

CT—*Chicago Tribune*

KC—King Center Archives at the Martin Luther King Jr. Center

KCM—The King Collection at Morehouse, Robert W. Woodruff Library

LAT—*Los Angeles Times*

LBJ—Lyndon Baines Johnson Presidential Library

MARBL—Manuscript and Rare Book Library at Emory University

NYT—*New York Times*

WAA—*Washington Afro-American*

WHDD—White House Daily Diary, Lyndon Baines Johnson Presidential
　　　Library archives

WP—*Washington Post*

WSB—The WSB Television Newsfilm Collection, University of Georgia
　　　Libraries Media Archives and Peabody Awards Collection

Prologue

1 *He's showing his strength*, and rest of Massell scene: Sam Massell interview, January 2008.
2 Lonnie King arrived: Lonnie King interview, May 2009.For the rest of the details in this chapter, see notes on chapter 6.

Chapter 1: Thursday, April 4, 1968

5 "Of all the weird ideas": Xernona Clayton interview, December 2007.
6 Calvin Craig: Robert M. Thomas Jr., "Calvin F. Craig, 64: Enigma in Klan and Civil Rights Work," NYT, April 24, 1998. Obituary, accessed online at nytimes.com.

8 *Have you heard:* Clayton interview, December 2007.
8 Description of the scene at the home and airport: Ibid., archival footage, WSB, item 53565; and "Atlantans Rally about Mrs. King," WAA, April 6, 1968, 13.
8 "Inevitably, mountain, memorial, and kitsch blend": Peter Range, "The Pinnacle of Kitsch, Southern Style," NYT, October 29, 1972, Travel and Resorts, XXX1.
10 "Doc just got shot": Coretta Scott King, *My Life with Martin Luther King, Jr.*, 293.
10 "I'm going to his wife" and rest of Allen dialogue in this scene: Ivan Allen with Paul Hemphill, *Mayor*, 196–202.
11 Description of behind-the-scenes planning for the Nobel dinner: Ibid., 95–99; Kevin Kruse, *White Flight*, 205–6; Mark Pendergrast, *For God, Country and Coca-Cola*, 286-87; Jacob Rothschild papers, Series 2, Box 6, folders 6 and 7, MARBL.
11 "You gather to honor a man": Sermon notes, Jacob Rothschild papers, Series 3, Box 15, Folder 1, MARBL.
11 "the difficult role you played": Letter from Cecil Alexander to Jacob Rothschild, January 28, 1965, Series 2, Box 6, Folder 6, Jacob Rothschild Papers, MARBL.
12 "After the dinner ended": Carbon copy of letter from Jacob Rothschild to Sidney Regner, dated February 2, 1965, Series 2, Box 6, Folder 6, Jacob Rothschild Papers, MARBL.
12 "My friend Sam Williams": Allen, *Mayor*, 98.
12 "generally forgotten by civic leaders": Chris Eckl, "In Vine City, Black Is White," *Georgia Bulletin*, August 4, 1966, http://www.georgiabulletin.org/local/1966/08/04/a/.
13 "Mrs. King, I have to inform you": Allen, *Mayor*, 200.
14 "I can't reach my parents" and rest of Clayton dialogue in scene: Clayton interview, December 2007.
15 "Let's go check on the Kings" and rest of dialogue in the scene with Mangham and family: Marvin Mangham interviews, September 2009.
17 "I do not believe that I should devote" and rest of Johnson quotes: "President Lyndon B. Johnson's Address to the Nation Announcing Steps to Limit the War in Vietnam and Reporting His Decision Not to Seek Reelection, March 31, 1968," LBJ, http://www.lbjlib.utexas.edu/johnson/archives.hom/speeches.hom/680331.asp.
18 "one of the best acts-of-God men": Charles Pou, "Sanders' Name Is Projected as Vice Presidential Choice," AJ, April 4, 1968, 1.
18 "I'm sorry you have to hear this": Carl Sanders interview, January 2008.
18 Johnson's Oval Office conversation: "Sanders with LBJ When Word of Killing Received," AJ, April 5, 1968, A4; Tom Johnson, personal interview, April 2009; and Sanders interview, January 2008.
18 They were debating what Johnson should do: Tom Johnson interview, April 2009; WHDD, April 4, 1968.
19 The sherry wager is discussed in Ramsey Clark, Oral History Interview IV, 14.
19 "until we have someone in the White House" and "save us from Stokely": Charles Pou, "Wallace Bid Opens with Racial Note," AJ, April 4, 1968, 1.
19 "Southerner who turned away from the ancestral vices": Eugene Patterson, "A Tale of Two Southerners," AC, April 5, 1968, 4.
20 For an insightful analysis of the speech delivered by Kennedy and its rhetorical impact, see Karl W. Anatol and John R. Bittner, "Kennedy on King: The Rhetoric of Control," *Today's Speech* 16, 1968, no. 3, 31–34. For a firsthand account, see John Lewis with Michael D'Orso, *Walking with the Wind*, 405–6.
20 "I have bad news for you" and rest of speech in this section: American Rhetoric, top one hundred speeches, sound recording at http://www.americanrhetoric.com/speeches/rfkonmlkdeath.html.
22 "There was stunned silence": Remer Tyson, "King's Death Stuns Negroes Attending Weltner Speech," AC, April 5, 1968, 2.

208 / Notes

23 "As soon as I'm back from Memphis": Ron English interview, October 2007.
23 "Martin Luther King has been shot!": Maria Saporta interview, February 2008.
24 "This is not a good neighborhood" and rest of Kathryn Johnson dialogue in this scene: Kathryn Johnson interview, February 2008.
24 jerky news footage: "Dr. Martin Luther King," CBS News clip, http://www.youtube.com/watch?v=cmOBbxgxKvo.
24 "overstepping the bounds of Christianity": Hartwell and Susan Hooper, "The Scripto Strike: Martin Luther King's 'Valley of Problems,' Atlanta, 1964–1965," *Atlanta History*, Fall 1999, 22. This article offers an excellent account of the strike, King's role in supporting the strikers, and the dynamics of the established black leadership in Atlanta and its relationship with King and the SCLC.
26 "We've got some difficult days ahead" and rest of "Mountaintop" speech: King Papers Project at Stanford. Audio and transcript accessed at <http://mlk-kpp01.stanford.edu/index.php/encyclopedia/documentsentry/ive_been_to_the_mountaintop/>.
27 "bundle" of evidence and reports of white Mustang: FBI, FOIA, Martin Luther King Jr. Main File, Section 103, 51–52, http://foia.fbi.gov/foiaindex/king.htm.
28 "The dreamer has been killed" and "No one wanted to hear from us": Andrew Young interview, May 2009.
28 "Let's not burn America down": Jeff Nesmith, "Williams Describes Dr. King's Last Moments," AC, April 5, 1968, 9. The *Atlanta Constitution* story was picked up by the AP and widely reported; for example, "Hosea Williams Appeals," Associated Press, NYT, April 5, 1968, 26.
28 "The black people have lost their Moses": TV clip of Jesse Jackson interview, *Eyes on the Prize*, http://www.pbs.org/wgbh/amex/eyesontheprize/story/15_poor.html#video.
29 "My grandmother is inside that building" and rest of LaFayette dialogue in this scene: Bernard LaFayette interview, February 2008.
29 "killer bees in a horror movie": Thomas Morgan, "Raging Riots on 14th St. Shattered Years' Dreams," WP, April 4, 1978, A8.
31 "These policemen also speak to PTAs": Crime Prevention Bureau Fact Sheet, *Newsweek* Collection, Segregation, Atlanta 1966 folder, Box 13, MARBL.
32 Description of Jenkins's role in the Kerner Commission: Herbert Jenkins, *Keeping the Peace*, 117–25.
32 "Segregation and poverty have created in the racial ghetto": *Kerner Report*, 2.
32 "You, as a member of the President's Commission": telegram from Martin Luther King Jr. to Herbert Jenkins, quoted in Jenkins, *Keeping the Peace*.
33 "Where, the critics demanded, were Stokely Carmichael": Tom Wicker, "Introduction," in *Kerner Report*, v.
33 "Reading it is an ugly experience": Ibid, xi.
34 "We've been through these situations before" and rest of conversation between Ivan Allen and the Johnsons: Recordings of Telephone Conversations, WH6804.01, track 12908, LBJ.
35 "Whatever you need" and "Ivan, the minute": Allen, *Mayor*, 205.

Chapter 2: Friday, April 5, 1968

36 Details of the planning of the meeting: WHDD, April 5, 1968; oral history interviews from the LBJ Library with Harry McPherson, Roy Wilkins, Whitney Young, and A. Philip Randolph; and the following files from the LBJ Library: Collection Confidential File, FE 3-1, Deaths-Funerals; FE 3-1/King, President's Appointment Diary (Backup), April 4–11; and Tom Johnson's Notes of Meetings, April 5, 1968.

37 "adored": Dennis Dickerson, *Militant Mediator*, 247.
37 "I would be glad to talk to President Johnson or anyone else": Ben A. Franklin, "Dr. King Hints He'd Cancel March If Aid Is Offered," NYT, April 1, 1968, 1.
38 "traditional" and "camp in": Simeon Booker, "As D.C. Burns," *Jet*, April 18, 1968, 38.
38 "That's not the question": Harry McPherson, Oral History Interview V, 11, LBJ.
38 "This is Senator So-and-So" and rest of dialogue from Clayton phone conversations in this section: Clayton interview, December 2007.
39 "Coordinator of the Celebrity Plane": Letter from Martin Luther King Jr. to Harry Belafonte dated July 23, 1963, Subseries 1:1, Correspondence A-D, KCM.
39 "practical necessity": Clayton interview, May 2009.
39 "We knew we were wiretapped": Harry Belafonte interview, *Voices of Freedom*, 339.
40 "one of our truest friends": Coretta Scott King, *My Life*, 133.
40 "I want to come down there tomorrow": Coretta Scott King, *My Life*, 297–98.
40 "I think there's something to that": Ramsey Clark, Oral History Interview IV, 12–13, LBJ.
41 For context and details on Khesanh, see Joseph Treaster, "Airdrops Are Khesanh's Lifeline," NYT, March 13, 1968, 1; "Nearly 1,000 Men Land at Khesanh; Marines Elated," NYT, April 7, 1968, 1; Associated Press, "Siege of Khesanh Declared Lifted; Troops Hunt Foe," NYT, April 6, 1968, 1; and "The Siege of Khe Sanh," in *1968: The Year That Changed the World*, 56–61.
42 "The only military academy I have ever been to": "Vo Nguyen Giap, North Vietnamese Commander," in *1968*, 25.
43 "discombobulating" and rest of scene at SCLC office: Tom Houck interview, November 2007.
43 "I really don't know what to say": Bill Goodwin, "Shock, Grief for Slain Leader," AJ, April 5, 1968, 9A.
44 "What I noticed when I moved here": Bunnie Jackson-Ransom interview, December 2009.
44 Statistics on the disparity between black and white income, homeownership, etc.: Harold Martin, *Atlanta and Environs*, 344–45.
45 "White slaves killed Dr. Martin Luther King in Memphis": Ralph McGill, "A Free Man Killed by White Slaves," AC, April 5, 1968, 1.
46 "I just want to say that the death of old King": Ralph McGill, "Evil Played into His Hands," AC, April 6, 1968, 1.
46 The letters quoted are a representative sample of the large volume of letters, notes, and telegrams found in the Ralph McGill papers collection, Series 2, Box 18, folders 7–9, MARBL.
47 "[King] was locked in a life-and-death struggle": Walker Lundy, "King's Assassination Gives Militants Impetus in Fight," AJ, April 5, 1968, 1.
47 "The strategy of Dr. King and the conference has varied little" and "angry statements": Steven V. Roberts, "Nonviolent View Voiced by SCLC," NYT, April 4, 1968, 25.
47 For details of the riots, I referred to contemporary newspaper reports and Ben Gilbert and the staff of the *Washington Post*, *Ten Blocks from the White House*.
47 "March! March! March!": Willard Clopton, "Curfew Imposed as Roving Bands Plunder and Burn," WP, April 6, 1968, A1.
48 "Trojan horses": Willard Clopton Jr. and Robert G. Kaiser, "11,500 Troops Confront Rioters; Three-Day Arrest Total at 2,686," WP, April 7, 1968, A1.
48 "It was one of the saddest sights you'll ever see": Ramsey Clark, Oral History Interview IV, 16, LBJ.
48 Talking points: Memo in President's Appointment File, Diary Backup, April 5, 1968, LBJ.

49 "The approach of another summer": Homer Bigart, "Cause of Slum Riots Uncorrected in 3-State Area, a Survey Finds," NYT, March 5, 1968, 1.

49 "Riots increase the fears": Jose Yglesias, "Dr. King's March on Washington, Part II," *New York Times Magazine*, March 31, 1968.

49 "If rioting continues": King *Look* article, quoted in "Dr. King Sees Period in Negroes Rioting," NYT, April 1, 1968.

50 "No man can fill Dr. King's shoes": Simeon Booker, "Rev. Abernathy 'To Get Moving on Job Left Behind by Martin,'" *Jet*, April 25, 1968, 49.

50 "We have decided that as he died for the poor": "Abernathy Takes SCLC Leadership," AJ, April 5, 1968, 4A.

50 "We have to take whatever precautions are necessary": Duane Riner, "Governor Places Guard on Alert," AC, April 6, 1968, 4.

51 Background on Maddox comes from several sources, including Bradley Rice, "Lester Maddox and the Politics of Populism," in *Georgia Governors in an Age of Change*, 193–210; Jim Tharpe, "Last Respects: 'Lester Maddox Understood and Loved Everyday Georgians,'" AJC, June 28, 2003, A1; Jennifer A. Schuchman, "Lester's Last Stand," AM, October 2003, 85–87, 116–19; Martin, *Atlanta and Environs*, 3:406; and the subject file on Maddox in the *Newsweek* Collection at MARBL.

51 "What a shame": Hartwell and Susan Hooper, "Scripto Strike," *Atlanta History*, 22–23.

51 "Actual Scene": *Atlanta Journal* advertisement, in Atlanta Mayor Run-Off folder, *Newsweek* collection, Box 1, MARBL.

52 "In that you are the silk-stocking candidate": Justin Nystrom, "Segregation's Last Stand," *Atlanta History*, 38.

52 "We're closed for good. I can't integrate": "Atlantan Shuts His Restaurant to Bar Patronage by Negroes," NYT, August 14, 1964, 25.

52 "I stand with Pickrick": Sample license plate in *Newsweek* Collection, Maddox folder, Box 9, MARBL.

52 "strange and hostile," "When white America killed Dr. King," and rest of quotes from Carmichael press conference: Phil Casey, "Carmichael Warns of 'Retaliation,'" WP, April 6, 1968, A1.

52 "If not for his well-publicized ranting": Rice, "Lester Maddox," 193.

54 "Stokely was very visible": John Lewis, *Walking with the Wind*, 177.

54 "stroll through Dixie in broad daylight": Gordon Parks quoted in Michael Kaufman, "Stokely Carmichael, Rights Leader Who Coined 'Black Power,' Dies at 57," NYT, November 16, 1998, B10.

54 "tear this place up": "Atlanta: Stokely's Spark," *Time*, September 16, 1966, time.com.

54 *He's picked the wrong preacher* and rest of Charles Black dialogue in this section: Charles Black interview, April 2009.

55 "attacked from all quarters," "insurrection," and "Powerful white forces": SNCC fund-raising letter, *Newsweek* Collection, SNCC folder, Box 16, MARBL.

55 "no one group": CHR report, in *Newsweek* Collection, "Segregation: Atlanta 1966" subject folder, Box 13, MARBL.

56 "The civil rights movement has not touched": Don Bender, "The Atlanta Riots," Mennonite Central News Service, September 30, 1966, Mennonite Church USA electronic archives, mcusa-archives.org.

56 "That's our trouble" and "dancing the boogaloo": "Cities: Recipe for Riot," *Time*, June 30, 1967, at time.com.

57 "We favor nonviolent, peaceful demonstration": Dixie Hills community petition, June 21, 1967, *Newsweek* Collection, Box 2, MARBL.

57 "In Atlanta, the Marriott Hotel" and rest of quotes from pamphlet in this section: "Perspective on the Atlanta Rebellion," pamphlet produced by the Afro-American News Service, Atlanta, *Newsweek* Collection, Box 2, MARBL.

58 "We're hip, black, and angry!": Raleigh Bryans, "Negroes Spurn Offer by Allen," AJ, April 5, 1968, 1.

58 "people were talking about 'How can we get violent?'": James Wilborn interview, October 2009.

58 "There was a real sense": Marvin Mangham interviews, September 2009.

58 "Violent retaliation is out!": Black Tiger Manifesto flyer, *Newsweek* Collection, Box 7, King folder, MARBL.

59 *If the world is falling apart, it's as good a time as any:* Charles Black interview, April 2009.

59 "We want to state clearly and unequivocally" and rest of quotes from the "Appeal for Human Rights": Clippings of the Appeal from March 9, 1960, Southern Regional Council collection, AARL.

60 "putrid mattresses": Charles Black interview, April 2009.

61 "suitcase full of votes": Clifford Kuhn, "'There's a Footnote to History!'" *Journal of American History*, September 1997, 587.

61 "the episode, linking the Kennedy and King families": Ibid., 584.

62 "a new and shining example": "Atlanta's Good Example," NYT, August 31, 1961, 26.

63 "old guard," "young Turks," "militants": Charles Black interview, April 2009.

63 "It was a seminar": Ibid.

64 "P.S. Hot dogs and Coca-Cola will be served": Letter from Ivan Allen to Robert Woodruff, June 14, 1961; Ivan Allen for Mayor confidential campaign memos from July 24, 1961, and August 3, 1961; "The glories of the Old South": Note from Ivan Allen to Robert Woodruff, December 11, 1961. All from the Robert Woodruff papers, Box 5, folder 6, MARBL.

65 "The top fifty" and "I think many of them": "Interview with Ivan Allen, Jr.," AM, January 1969, 84–86, 88–92.

65 "was hailed in the world press": James Townsend, *Dear Heart*, 162.

66 "We drove the multicolored, multiracial": Abram, Oral History Interview II, 6–7, LBJ.

66 "ordinary circumstances": SCLC statement, Harry Belafonte correspondence files, Box 4, folder 17, KC.

66 "I remember going through the section of the city": Ibid., 7.

67 Greater Atlanta Council on Human Relations lists: Memo states, "This list is accurate as of October 1963": Ibid.

67 "It is safe to say that fewer": Ibid.

68 "They stood there, unflinching": Christine Farris, *Through It All*, 133.

68 "work of just one man": "Getting Very Close to Killer, Clark Says of Dr. King's Murder," AJ, April 5, 1968, 1.

69 "I asked you here for your support as responsible Negro leaders" and all other dialogue from the meeting: Tom Johnson's Notes of Meetings, Box 3, folder "April 5, 1968: 11:10 a.m. President's meeting with Negro leaders after death of Martin Luther King," LBJ.

69 "It seems apparent that McKissick will not come": President's Appointment File, Diary Backup, April 5, 1968, LBJ.

70 Higginbotham sensed that the president was afraid, and Higginbotham's participation in dinner at the White House that night: A. Leon Higginbotham Jr., Oral History Interview I, 5–7, LBJ.

71 "Forgive us our individual and our corporate sins": Nan Robertson, "Johnson Leads U.S. in Mourning," NYT, April 6, 1968, 25.

72 Jesse Jackson, blood on shirt and jacket: Discussed in detail in Frady biography, 228–34. Gary Wills quotes, Reverend Kyles saying Jackson "definitely handled the

body," *GQ*, February 1984, 46–48. In Frady's interview notes, Kyles says Jackson was there and the press came, but Jackson did not call a press conference. Frady papers, Box 40, MARBL.

71 "I come here with a heavy heart" and other Jackson quotes: "Aide of Dr. King Vows to Try to Restore Calm to Chicago," CT, April 6, 1968, N5.

72 "shadow has fallen": Ward Just, "The City Besieged: A Study in Ironies and Contrasts," WP, April 6, 1968, A14.

72 "Stay off the streets if you don't have a gun": Ibid.

73 "including the militant ones": Alex Coffin, "King's Body Comes Home; Funeral Set for Tuesday," AC, April 6, 1968, 1.

73 "Daddy's breathing": Bernice King interview, February 2008.

74 "He looked so peaceful": Maria Saporta interview, February 2008.

74 "No, let's not get into this" and rest of description of Marvin Mangham: Mangham interviews, September 2009.

74 "pulsating drama": Marion Jackson, "The King Is Dead," ADW, April 6, 1968, 1.

74 "We have brought our leader home": "King's Body Flown to Atlanta," WP, April 6, 1968, A4.

75 "huge platters and trays": Elizabeth Oliver, "How Is Mom Holding Up?" WAA, April 13, 1968, 1.

75 "one of the hardest things I've ever had to do": Andrea Young interview, June 2009.

75 "flashbulbs going off all the time": Bernice King interview, February 2008.

76 "This is a household" and "There was a keen sense": Bob Fitch interview, May 2009.

77 "I can find *that* entrance" and rest of dialogue in this scene: Xernona Clayton interview, December 2007.

77 For a concise summary of the FBI's use of the Levison-King connection as rationale for wiretapping King and the SCLC, see David Garrow, "The FBI and Martin Luther King," *The Atlantic*, July/August 2002.

78 "I need your help" and rest of press conference: President's Appointment File, Diary Backup, April 5, 1968, LBJ.

78 "All right. You want a chance?" and rest of dialogue in *Chicago Daily News* scene: Diane (Monk) McLelland interview, September 2009.

79 "James, James": Douglas Belkin, "Some Say Hub Owes Debt to James Brown," *Boston Globe*, December 26, 2006, http://www.boston.com/news/local/massachusetts/ articles/2006/12/26/some_say_hub_owes_debt_to_james_brown. See also "James Brown Helps Boston 'Cool It,'" WP, April 17, 1968, D13.

81 "In view of the president's desire": Message for Marvin Watson, FE 3-1/King, Box 5, LBJ.

81 "I hate to nitpick": Memo from Barefoot Sanders to Marvin Watson, April 5, 1968, FE 3-1/King, LBJ.

81 "Go commercial": Memo from Jim Jones, April 5, 1968, FE 3-1/King, LBJ.

82 "vitally affecting the lives of all our Negro citizens" and "It is not enough for the American nation": Richard Witkin, "Rockefeller Asks for 'Memorial Laws,'" NYT, April 6, 1968, 24.

82 "Pray for the trigger-happy and those that don't think": Philip Gailey, "All Night They File Silently In," AC, April 6, 1968, 5.

82 "young and old of both races": Keeler McCartney and Dick Hebert, "Non Violent Leaders Plead for All to Show the World," AC, April 6, 1968, 5.

82 "Let's demonstrate to the world": Ibid.

83 "Let's show the people who believe in the sword": Ibid.

83 "We need the help of the white leadership": Ibid.

Chapter 3: April 6, 1968

86 "Ralph Abernathy is expected to be confirmed": "Selected Racial Disturbances," Teletype from Hoover, April 6, 1968, President's Appointment File (Diary Backup), folder "April 4–11, 1968 Death of Martin Luther King and Riots in Major Cities II," LBJ.

87 "No. No. No": Tom Houck interview, December 2009.

87 "gamboled in makeshift showers": "Victory at Khe Sanh," *Time*, April 12, 1968, time.com

88 "I understand you had a little trouble yourself": "President Briefed by Westmoreland," NYT, April 7, 1968, 1.

88 "precious family time or golf time" and rest of dialogue: Randy Taylor interview transcript. The accounts of Central Presbyterian's role in the funeral are from the Taylor interview; "The Civil Rights Movement Comes to Central," history by Norm Kohn; Allen, *Mayor*, 212–13; and my interviews with Norm and Kathy Kohn and Don Carl Robinson, February 2008.

89 "Is there anything we can do?" and rest of dialogue between Clayton and mortician: Xernona Clayton interview, December 2007.

90 "Stop!" and "Now, let them come in": Ron English interview, October 2007.

90 *It's hard, just different-looking*: Marvin Mangham interviews, September 2009.

91 "He is going to blow your minds": Thaddeus Stokes, "We Shall Overcome," ADW, April 9, 1968, 4.

91 "Black power without black action is rhetoric": Flyer, *Newsweek* Collection, Box 7, King folder, MARBL.

91 "selected racial developments and disturbances" and quotes from J. Edgar Hoover memo in rest of section: Teletype from Hoover, April 6, 1968, President's Appointment File (Diary Backup), folder "April 4–11, 1968 Death of Martin Luther King and Riots in Major Cities, II," LBJ.

92 "like any home in the South" and rest of dialogue between Moses, Mullá, and Coretta King: Linda Mullá interview, February 2008.

93 "wrapped in grief": Kathryn Johnson interview, February 2008.

94 "There was a sense we were seeing history": Bob Fitch interview, May 2009.

94 The general description of the letters, telegrams, and other materials is from looking through two key sources: Series 1.3: Correspondence: Condolences and Letters Received After Assassination, KCM; and subject files, "funeral," KC.

94 "just written a letter to the House Rules Committee": Letter from Jane and Charles Kmosko to Coretta Scott King, April 6, 1968. Ibid.

94 "Do not be sad Mrs. King": Letter from Socovo Santos, included in a thirty-five-page package sent by Sister Ann Thaddeus to Coretta Scott King, April 7, 1968. Ibid.

94 "Hush little Bernice": Poetry booklet from the Wogaman School, Dayton, Ohio. Funeral folder, KC.

94 "Dear Friend: Your recent letter has been received": Form letter titled "Acknowledgment of Meaningful Letters of Condolences," Series 1.3: Correspondence: Condolences and Letters Received After Assassination, KCM.

95 "could express and interpret" and rest of press conference statements by Coretta Scott King: WSB, clip 53564.

96 "Inside SCLC, members of Mr. Abernathy's inner circle": Earl Caldwell, "After King," NYT, April 21, 1968, E3.

96 "In many ways they complemented each other": "Trusted Successor to Dr. King," NYT, April 6, 1968, 25.

96 "mantle of leadership" on the "reluctant shoulders": Achsah Nesmith, "Rev. Ralph D. Abernathy Sadly Takes SCLC Reins," AC, April 6, 1968, 1.

96 "quiet, expressionless man" and "beefy shouldered": Simeon Booker, "Rev. Abernathy 'To Get Moving on Job Left Behind by Martin,'" *Jet*, April 25, 1968, 49, 50.

96 "He has taken liquid nourishment": Jack Nelson, "Abernathy Says King's Protests Will Continue," LAT, April 11, 1968, 6.

97 "As an organizer, it is doubtful": "Can the SCLC overcome the loss of its principal leader?" CSM, April 6, 1968, B19.

97 "was involved just then in a struggle": Lerone Bennett Jr., "The Martyrdom of Martin Luther King," *Ebony*, May 1968, 176.

97 "I'm surprised they didn't take out at least another five": Bernard LaFayette interview, February 2008.

98 "There was an intensity and a fury" and "We don't believe in conciliation and negotiation": Simeon Booker, "As D.C. Burns, President Moves to Head Off Race Confrontation," *Jet*, April 18, 1968, 40.

98 "I'm here to pick up the clothes" and rest of dialogue: Xernona Clayton interview, December 2007.

99 "Mr. President. We're in trouble" and rest of dialogue between Daley and the president: Recordings of Telephone Conversations, WH6804.01, tracks 12910 and 12911, LBJ.

99 "We are beginning the movement of troops" and conversation between Clark and Johnson: Ibid., track 12912.

100 "shoot to kill": "Riots Go On," CT, April 7, 1968, 1.

100 "Here we were, two white": Allen, *Mayor*, 210.

101 "Help us with calls" and description of scene at church: Winifred Green interview, June 2009.

101 "It's all long distance" and rest of conversation between Allen and Abernathy: Allen, *Mayor*, 211.

Chapter 4: Palm Sunday, April 7, 1968

103 "There are so many people" and rest of dialogue between Taylor and the SCLC and Taylor and Allen: Taylor interview transcript.

104 "response of white churches": Telex from Atlanta *Newsweek* bureau to New York office, April 12, 1968, *Newsweek* Collection, Box 7, King folder, MARBL.

105 "At eleven on Sunday morning": Transcript of session, Western Michigan archives, http://www.wmich.edu/library/archives/mlk/q-a.html.

105 "I strongly object to the use": Letter from Robert Brown to Sanford Atwood, April 8, 1968, Emory University, Office of the President, Sanford Atwood, Office Files, Series 002, Box 17, folder 8, MARBL.

105 "known Communist": Letter from John McLaren to Sanford Atwood, April 20, 1968, ibid.

105 Honeywell charter: Letter from Fred Kaiser, Vice President, Southern Area, to Herbert Jenkins, April 12, 1968, Jenkins papers, Box 18, folder 14, AHC.

105 "Somewhere, sometime, we all got to sit down together": Bernard Weinraub, "Rioting Disquiets G.I.'s in Vietnam," NYT, April 8, 1968, 35.

106 "trail had lengthened" and rest of *Meet the Press* show: Martin Waldron, "Dr. King's Assassin on Run, Clark Says," NYT, April 8, 1968, 1.

106 "Every time M.L. would be scheduled to speak": Ron English interview, October 2007.

106 "America is a dying nation today": Walker Lundy, "Crowded Church Empty of Its Voice," AJ, April 8, 1968, 2.
107 "I want you to know, Martin" and rest of Abernathy sermon: Margaret Hurst, "Abernathy Reads Letter to Dr. King at Church," AC, April 8, 1968, 1.
107 "His life is in our hands": Sermon notes, Jacob Rothschild papers, Series 3, Box 15, folder 18, MARBL.
107 "The indictment against white America": Ibid.
107 "Ministers Manifesto": Regional Council of Churches of Atlanta, http://www.rccatl.org/tiki-read_article.php?articleId=34.
108 "A glance at the names": "What Follows?" editorial, AJ, April 8, 1986, 18A.
108 "White America, too, confronts a challenge": Jacob Rothschild papers, Series 3, Box 15, folder 18, MARBL.
108 "Atlanta must face the fact": "What Follows?" AJ.
108 "a sinful pastime": "Civil Disobedience a Sin, Maddox Says," AC, April 8, 1968, 12.
109 outdoor memorial service: "King Memorial Conducted in Kirkwood Park," AC, April 8, 1968, 16.
109 "I'm afraid, Walter": Willard Clopton Jr. and Robert G. Kaiser, "Fires Dying Out; Arrests Decline, Curfew Continues," WP, April 8, 1968, A1.
110 "This one's headed for downtown!" and rest of scene with buses at the airport: Pete Kilgo interview, January 2008.
110 *King paraphernalia:* Jesse Jackson interview, February 2008.
111 *What have we done?* and rest of dialogue with Kohns at SCLC and church: Norm and Kathy Kohn interviews, February 2008 and November 2009.
112 "It was the first time I'd ever carved": Eugene Patterson, "Mrs. Tuttle Sliced the Ham," AC, April 12, 1968, 4.
112 "I've got a gig for you": Marvin Mangham interviews, September 2009.
114 "open grassy area": Diagram, Box 14, FE 3-1, Document 8g, LBJ.
114 "What can we do to help?" and rest of dialogue in scene at senior King home: June Dobbs Butts interview, November 2007.
116 "That image is seared": Tom Johnson interview, April 2009.
116 Descriptions of the divvying up of responsibilities between the King family and SCLC, and other elements of planning for the funeral's various events, come from my interviews with Lonnie King, Xernona Clayton, Isaac Farris, Ron English, Tom Houck, Joseph Lowery, and Bernard LaFayette; memoirs by Coretta Scott King and Christine King Farris; the Funeral subject file, KC; and Steve Morris, "Birmingham Strategist Called to Direct King Funeral," *Jet*, April 25, 1968, 18–21.
116 "You know, M.L. has already preached his own eulogy": Farris, *Through It All*, 131.
116 Stein's role in the *Martin Luther King Jr. Speaks* program is outlined in an SCLC memo from public relations director Tom Offenberger to the executive staff, January 22, 1968. In Offenberger files, KC.
117 "I really can't bring myself to do it" and rest of dialogue: Xernona Clayton interview, December 2007.

Chapter 5: Monday April 8, 1968

119 Participation by Cosby and Culp also is noted in David Nordan, "Mrs. King, Others Leave for March," AJ, April 8, 1968, 11A.
120 *Whoever wanted King killed has already done their job:* Jesse Jackson interview, February 2008.
120 "In spite of the times that he had to be away" and rest of speech by Coretta Scott King: Coretta Scott King, *My Life*, 311–14.

120 "the Black Madonna of Grief": Simeon Booker, "Returns to Walk in Footsteps of Husband Felled by Assassin," *Jet*, April 25, 1968, 6.

121 "wearing a simple black dress": J. Anthony Lukas, "Mrs. King Asks 'Peaceful Society,'" NYT, April 9, 1968, 1.

121 "impassioned inaugural speech" and "We are bound": Vincent Burke and Ed Meagher, "Mrs. King Leaders Memphis March, Pleads for Poor," LAT, April 9, 1968, 1.

121 "bundle" and tracing of gun to Birmingham shop: Thomas Powers, "Learn King Murder Rifle from Alabama," CT, April 9, 1968, 1.

122 "asked that I relay to you his hope": Memo from Mike Manatos to Lyndon Johnson, April 8, 1968, FE 3-1/King, LBJ.

122 "The country knows the president has done enough": Memo from Marvin Watson to Lyndon Johnson, April 8, 1968, ibid.

122 "I frankly don't think it is safe": Phil Landrum quoted in memo from Marvin Watson to Lyndon Johnson, April 8, 1968, ibid.

123 "large number of secret service agents": Memo from Thomas Johns to Marvin Watson, April 8, 1968, Box 14, FE 3-1, Document 8a, LBJ.

123 "Give V.P. whatever he needs": Note on memo from Marvin Watson to Lyndon Johnson, April 8, 1968, ibid.

123 "a preacher friend of his": Memo from Barefoot Sanders to Jim Jones, April 8, 1968, ibid.

124 "center of the universe": Maria Saporta interview, February 2008.

125 "We have to deal with the injustices": WSB, clip 42464.

125 "That Thunderbird won't do" and "When they come to mourn": Remer Tyson, "Kennedy's Aides Turn in Thunderbird for a Ford," AC, April 9, 1968, 1.

126 "The skyline of urban America in the past week has been a desolating one": Max Lerner, "Skyline of Tragic America," LAT, April 10, 1968, A5.

126 "Go see what condition it's in" and rest of dialogue in scene with Jo Freeman: Freeman interview, May 2009.

127 "spirituous liquors": Mayoral proclamation, Jenkins papers, Box 18, folder 14, AHC.

127 "The executive heads": Mayoral proclamation, April 8, 1968, ibid.

129 "I saw my son yesterday" and scene at Davis funeral: Associated Press, "King Sr. Conducts Rites of Son's Teacher," AJ, April 9, 1968, 8A.

129 *How strange:* Isaac Farris interview, August 2009.

130 "Do you think Marty King is going to be here?" and rest of dialogue in this scene: Jim Peppler interview, September 2009.

130 "fix his head" and "Don't stare": Cynthia Patterson-Lewis interview, October 2009.

131 *This is unreal:* Lewis, *Walking with the Wind*, 411.

131 "Those of us who are left," and rest of quotes from SCLC meeting with Robert Kennedy, Young, *An Easy Burden*, 486.

132 "I've got two jobs for you": Mickey Shur interview, July 2009.

132 Williams had struggled to find the right wagon, and rest of anecdote about wagon: Abernathy, *And the Walls*, 458; and Jim Auchmutey, "We Lost a Hero but Kept the Peace," AJC, March 30, 2008, A1.

132 "He's one of the only people in the world to know the ingredients": Peter Geffen interview, May 2009.

133 "Police said they had never seen a case": Martin Waldron, "Hunt for Killer Spans Wide Area," NYT, April 10, 1968, 31.

133 "What was that?" and rest of dialogue in scene in church: Norm Kohn interview, February 2008.

Chapter 6: Tuesday, April 9, 1968

136 *Could she possibly think that the Kings:* Kathryn Johnson interview, February 2008.

136 *They are communicating in spirit:* Xernona Clayton interview, December 2007.

136 *I can't carry everything:* Kathryn Johnson interview, February 2008.

137 "The enemy intended to overrun the base at Khesanh": "Johnson's Troop Message," NYT, April 9, 1968, 2.

137 "A small fortress": Tom Greene and Steve Ball Jr., "160 Troopers Guard Capitol," AJ, April 9, 1968, 2A.

137 "A few months": NYT, "Book Tells of Stern Maddox Order on Marchers," July 6, 1968, 19.

138 "armed camp" and "segregationist hashslinger": George Collins, "Poor Prominent at King Funeral," WAA, April 13, 1968, 1.

138 "sitting in his office under heavy guard": Homer Bigart, "Leaders at Rites," NYT, April 10, 1968, 1.

138 "helmeted, machine-gun-armed cops": "King's Last March," *Time*, April 19, 1968, time.com.

138 "What are you doing" and rest of exchange: Don Robinson interview, February 2008.

139 "hushed room": Terry Kay, "Performers Plan Tribute to King," AJ, April 9, 1968, 16A.

140 "You can't take those things!" and rest of scene at SCLC offices: Bernard LaFayette interview, February 2008.

141 *That's obviously a fantasy!:* Jo Freeman interview, May 2009.

141 "like a daze—like being underwater": Winifred Green interview, June 2009.

142 "My friends, this is Ralph Abernathy" and rest of scene: Charles Black interview, April 2009; Paul Hemphill interview, February 2008; and Paul Hemphill, "Bizarre Time of Frenzy," AJ, April 10, 1968, 2A.

143 "Hello, Jackie!": Thaddeus Stokes, "For World Peace," ADW, April 10, 1968, 4.

143 Compilation of notable attendees from various newspaper accounts, including "Who's Who Attending Funeral," AC, April 10, 1968, 14; Nicholas von Hoffman and Bernadette Carey, "Mule Wagon Leads March," WP, April 10, 1968, 1; Thaddeus Stokes, "They All Came," ADW, April 12, 1968, 6; George Collins, "Poor, Prominent at King funeral," WAA, 1; Homer Bigart, "Leaders at Rites," NYT, April 10, 1968, 1.

145 "there were so many people": Lonnie King interview, May 2009.

145 *"People lined up like a human carpet"* and other dialogue from entering the church: June Dobbs Butts interview, November 2007.

145 "wrong with the scene" and "I realized: This was Ebenezer": Abernathy, *And the Walls*, 461.

145 "When the King family and others": C. R. Fairall to Herbert Jenkins, Jenkins papers, Box 18, folder 14, AHC.

146 "strange level of celebrity" and other dialogue from Peppler: Peppler interview, September 2009.

146 "We're not going to get in the church" and rest of Patterson family experience in this chapter: Cynthia Patterson-Lewis interview, October 2009.

147 "Who's in there?" and rest of scene with the celebrity bus: Pete Kilgo interview, January 2008.

148 OBSEQUIES MARTIN LUTHER KING JR. and rest of quotations from the funeral program: KC.

148 "O God, our leader is dead" and rest of English prayer: "Transcripts," NYT, April 10, 1968, 32.

149 Allen anecdote about man in yellow jacket: Allen, *Mayor*, 217–18. Confirmed with Lee Walburn, October 2009.

149 "Martin Luther King spoke with the tongues": "Transcripts," NYT.
150 "Mrs. King has requested": News-footage clip, http://www.youtube.com/watch?v=lQbLW9mDdbI.
150 "I'd like somebody": From the "Drum Major Instinct" sermon, Funeral folder, KC.
150 King's notes for "Drum Major" and the manila folder from the Ivan Allen Company in which they were filed are among the documents in the King Collection at Morehouse College, Series 2: Writings by Martin Luther King, Jr., Sub-Series "Sermons."
150 Representative media previews of "Drum Major" include "King Gave Outline for Eulogy," WP, April 7, 1968, A5, and "Rev. King Preached Own Funeral Before Death," *Jet*, April 18, 1968, 24.
152 "If you don't move back": Remer Tyson, "Nowhere to Move in Crowd Like That," AC, April 10, 1968, 7.
152 "honorary pallbearers" and details: Memo "Order of Procession," Funeral subject folder, KC.
153 "frighteningly enormous": Young, *An Easy Burden*, 478.
153 "Today, there was only the clop, clop, clop": John Goldman, "For Marchers, Nonviolence Was Order of Their Sad Day," LAT, April 10, 1968, 2.
153 "Everybody was crying. Everybody": Sam Williams interview, February 2008.
153 "We kept it quiet": Bernard LaFayette interview, February 2008.
153 "Sammy Davis is back here!" and rest of exchange: WSB, clip 38278.
154 *How many of these people were with us:* Jesse Jackson interview, February 2008.
154 "Even if we grant that they were at their highest point of courtesy": Letter from Neva Bethel to Herbert Jenkins, dated April 11, 1968, Jenkins papers, Box 18, folder 14, AHC.
155 "scared to death, peering out at us": Paul Hemphill interview, February 2008.
155 "We were the center of liberal America": Sam Massell interview, January 2008.
156 "make way for Senator Robert Kennedy": Marion Gaines, "Humble Throng Endured Long, Hot Wait for Funeral," AC, April 10, 1968, 10.
157 "Everyone take ten steps backward!" Ibid.
157 "It is now for us": "Transcripts, of Prayer, Tribute, and Eulogy Delivered at Services for Dr. King," NYT, April 10, 1968, 32.
157 "I regretted very much": Joseph Lowery interview, February 2008.
157 "Help us work for that day when": "Transcript of Rev. Lowery's Inaugural Benediction," WP, http://voices.washingtonpost.com/inauguration-watch/2009/01/transcript_of_rev_lowerys_inau.html.
158 "On another day, perhaps a cooler one": Lewis, *King*, 392.
158 "the entire city appears to be quiet" and "church was very much over-crowded": Teletype from Special Agent Livingood to Special Agent in Charge Hill, April 9, 1968, President's Appointment File (Diary Backup), folder "April 4–11, 1968, Death of Martin Luther King and Riots in Major Cities, II," LBJ.
159 "Ada and Bell—the epitome of poverty": Collins, "Poor, prominent," WAA.
159 "One has to go back more than ten decades": Lerone Bennett, "The Martyrdom," *Ebony*, May 1968, 174.
159 "I just thought I'd like you": Leslie Harper to Coretta Scott King, April 9, 1968, Series 1.3: Correspondence: Condolences and Letters Received After Assassination, KCM.
160 "You have today made yourself": Mrs. Lawrence Greene to Coretta Scott King, April 9, 1968, ibid.
160 "My class and I watched": Sister Mary Bonaventure to Coretta Scott King, April 9, 1968, ibid.
160 "Just who did you think": Unsigned letter, April 9, 1968, ibid.

160 "I am so sorry" and rest of dialogue: Kathy Kohn interview, February 2008.

161 *He must not have slept more than a few hours:* Christine King Farris, *Through It All*, 137.

161 "a leader to heal": Margaret Hurst, "Cemetery Is Called Too Small for His Spirit," AC, April 10, 1968, 8.

161 "weeping and wailing": June Dobbs Butts interview, November 2007.

162 "clicking grotesquely, like teeth": Reporters' notes, *Newsweek* Collection, King funeral folder, Box 7, MARBL. Jim Peppler in his interview with me also remarked on the large number of photographers and has photographs of the crane above the grave and the photographers perched on nearby tombs and monuments.

162 *I now know Martin Luther King is dead:* Tom Houck interview, November 2007.

Chapter 7: Wednesday, April 10, 1968

176 "last assignment": Morris Shelton, "White, Negro Visitors Pass King's Grave," AJ, April 11, 1968, 4A.

176 "You need to fix me a bill": Pete Kilgo interview, January 2008.

176 "I orchestrated a series": Christine King Farris, *Through It All*, 138–39. A description of one transfer is described in Ralph Abernathy's memoir, *And the Walls Came Tumbling Down*, 465–66.

177 only forty arrests occurred: Speech given by Herbert Jenkins to the Georgia State Chamber of Commerce, April 17, 1968, at the Regency Hyatt, Atlanta, Jenkins papers, Box 15, folder 2, p. 16, AHC.

177 $100,000 just in extra pay: Raleigh Bryans, "Allen Praises City Attitude," AJ, April 10, 1968, 2A.

177 "pay expenses incurred by the city related": City of Atlanta Board of Aldermen minutes, vol. 11, p. 668, lines 40–41, AHC.

177 "such a tense situation": Duane Riner, "Maddox and Smith Pat City on Back," AC, April 11, 1968, 5.

177 "It is this kind of high performance": Samuel Williams to Herbert Jenkins, April 17, 1968, Jenkins papers, AHC, Box 18, folder 14.

177 The annual reports: Jenkins papers, Box 3, folder 3, AHC. The photograph of the King funeral is on page 28 of the 1968 annual report.

178 "services rendered": Narvie J. Harris to Herbert Jenkins, April 11, 1968, ibid.

178 "others of goodwill": John Middleton to Herbert Jenkins, April 15, 1968, ibid.

178 "You have done yourselves proud": F. Burt Vardeman to Herbert Jenkins, April 11, 1968, ibid.

178 "I had a great feeling": Tom LeLand to Herbert Jenkins, April 11, 1968, ibid.

178 "Chief: you did a magnificent job": Charles Weltner to Herbert Jenkins, April 10, 1968, ibid.

178 "The possibilities which loomed": Theta M. Miller to Herbert Jenkins, April 11, 1968, ibid.

178 "superb performance": Robert W. Bivens to Herbert Jenkins, April 15, 1968, ibid.

178 Also, letters to Jenkins from George Erwin, April 11, 1968; J. W. "Bill" Pinkston Jr., April 10, 1968; W. O. Duvall, April 10, 1968; Harold Brockey, April 12, 1968; Marvin C. Goldstein, April 15, 1968; and George E. Manners, April 16, 1968. Ibid.

179 "I shudder to think": George T. Smith to Herbert Jenkins, April 11, 1968, ibid.

179 "Everybody was busy congratulating everybody else" and rest of editorial: "The People Behind the Tributes," AC, April 11, 1968, 4.

179 "I know you are utterly exhausted": Helen Bullard to Ivan Allen, April 9, 1968, Helen Bullard papers, Series 1, Box 1, folder 6, MARBL.

179 "put up job": From Robert L. Noble to Ivan Allen, April 10, 1968, rerouted with memo slip to Herbert Jenkins, Jenkins papers, Box 18, folder 14, AHC, and attached to clip "He was a moment in the conscience of man," *New York Daily News*, April 10, 1968, 29.

180 "Jean articulated": Minutes, April 1968, Wednesday Morning Study Club Records, Box 3, folder 3, AHC.

180 *They must have been there:* Cynthia Patterson-Lewis interview, October 2009.

181 "Eighty-two percent of the people in my district": Art Pine, "Georgians All Vote Against," AC, April 11, 1968, 1.

181 General background on Open Housing bill of 1968 and its passage: "President Signs Civil Rights Bill; Pleads for Calm," NYT, April 12, 1968, 1.

182 "Nothing could be a greater memorial": "Senate Bars Cut in Funds for Jobs," NYT, April 11, 1968, 34.

182 "We have passed many": "Transcript of Johnson's News Conference," NYT, April 11, 1968, 18.

182 "I come this afternoon with Dr. Martin Luther King" and rest of scene at press conference: WSB, clip 53566.

182 the board's members had voted: Harmon Perry, "SCLC Board Elects Widow, Belafonte," AJ, April 11, 1978, 2A.

184 "There was never any debate or question": Joseph Lowery interview, February 2008.

184 "movement twins": Bernard LaFayette interview, February 2008.

184 "About the delay of two days" and other dialogue from Academy Awards: "'In Heat of Night' Wins Oscar as Best Film," NYT, April 11, 1968, 52.

184 "In the forty years": Dyson, *April 4, 1968*, 170.

Epilogue: January 15, 1969

186 "Today my husband would have been": Press release with statement by Coretta Scott King, January 15, 1969, Vincent Harding papers, Box 11, folder 4, MARBL.

186 Description of planned memorial and background on fund-raising efforts: Vincent Harding papers, Boxes 9–11, MARBL.

187 "private arrangement": Kathy McGrath, "King Widow Silent on Book Advance," AC, January 16, 1969, 22.

187 "advised recently that Stanley Levison": Memo from J. Edgar Hoover to Special Agent in Charge, Atlanta Bureau, FBI, "Coretta King," April 23, 1968. See also memo from G. C. Moore to W. C. Sullivan, "Martin Luther King, Jr., Security Matters—Communist," October 6, 1969, in Coretta Scott King FBI file, accessed through FBI FOIA, http://foia.fbi.gov/foiaindex/kingcorettascott.htm.

188 "Millions of dollars came into SCLC after King died": Tom Houck interview, December 2009.

188 "friction": Ben A. Franklin, "Friction Is Developing over Abernathy Leadership," NYT, June 2, 1968, 88.

188 "You know they won't sell mules to black people": Winifred Green interview, June 2009.

189 "I cannot turn to white America": SCLC fund-raising letter signed by Ralph David Abernathy, January 2, 1969, Rothschild papers, Series 2, Box 8, folder 7, MARBL.

189 "a good idea" and "He was a fine man": Roger Porter, "Most Agree on Honor for King," Roger AJ, January 14, 1969, 5A.

190 "His life and work will stand as testimony": Duane Riner, "Senate Applauds Tribute to King," AJ, January 16, 1969, 1.

190 "I wouldn't want to see this in the paper": Remer Tyson, "Fellow Lawmakers Think When Ward Speaks Up," AC, January 16, 1969, 11.

190 "In reaffirmation of those principles": Diane Stepp, "Central Church Unveils King Plaque," AC, August 29, 1968.

190 "Let it be sufficient to say": Ibid.

190 "We thank thee God": Ibid.

191 "To achieve the goals of the Housing Act" and rest of speech: "President Lyndon B. Johnson's Annual Message to the Congress on the State of the Union, January 14, 1969," LBJ, http://www.lbjlib.utexas.edu/johnson/archives.hom/speeches.hom/690114 .asp.

191 "a richness and timbre it has often lacked": Neil Sheehan, "Johnson Calls on Nation to Continue Peace Quest and His Social Programs," NYT, January 15, 1969, 1.

192 "white mind-set": "Nixon Hears Dissent—After Negro Visit," AJ, January 14, 1969, 17A.

192 "Nixon put the black people and the nation a step backward": Ibid.

192 "We call on good people everywhere": Alex Coffin, "Spare King's Killer, Rev. Abernathy Asks," AC, January 16, 1969, 1.

193 "honored to be here": Ibid.

193 "O Lord, we dedicate this hallowed": Liturgy handout from dedication, Funeral folder, KC.

194 "Start Atlanta Now!": "300 Sign Up to Take Tours of Poor Areas," AC, January 16, 1969.

194 "I am speaking now as a private Atlanta citizen": WSB, clip 44605.

196 "more militancy" and the Miami survey: Philip Meyer, "Aftermath of Martyrdom," 165.

197 "These proportions demonstrate once again": "A Report of Certain Reactions by the Atlanta Public to the Death of the Reverend Doctor Martin Luther King, Jr.," Emory University Center for Research in Social Change, April 1969, 17.

197 "had little impact on whites": C. Richard Hofstetter, "Political Disengagement," 179.

GLOSSARY OF ORGANIZATIONS

A. Philip Randolph Institute (APRI). Named for A. Philip Randolph, early civil rights activist and organizer of the 1963 March on Washington, this group, founded in 1965 by Randolph and Bayard Rustin, coordinated efforts between civil rights groups and the labor movement.

Atlanta Community Relations Commission (ACRC). Created in 1966 by Mayor Ivan Allen, this twenty-member group was appointed to study race relations in the city and make recommendations to the mayor.

Black Panther Party. Formed in Oakland, California, in 1966 by Huey Newton and Bobby Seale, it took its name from the black panther emblem that Stokely Carmichael promoted during voter registration drives in Lowndes County, Alabama. Organizers called for an end to police brutality in black neighborhoods and also implemented community-service programs such as providing food for low-income children. By 1968, the party was associated with ideas of militancy and black nationalism.

Brotherhood of Sleeping Car Porters. Founded in 1925, it was the first African-American labor union to negotiate a collective agreement with a major company. A. Philip Randolph was the president for many years.

Chicago Freedom Movement (CFM). An ambitious alliance between the SCLC and CCCO launched in 1965 with the goal of abolishing slums in Chicago. This was the largest civil rights effort in a Northern city. During the CFM, King moved to a Chicago tenement to highlight living conditions there.

Committee on the Appeal for Human Rights (COAHR). Student movement founded in 1960 at the historically black colleges of the Atlanta University Center that published a statement about racial discrimination and lack of economic opportunity for Atlanta's blacks. The students led sit-ins in Atlanta. Many leaders of COAHR, such as Julian Bond, went on to be involved in SNCC.

Congress of Racial Equality (CORE). Founded in the 1940s and based on the Gandhian ideas of nonviolent resistance, it pioneered early attempts to desegregate interstate travel. By the early 1960s, there were CORE chapters throughout the country. CORE worked with SNCC and SCLC on the 1961 Freedom Rides. In 1968, under the direction of Roy Ennis, the organization became more conservative.

Coordinating Council of Community Organizations (CCCO). Founded in Chicago in the early 1960s, a biracial organization concerned with public school policy, particularly reform of poor schools in the city's black communities.

Model Cities Program. An element of Lyndon Johnson's War on Poverty and Great Society programs, it was launched in 1966. The goal was to develop jobs and opportunities in blighted areas and to involve citizens in the process. Under the Nixon administration the citizen-involvement element was disbanded, and the program ended in 1974.

National Association for the Advancement of Colored People (NAACP). Founded in 1909 with the goals of universal voting rights and civil rights. Early work focused on antilynching efforts, then legal battles against segregation and discrimination, including the 1954 *Brown v. Board* school integration case. The NAACP focused on work through the legal system, not direct action as did SCLC and other groups, but supported many efforts of the modern civil rights movement and was involved in passage of key laws. Roy Wilkins was head of the NAACP in 1968.

National Council of Negro Women (NCNW). Founded in 1935, it initially focused on voting and education rights. In the 1960s, its efforts addressed housing rights, including open-housing laws, integration of public housing, and housing discrimination. Dorothy Height was its head in 1968.

National Urban League (NUL). Founded in 1910 (and initially called the Committee on Urban Conditions Among Negroes), the league's focus was the poor conditions of blacks who migrated from the South to the North. In 1968, the NUL was headed by Whitney Young, who partnered with SCLC and other civil rights organizations. The NUL has more than one hundred chapters today.

Operation Breadbasket. An arm of the SCLC launched in 1962, it focused on black economic empowerment, encouraging boycotts of companies that did not hire blacks or stock products produced by black-owned manufacturers. The most successful campaign was run by Jesse Jackson, who oversaw Operation Breadbasket in Chicago at the time of King's death.

Southern Christian Leadership Conference (SCLC). Cofounded in 1957 by Martin Luther King and other ministers and activists, including Ralph Abernathy, C. K. Steele, Joseph Lowery, Bayard Rustin, and Ella Baker. A national, Atlanta-based board governs SCLC, which partnered with affiliates in other cities.

Student Nonviolent Coordinating Committee (SNCC). Emerging in 1960 out of meetings that SCLC's former director Ella Baker held with students at Shaw University in Raleigh, North Carolina, SNCC (commonly called Snick) became one of the leading civil rights groups of the 1960s, with members participating in the Freedom Rides, sit-ins, boycotts, voter-registration drives, and other key direct-action programs. In the mid-1960s, SNCC became split over direction and moved in a more militant, black nationalist direction when Stokely Carmichael became president in 1966. Carmichael left in 1967 to join the Black Panther Party and was replaced by H. Rap Brown, who changed the group's name to the Student National Coordinating Committee. SNCC dissolved in the early 1970s.

Summer Community Organization and Political Education Project (SCOPE). A 1965–66 effort that relied on mostly student volunteers to educate voters and monitor the recently passed Voting Rights Act. Some five hundred students from one hundred colleges worked in ninety Southern counties. Many of the SCOPE volunteers were whites.

SELECTED BIBLIOGRAPHY

Newspapers

Atlanta Constitution
Atlanta Daily World
Atlanta Inquirer
Atlanta Journal
Atlanta Journal-Constitution
Atlanta Voice
Chicago Tribune
Christian Science Monitor
Great Speckled Bird
Los Angeles Times
Memphis Commercial Appeal
Memphis World
New York Times
Wall Street Journal
Washington Afro-American
Washington Post

Manuscript Collections

Atlanta Life Insurance Collection, Auburn Avenue Research Library on African-American Culture and History, Atlanta.

Helen Bullard papers, Manuscript and Rare Book Library, Emory University, Atlanta.

Calvin Craig papers, Manuscript and Rare Book Library, Emory University, Atlanta.

Marshall Frady papers, Manuscript and Rare Book Library, Emory University, Atlanta.

Great Speckled Bird papers, Manuscript and Rare Book Library, Emory University, Atlanta.

Vincent Harding papers, Manuscript and Rare Book Library, Emory University, Atlanta.

Herbert Jenkins papers, Kenan Research Center, Atlanta History Center, Atlanta.

Martin Luther King Jr., correspondence files, King Center Archives, Atlanta.

Martin Luther King Jr., subject files, King Center Archives, Atlanta.

King Collection at Morehouse, Robert Woodruff Library, Atlanta University Center, Atlanta.
King Papers Project at Stanford University. Accessed digitally at http://www.stanford. edu/group/King/.
Ralph McGill papers, Manuscript and Rare Book Library, Emory University, Atlanta.
Newsweek Atlanta bureau collection, Manuscript and Rare Book Library, Emory University, Atlanta.
Eliza Paschall papers, Manuscript and Rare Book Library, Emory University, Atlanta.
Jacob Rothschild papers, Manuscript and Rare Book Library, Emory University, Atlanta.
Southern Christian Leadership Conference (SCLC) files, 1957–68, King Center Archives, Atlanta.
Southern Regional Council papers, Auburn Avenue Research Library on African-American Culture and History, Atlanta.
White House Daily Appointment Diaries, Lyndon Baines Johnson Presidential Library and Museum, Austin, Texas.
Hosea Williams papers, Auburn Avenue Research Library on African-American Culture and History, Atlanta.
Robert W. Woodruff papers, Manuscript and Rare Book Library, Emory University, Atlanta.

Digital Photo and Video Archives

ABC News. http://ugv.abcnews.go.com/player.aspx?id=2733547.
AP Photos. apimages.com.
Atlanta in the Civil Rights Movement. Atlanta Regional Consortium for Higher Education. http://www.atlantahighered.org/civilrights/.
Corbis. http://pro.corbis.com.
Eyes on the Prize. http://www.pbs.org/wgbh/amex/eyesontheprize/story/15_poor. html#video.
Getty Images. http://www.gettyimages.com.
Dr. King and the 1968 AFSCME Memphis Sanitation Strike. Published by AFSCME at http://www.afscme.org/about/1029.cfm.
Life magazine photographs from Memphis, April 4, 1968. http://www.life.com/image/51419416/in-gallery/24651.
Floyd Jillson Photographic Collection. Atlanta History Center. atlantahistorycenter. com.
The Jim Peppler Southern Courier Photographic Collection. Alabama Department of Archives and History. http://216.226.178.196/cdm4/peppler.php.
Bill Wilson Photographic Collection. Atlanta History Center. atlantahistorycenter. com.
WSB-TV Newsfilm Collection. Walter J. Brown Media Archives and Peabody Awards Collection, University of Georgia. Accessed through the Civil Rights Digital Library, http://crdl.usg.edu/.

Sound Recordings

Dr. Martin Luther King, Jr. 1929–1968. Sound Recording. Brotherhood Records, 1968.
Selected recordings of White House phone calls, April 1968. Lyndon Baines Johnson Presidential Library.

Interviews

Bell, Eldrin. Telephone interview, January 9, 2008.
Black, Charles. Personal interviews, April 17, 2009.
Butts, June Dobbs. Personal interviews, November 5, 2007, and August 7, 2009.
Clayton, Xernona. Personal interviews, December 6, 2007, and May 2009.
Dodd, Marie. Telephone interview, February 4, 2008.
English, Jethro. Personal interview, October 31, 2007.
English, Ron. Personal interview, October 31, 2007.
Farris, Isaac, Jr. Personal interview, August 21, 2009.
Fitch, Bob. Telephone interview, May 29, 2009.
Freeman, Jo. Telephone interview, May 29, 2009.
Geffen, Peter. Telephone interview, May 25, 2009.
Green, Winifred. Telephone interview, June 8, 2009.
Hemphill, Paul. Personal interview, February 13, 2008.
Houck, Tom. Personal interviews, November 6, 2007, and December 8, 2009.
Jackson, Jesse. Telephone interview, February 28, 2008.
Jackson-Ransom, Bunnie. Personal interview, December 11, 2009.
Johnson, Kathryn. Telephone interview, February 22, 2008.
Johnson, Tom. Personal interview, April 22, 2009.
Johnson, Winston. Telephone interview, January 28, 2008.
Kilgo, Pete. Telephone interview, January 30, 2008.
King, Bernice. Telephone interview, February 28, 2008.
King, Lonnie. Personal interview, May 25, 2009.
Kohn, Kathy. Personal interviews, February 10, 2008, and November 18, 2009.
Kohn, Norm. Personal interviews, February 10, 2008, and November 18, 2009.
LaFayette, Bernard. Telephone interview, February 5, 2008.
Latimore, Patricia. Telephone interview, February 25, 2008.
LeFever, Harry. Telephone interview, May 28, 2009.
Lowery, Joseph. Telephone interview, February 25, 2008.
Mangham, Marvin. Telephone interviews, September 19 and 22, 2009.
Massell, Sam. Personal interview, January 14, 2008.
McClelland, Diane (Monk). Telephone interview, September 23, 2009.
Mullá, Linda. Telephone interview, February 5, 2008.
Omilami, Elizabeth. Telephone interview, February 21, 2008.
Patterson-Lewis, Cynthia. Personal interview, October 8, 2009.
Peppler, Jim. Telephone interview, September 23, 2009.
Robinson, Don Carl. Personal interview, February 10, 2008.
Sanders, Carl. Telephone interview, January 29, 2008.
Saporta, Maria. Personal interview, February 14, 2008.
Shur, Rabbi Mickey. Telephone interview, July 6, 2009.
Wilborn, James. Telephone interview, October 21, 2009.
Williams, Sam. Telephone interview, February 28, 2008.
Young, Andrea. Telephone interview, June 17, 2009.
Young, Andrew. Telephone interview, May 22, 2009.

Oral History Transcripts

Abernathy, Ralph. Interview conducted by Blackside Inc. on November 6, 1985, for *Eyes on the Prize: America's Civil Rights Years* (1954–65). Henry Hampton Collection, Film and Media Archive, Washington University Libraries.
Abram, Morris. Oral History Interview II, 5/3/84, by Michael L. Gillette. Transcript. Internet copy, LBJ Library.
Clark, Ramsey. Oral History Interview IV, 4/16/69, and Interview V, 6/3/69, by Harri Baker. Internet copy, LBJ Library.
Clifford, Clark. Oral History Interview VI, 4/24/70, by Joe B. Frantz. Internet copy, LBJ Library.
DeLoach, Cartha D. "Deke." Oral History Interview I, 1/11/91, by Michael L. Gillette. Transcript. Internet copy, LBJ Library.
Higginbotham, A. Leon, Jr. Oral History Interview I, 10/7/76 by Joe B. Frantz. Transcript. Internet copy, LBJ Library.
McPherson, Harry. Oral History Interview V, 4/6/69, by T. H. Baker. Internet copy, LBJ Library.
Randolph, A. Philip. Oral History Interview I, 10/29/69, by Thomas H. Baker. Internet copy, LBJ Library.
Taylor, Randall A. Interview with Dean Thompson. Transcript courtesy of Arline Taylor via Don Carl Robinson, music minister, Central Presbyterian Church, Atlanta.
Wilkins, Roy. Oral History Interview I, 4/1/69, by Thomas H. Baker. Internet copy, LBJ Library.
Young, Andrew. Oral History Interview I, 6/18/70, by Thomas H. Baker. Internet copy, LBJ Library.
Young, Whitney. Oral History Interview I, 6/18/68, by Thomas H. Baker. Internet copy, LBJ Library.

Books

1968: The Year That Changed the World. New York: Time Books, 2008.
Abernathy, Ralph David. *And the Walls Came Tumbling Down: An Autobiography.* New York: Harper & Row, 1989.
Allen, Ivan, Jr., with Paul Hemphill. *Mayor: Notes on the Sixties.* New York: Simon & Schuster, 1971.
Black, Earl. *Southern Governors and Civil Rights.* Cambridge, Mass.: Harvard University Press, 1976.
Branch, Taylor. *Parting the Waters: America in the King Years: 1954–1963.* New York,: Simon & Schuster, 1988.
———. *Pillar of Fire: America in the King Years: 1963–1965.* New York: Simon & Schuster, 1998.
———. *At Canaan's Edge: America in the King Years: 1965–1968.* New York: Simon & Schuster, 2006.
Carson, Clayborne, ed. *The Autobiography of Martin Luther King, Jr.* New York and Boston: Intellectual Properties Management. with Warner Books, 1998.
Clayton, Xernona. *I've Been Marching All the Time: An Autobiography.* Athens, Ga.: Longstreet Press, 1991.

Dallek, Robert. *Flawed Giant: Lyndon Johnson and His Times, 1961–1973.* New York: Oxford University Press, paperback ed., 1998.
_____. *Lyndon Johnson: Portrait of a President.* New York: Oxford University Press, 2005.
Dickerson, Dennis C. *Militant Mediator: Whitney M. Young Jr.* Lexington: University Press of Kentucky, 2004.
Farris, Christine King. *Through It All: Reflections on My Life, My Family, and My Faith.* New York, London, Toronto, and Sydney: Atria Books, 2009.
Frady, Marshall. *Jesse: The Life and Pilgrimage of Jesse Jackson.* New York: Simon & Schuster Paperbacks, 2006.
Garrow, David J. *Bearing the Cross: Martin Luther King, Jr., and the Southern Christian Leadership Conference.* New York: Random House, Vintage Books ed., 1988.
Gilbert, Ben, and the staff of the *Washington Post. Ten Blocks from the White House: Anatomy of the Washington Riots of 1968.* New York: Praeger, 1969.
Hansen, Drew D. *The Dream: Martin Luther King, Jr., and the Speech That Inspired a Nation.* New York: Harper Collins, 2003.
Jenkins, Herbert. *Keeping the Peace: A Police Chief Looks at His Job.* New York: Harper & Row, 1970.
Johnson, Charles, and Bob Adelman. *Remembering Martin Luther King Jr. 40 Years Later: His Life and Crusade in Pictures.* New York: Life Books, 2008.
The Kerner Report: The Complete Text. 21st printing. New York, Toronto, and London: Bantam Books, 1968.
King, Coretta Scott. *My Life with Martin Luther King, Jr.* Rev. ed. New York and London: Puffin Books, 1993.
King, Dexter, with Ralph Wiley. *Growing Up King: An Intimate Memoir.* New York: Warner Books, 2003.
Kruse, Kevin. *White Flight: Atlanta and the Making of Modern Conservatism.* Princeton and Oxford: Princeton University Press, 2005.
Lassiter, Matthew. *The Silent Majority: Suburban Politics in the Sunbelt South.* Princeton and Oxford: Princeton University Press, 2006.
Lentz, Richard. *Symbols, the News Magazines, and Martin Luther King.* Baton Rouge and London: Louisiana State University Press, 1990.
Lewis, David L. *King: A Critical Biography.* New York and Washington: Praeger Publishers, 1970.
Lewis, John, with Michael D'Orso. *Walking with the Wind: A Memoir of the Movement.* San Diego, New York, and London: Harvest Books, paperback ed., 1998.
Martin, Harold H. *Atlanta and Environs, Vol. III: A Chronicle of Its People and Events, Years of Change and Challenge, 1940–1976.* Athens, Ga., and London: University of Georgia Press with the Atlanta Historical Society, 1987.
Mays, Benjamin. *Born to Rebel: An Autobiography.* Athens and London: University of Georgia Press, paperback ed., 2003.
Pendergrast, Mark. *For God, Country and Coca-Cola: The Unauthorized History of the Great American Soft Drink and the Company That Makes It.* New York: Scribner, 1993.
Pomerantz, Gary. *Where Peachtree Meets Sweet Auburn: A Saga of Race and Family.* New York: Penguin, 1996.
Roberts, Gene, and Hank Klibanoff. *The Race Beat: The Press, the Civil Rights Struggle, and the Awakening of a Nation.* New York: Alfred A. Knopf, 2006.
Sunnemark, Fredrik. *Ring Out Freedom! The Voice of Martin Luther King, Jr., and the Making of the Civil Rights Movement.* Bloomington and Indianapolis: Indiana University Press, 2004.

Townsend, James L. *Dear Heart*. Atlanta: Peachtree Publishers, 1980.
Washington, James M., ed. *A Testament of Hope: The Essential Writings and Speeches of Martin Luther King, Jr.* San Francisco: HarperCollins San Francisco, 1986.
Young, Andrew. *An Easy Burden: The Civil Rights Movement and the Transformation of America*. New York: HarperCollins, 1996.

Articles and Essays

Anatol, Karl W., and John R. Bittner. "Kennedy on King: The Rhetoric of Control." *Today's Speech* September 1968, 16, no. 3: 31–34.
Bal, Vidula V. "Martin Luther King, Jr., Assassination." In *Museum of Broadcast Communications Encyclopedia of Television*, vol. 2, 1997.
Bennett, Lerone, Jr. "The Martyrdom of Martin Luther King." *Ebony*, May 1968, 174–81.
Booker, Simeon. "As D.C. Burns, President Moves to Head Off Race Confrontation." *Jet*, April 18, 1968, 38–41.
_____. "Returns to Walk in Footsteps of Husband Felled by Assassin." *Jet*, April 25, 1968, 6–17.
_____. "Rev. Abernathy 'To Get Moving on Job Left Behind by Martin.'" *Jet*, April 25, 1968, 48–51.
Burns, Rebecca. "Funeral." *Atlanta*, April 2008, 96–101, 133–43.
_____. "Atlanta Student Movement: 50 Years Later." *Atlanta*, March 2010, 75–79, 119–20.
Cleghorn, Reese. "Notes on a Native Son." *Atlanta*, June 1968, 52–55, 68–71.
Cummings, Melbourne S., and Lyndrey Niles. "King as Persuader: Facing the Ultimate Sacrifice." *Journal of Religious Thought* (1992): 49–57.
Darman, Jonathan. "1968: The Year That Changed Everything." *Newsweek*, November 19, 2007, 42–43.
Dayan, Daniel, and Elihu Katz. *Media Events: The Live Broadcasting of History*. Cambridge, Mass.: Harvard University Press, 1992.
Daynes, Gary. "Fighting for an Authentic Past: The Commemoration of Martin Luther King, Jr., in Atlanta, Georgia." *Atlanta History* 41, no. 1 (Spring 1997): 5–26.
Garrow, David. "The FBI and Martin Luther King." *Atlantic*, July/August 2002. http://www.theatlantic.com/doc/200207/garrow.
Hein, Virginia H. "The Image of 'A City Too Busy to Hate': Atlanta in the 1960s." *Phylon* 33, no. 3 (1972): 205–21.
Hemphill, Paul. "Summerhill: Then and Now." *Atlanta Journal and Constitution Magazine*, April 7, 1968, 14, 17–19.
Higgins, Christopher. "Show Biz Stars Loved King; Raised Funds," *Jet*, April 18, 1968, 60–63.
Hoffman, Scott W. "Holy Martin: The Overlooked Canonization of Dr. Martin Luther King, Jr." *Religion and American Culture* 10, no. 2 (2000): 123–48.
Hofstetter, C. Richard. "Political Disengagement and the Death of Martin Luther King." *Public Opinion Quarterly* 33, no. 2 (1969): 174–82.
Hon, Linda Childers. "To Redeem the Soul of America: Public Relations and the Civil Rights Movement." *Journal of Public Relations Research* 9, no. 3 (1997): 163–212.
Hooper, Hartwell, and Susan Hooper. "The Scripto Strike: Martin Luther King's 'Valley of Problems,' Atlanta, 1964–1965." *Atlanta History* 43, no. 3 (Fall 1999): 5–34.

Huie, William Bradford. "James Earl Ray: The Final Wail of a Lonely Loser." *Atlanta*, January 1979, 35–37.

"Interview with Ivan Allen, Jr." *Atlanta*, January 1969, 84–86, 88–92.

"Ivan Ho!" *Time*, September 17, 1965, accessed online at time.com.

Kuhn, Clifford M. "'There's a Footnote to History!' Memory and the History of Martin Luther King's October 1960 Arrest and Its Aftermath." *Journal of American History*, September 1997, 583–95.

Lynch, Christopher. "Reaffirmation of God's Anointed Prophet: The Use of Chiasm in Martin Luther King's 'Mountaintop' Speech." *Howard Journal of Communications* 6, nos. 1 and 2. (1995): 12–31.

Meyer, Philip. "Aftermath of Martyrdom: Negro Militancy and Martin Luther King." *Public Opinion Quarterly* 33, no. 2 (1969): 160–74.

Miller, Keith D. "Alabama as Egypt: Martin Luther King, Jr., and the Religion of Slaves." In *Martin Luther King, Jr., and the Sermonic Power of Public Discourse*, eds. Carolyn Calloway-Thomas and John Louis Lucaites, 18–32. Tuscaloosa: University of Alabama Press, 1993.

Morris, Steve. "Birmingham Strategist Called to Direct King Funeral." *Jet*, April 25, 1968, 18–21.

Nystrom, Justin. "Segregation's Last Stand: Lester Maddox and the Transformation of Atlanta." *Atlanta History* 45, no. 2 (Summer 2001): 34–51.

Pach, Chester, Jr. "TV's 1968: War, Politics, and Violence on the Network Evening News." *South Central Review* 16, no. 4 (1999): 29–42.

Reed, Harry A. "Martin Luther King, Jr.: History and Memory, Reflections on Dreams and Silences." *Journal of Negro History* 84, no. 2 (1999): 150–66.

Reed, Roy. "The Southern Demagogue: Death of a Breed." In *The Prevailing South*, ed. Dudley Clendinen, 76–88. Atlanta: Longstreet Press, 1993.

"Rev. King Preached Own Funeral Before Death." *Jet*, April 18, 1968, 24.

Rice, Bradley R. "King, Martin Luther, Jr." In *Dictionary of Georgia Biography*, ed. Kenneth Coleman and Charles Stephen Carr, 577–79. Athens: University of Georgia Press, 1983.

Riley, Betsy. "A Separate Peace." *Atlanta* magazine, May 2010, 75–79, 92–99.

Sharman, Nick. "Remaining Awake Through a Great Revolution: The Rhetorical Strategies of Martin Luther King Jr." *Social Semiotics* 9, no. 1 (1999): 85–106.

Thomas, Evan. "The Worst Week." *Newsweek*, November 19, 2007, 44–48.

Williams, Roger. "The Negro in Atlanta: An Analysis of the Facts, Forces, and Frustrations that Shape the Lives and Future of Atlanta's Negro Community." *Atlanta*, June 1963, 25–30.

Wills, Gary. "Jesse Jackson Over the Rainbow." *GQ*, February 1984.

Theses and Dissertations

Burns, Rebecca. "Mourning and Message: Martin Luther King Jr.'s 1968 Atlanta Funeral as an Image Event." Dissertation, Georgia State University, 2008.

Dyson, Michael Eric. "Uses of Heroes: Celebration and Criticism in the Interpretation of Malcolm X and Martin Luther King, Jr." Dissertation, Princeton University, 1993.

Godboldte, Catherine. "Ancient African Traditional Funeral Ceremonies and the Funeral Ceremonies of the Historic African-American Church." Dissertation, Temple University, 1995.

Kane, Thomas Henry. "Last Acts: Automortography and the Cultural Performance of Death in the United States, 1968–2001." Diss., University of Virginia, 2003.

White Papers, Government Reports, and Other Documents

Crawford, Fred, Harvey Gates, and James Conyers. "Civil Aggression and Urban Disorders, Atlanta, Georgia, 1967." Atlanta: Emory University Center for Research in Social Change, 1968.

Crawford, Fred, Roy Norman, and Leah Dabbs. "A Report of Certain Reactions by the Atlanta Public to the Death of the Reverend Doctor Martin Luther King, Jr." Atlanta: Emory University Center for Research in Social Change, 1969.

DeWolf, L. Harold. "Funeral Tribute to Martin Luther King, Jr., Ebenezer Baptist Church, April 9, 1968." Transcript. Religion & Ethics Newsweekly online. http://pbs.org.wnet/religionandethics/week920/tribute.html.

Dr. Martin Luther King Jr. Assassination Investigation. Online archive published by the Shelby County Register of Deeds, Memphis, Tennessee. http://register.shelby.tn.us/mlk/.

Federal Bureau of Investigation. Freedom of Information and Privacy Act Special Reports. Subject: Stokely Carmichael. File: HQ 100-446080, Section 1.

———. Freedom of Information and Privacy Act Special Reports. Subject: Martin Luther King Jr. File: 100-106670, Section 103.

———. Freedom of Information and Privacy Act Special Reports. Subject: Coretta Scott King.

Jenkins, Herbert. "Forty Years on the Force: 1932–1972; Herbert Jenkins Reminisces on His Career with the Atlanta Police Department." Atlanta: Emory University, Center for Research in Social Change, 1973.

Kohn, Norm. "The Civil Rights Movement Comes to Central." History prepared for the sesquicentennial of Central Presbyterian Church.

Report of the Select Committee on Assassinations of the U.S. House of Representatives: Findings in the Assassination of Dr. Martin Luther King, Jr. Accessed online through the National Archives. http://www.archives.gov/research/jfk/select-committee-report/part-2-king-findings.html.

INDEX

Page numbers in *italics* refer to illustrations.

234 / *Index*

ABOUT THE AUTHOR

Rebecca Burns is an author and journalist who focuses on Southern history and the intersection of race, religion, and politics. She was editor in chief of *Atlanta* magazine for seven years and is the author of *Rage in the Gate City: The Story of the 1906 Atlanta Race Riot,* which was a finalist for the 2007 Georgia Author of the Year Awards. She wrote the Atlanta edition in the Yesterday and Today book series and is a frequent speaker at colleges and community groups. Find out more at www.rebecca-burns.com.

Printed in the United States
By Bookmasters